About Island Press

Since 1984, the nonprofit organization Island Press has been stimulating, shaping, and communicating ideas that are essential for solving environmental problems worldwide. With more than 1,000 titles in print and some 30 new releases each year, we are the nation's leading publisher on environmental issues. We identify innovative thinkers and emerging trends in the environmental field. We work with world-renowned experts and authors to develop cross-disciplinary solutions to environmental challenges.

Island Press designs and executes educational campaigns, in conjunction with our authors, to communicate their critical messages in print, in person, and online using the latest technologies, innovative programs, and the media. Our goal is to reach targeted audiences—scientists, policy makers, environmental advocates, urban planners, the media, and concerned citizens—with information that can be used to create the framework for long-term ecological health and human well-being.

Island Press gratefully acknowledges major support from The Bobolink Foundation, Caldera Foundation, The Curtis and Edith Munson Foundation, The Forrest C. and Frances H. Lattner Foundation, The JPB Foundation, The Kresge Foundation, The Summit Charitable Foundation, Inc., and many other generous organizations and individuals.

Overbuilt

Overbuilt

THE HIGH COSTS AND LOW REWARDS OF US HIGHWAY CONSTRUCTION

Erick Guerra

ISLANDPRESS | Washington | Covelo

FSC
www.fsc.org
MIX
Paper | Supporting responsible forestry
FSC® C005010

Library of Congress Control Number: 2024948137

All Island Press books are printed on environmentally responsible materials.

Manufactured in the United States of America
10 9 8 7 6 5 4 3 2 1

Keywords: American Association of State Highway and Transportation Officials (AASHTO), Boston's Big Dig, Boston's Central Artery, carbon emissions, cost-benefit analysis, Dallas's Central Expressway, displacement, expressway, Federal Highway Act, Federal Highway Administration, gas tax, highway, highway trust fund, induced demand, Intermodal Surface Transportation Efficiency Act (ISTEA), Interstate and Defense Highways Act, Interstate Highway System, racial injustice, road safety, surface transportation policy, traffic congestion, traffic engineering, traffic fatalities, transportation finance, transportation policy, urban renewal

For Sunny and Eddie

Contents

CHAPTER 1

Introduction

In his Grand Plan, President Eisenhower envisioned each level of government contributing to the upgrade of the Nation's entire road network. His goal was the creation of a system to improve safety, reduce traffic jams, increase economic efficiency, and provide for the national defense.—Richard Capka, administrator of the Federal Highway Administration (2006–2008), Remarks to Congress

Like many Americans, I grew up in the distant wake of interstate and other highway construction.* My family slowly moved from an old mill town off Interstate 495 in Massachusetts, to an even older manufacturing town off Route 128, to a town just west of Cambridge, and eventually to an old German brewer's home off a linear park that had been cleared for a federally funded highway through southwest Boston. That

* Throughout this book, I make numerous references to interstate construction, individual interstates, the general interstate construction program, and specific laws and policies. I capitalize the word *interstate* when referring to specific interstates (e.g., Interstate 495), the officially designated Interstate Highway System (Interstate System for short), and legal or document titles. I also default to the capitalization used in quotations from source material, including transcripts of recorded interviews. In these instances, the source materials frequently use *Interstate* to refer to the Interstate Highway System, but also the interstate highway program or interstates more generally.

Interstate 95 and Route 128 were the same road felt like a local quirk. It was no different from the locals knowing that a frappe comes with ice cream but a milkshake does not. Going to the see the Bruins and Celtics, my dad and I would walk under the shadows of the Central Artery, one of the first major elevated expressways in the United States, in an environment that felt like something out of one of the darker versions of Batman's Gotham City. The structures looked old, dark, and eternal.

Staring down at us while sitting in traffic on a highway that erased one neighborhood was a billboard for apartments on the site of another erased neighborhood announcing that if we lived there, we'd be home now. After high school, my closest friends moved into a house together in a neighborhood that was nearly razed to build another urban expressway. A mural by what would become my neighborhood grocery store a decade later showed heroic neighbors and activists facing down federal bulldozers (figure 1-1). At the time, I did not realize that a freeway had been planned to run through the neighborhood. The neighborhood was convenient and filled with a rich diversity of houses and shops. The idea of spending hundreds of millions of dollars to replace it all with just another highway seemed crazy. There already seemed to be plenty of roads and highways to get around.

Not until graduate school did I learn how much damage urban highways had done or the callous disregard with which state and federal highway officials had built them. Class readings and lectures on slum clearance and urban highways played a part in my growing understanding. More than anything, Fred Salvucci, former Massachusetts secretary of transportation and MIT professor, telling the story of how his grandmother's home was taken to build the Mass Turnpike, changed my connection to my built environment. Like so many others during the time, his grandmother, a seventy-year-old widow, was given a dollar and told she had to vacate her house for a highway project.[1] Officials sent a letter assuring her that the government would assess her home's value

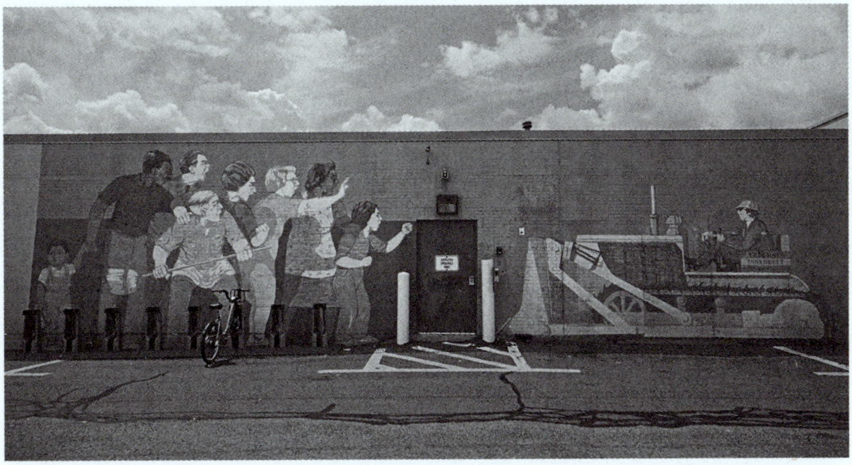

Figure 1-1. *Beat the Belt*, 1980 mural by Bernie LaCasse. (Photo by Chris Bell.)

and reimburse her later. The only analysis that had been done to justify her home's taking was a rudimentary traffic flow study predicting how many people were likely to drive on the roadway. These types of stories permeate and linger on the structures, buildings, and monuments of the cities and towns of my childhood and adult life.

Decades of reforms would force the highway builders to treat people and the environment with more respect. Many highway builders resented these new social protections. Some continue to resent them. Most would reflect that the Interstate Highway System could not have been built with today's protections in place. The first Federal Highway administrator, Bertram Tallamy, lamented three decades later, "The only observation that I see and I am sure everybody knows, that the red tape that is involved now by the federal government, by the state government, by the local agencies, hinder actual accomplishment.... We could not build the Interstate today."[2]

The assumption is that all the destruction from building highways—including the disproportionate impact on Black, Brown, immigrant, and low-income communities—was worth it. The Interstate System and the hundreds of thousands of miles of supporting state highways and arterials are frequently hailed as a marvel and triumph of engineering, the world's largest public works investment visible from space, a critical component of the American way of life, and a fundamental component of economic competitiveness.[3] Politicians frequently hail President Dwight Eisenhower's 1956 National Interstate and Defense Highways Act and subsequent highway acts as models of successful bipartisanship. Federal Highway administrator Richard Capka's reference to Eisenhower's *Grand Plan* (capital G, capital P) imbues the highway program with a mythic, near religious status.[4] Some eggs were broken. Society benefits from the omelet.

Conversations about the effects of the original program also ignore that the finance, governance, and construction models established by the 1956 National Interstate and Defense Highways Act continue to influence what gets built today. Of the inflation-adjusted $2.5 trillion spent on highways from the Highway Trust Fund since its inception in 1956, about 60 percent has been spent since completing the last bit of the originally planned Interstate System in 1992.[5] About 75 percent has been spent since the system was supposed to have been completed in 1969. State and local governments have spent trillions more on road investments and repairs over the same period.

Though fewer homes and businesses are destroyed, highway planners are still breaking eggs to make omelets—extremely expensive omelets. There are nearly twice as many lane miles of urban interstate and 55 percent more secondary highways and arterials today as there were in 1990.[6] Few Americans have a sense of how much the government spends on roadways or how, why, or where roads get built. The better informed generally understand that the federal government and states raise dedicated transportation funds through a gas tax. And these funds are primarily spent to build, widen, upgrade, and maintain major highways and arterials.

Many citizens likely understand that highway planners and politicians largely promoted the Interstate System for national defense, interstate commerce, and even abstract concepts like promoting American family life. By contrast, few probably know that the engineers, planners, and administrators who designed and built the system focused on building roads that encouraged more driving to raise additional gas tax revenues. There is a reason highway planners bulldozed their way through cities before focusing on connecting them: those urban highways would carry the most traffic and generate the most revenues. Fewer still probably realize just how unsuccessful highway builders have been at reducing congestion or improving traffic safety, the two primary stated goals of nearly every large federal and state funding package since the National Interstate and Defense Highways Act.

Despite all the spending and stated policy goals, congestion and traffic deaths remain endemic. One popular source indicates that Americans now spend three times as much time in traffic as they did in 1991. The average time spent in traffic per car commuter increased from twenty-nine hours in 1991 to fifty-four hours in 2019.[7] More than a million people have died on US roads since the completion of the Interstate Highway System. The US traffic fatality rate is two to four times higher than in Canada or wealthy European countries and has improved much more slowly over time than in peer countries. At an average economic cost of $1.5 million per fatality, fatal traffic collisions have cost nearly $2 trillion in lost wages and medical expenses since 1991.[8] Millions more crashes involving serious and moderate injuries cost hundreds of billions more. These estimates generally ignore the social and personal costs of millions of shattered lives, lost loved ones, and traumatized families.

Perhaps the biggest effect of highway investments since the 1990s has been to make the United States ever more car dependent. Residents and visitors have driven around ninety trillion miles since 1991, producing more carbon emissions than any other country barring China from the transport sector alone. Outside of a handful of cities, Americans without cars—due to income, health, age, or other reasons—struggle to access employment, shops, hospitals, and other daily needs. Losing a car due to changes in life circumstances, like a crash or mechanical failure, is associated with decreases in income, happiness, health, and employment. As a result, people go to great lengths to maintain access to a personal car, taking on debt, driving without insurance, or purchasing an older poorly maintained vehicle that is not only less safe but contributes substantially to local air pollution. After housing, US households spend more on transportation than any other type of expenditure, including food, health, or education,[9] leaving many families and the overall economy vulnerable to even modest increases in gas prices.

Looking across cities and urban areas, the legacy of the past decades of road investments is unimpressive. The places that seem to be doing best in terms of economic efficiency, traffic safety, social equity, and environmental sustainability are frequently the places with the fewest highways and major arterials per capita. These towns and cities are much likelier to be more densely populated and have grown less around freeways and large auto-oriented arterials than the rest of the country. They are also the places where having a car is less of a prerequisite for everyday access to basic economic and social opportunities. While good accessibility is hardly universal, many more people can and do get to work and other important destinations by bus, train, foot, and bike.

In this book, I argue that the US roadway system is overbuilt. There are so many high-capacity urban interstates, highways, and arterials that the costs of adding new roadway capacity generally outweigh the benefits. This claim is somewhat controversial. Transportation is necessary for a functioning modern society and economy. Without streets and highways, there is severely constrained access to employment, food, and other necessities. Businesses have a difficult time attracting employees and receiving or shipping goods. However, too much roadway is also problematic. The inverse of a dysfunctional place without streets or highways is a somewhat absurd place composed entirely of streets and highways. Roadways connect places but they also replace other land uses, like houses, businesses, parks, and schools. Somewhere between no roadway and only roadway lies some optimum. Below this optimum, a roadway system is underbuilt. New investments in highways and arterials will tend to spur economic activities, improve accessibility, and produce social and economic benefits. The first major roadway connecting through a city, for example, confers enormous benefits. Each new roadway investment will tend to confer smaller and smaller benefits. While there is a fair amount of disagreement over the absolute benefits of highway investments in the United States, there is generally consensus that newer investments produce fewer benefits than the older ones. At a certain point, the fiscal, environmental, and social costs of road investments outweigh the benefits. The road system becomes overbuilt. New investments have smaller benefits and tend to distort and shuffle economic activities rather than produce new ones.

While the optimal amount of roadway will vary by geography, culture, and economy, the US roadway system is well beyond the optimal level of investment. Most national transportation problems stem from having too much road infrastructure rather than too little. The desired increased economic activity or reduced congestion from building more highways or expanding existing ones rarely materialize. More than anything, more highways lead to more driving, which produces more pollution, more traffic fatalities, and more auto-centric cities and towns that require more driving to participate in basic civic, social, and economic activities.

Even narratives about crumbling infrastructure and a diminishing Highway Trust Fund stem from this more fundamental problem. As the national highway system has expanded and aged, the annual costs of repaving, repairing, and rebuilding roads, bridges, and interchanges have also skyrocketed. The original National Interstate and Defense

Highways Act had never envisioned these kinds of ongoing costs. There are more highways and major roads than anyone really cares to pay to maintain or reconstruct. There is also so much road infrastructure that new transit, bicycle, or pedestrian investments do little to shape overall national or even local travel behavior. The 2021 Bipartisan Infrastructure Law announced the largest ever federal spending package on public transportation. While many of these investments may be beneficial, they will do nothing to resolve the fundamental problem of an overbuilt national roadway system. And still, policymakers, planners, and engineers continue to prioritize building and upgrading road infrastructure.

Over the course of this book, readers will learn about how the US roadway system became overbuilt, how public policy continues to encourage overbuilding, what the scale and consequences of overbuilding are, and how policymakers can stop and begin to correct overbuilding. The emphasis is on urban highways. More than half of the initial interstate financing and most of the early construction projects went into cities. Gas tax revenues from urban traffic then financed the rural parts of the system. The largest social, economic, and environmental effects of the highway system, moreover, have happened in cities and their suburbs. Urban areas account for just under half of interstate lane miles but more than two-thirds of interstate vehicle travel. While early arguments for subsidizing highways often emphasized connecting the country and making it easier for farmers to get goods to market, fewer than one in five US residents live in rural areas today. By the time construction began on the first miles of the Interstate System, planners and engineers had abandoned their rural emphasis and instead focused on eliminating urban congestion and facilitating car travel.

The national propensity to build roadways is no longer official or intentional policy. Instead, overbuilding stems from the institutions, finance mechanisms, and evaluation metrics developed in the first half of the twentieth century to finance and build the Interstate System and roughly four million miles of supporting highways, arterials, and secondary roads that make up the Federal-Aid Highway network. In the leadup to the 1991 Intermodal Surface Transportation Efficiency Act (ISTEA), the first major federal transportation law focused on transportation policy after completing the Interstate System, policymakers recognized the need for a drastic shift in highway policy. As President George H. W. Bush framed the issue, "We've got to take full advantage of our present opportunity to create a surface transportation program that will meet our present and future needs, not our past problems."[10] Indeed, ISTEA (pronounced like the beverage) opened with lofty statements about economic efficiency, environmental soundness, energy efficiency, fiscal responsibility, multimodality, and the mobility needs of the poor, elderly, and physically disabled.

Despite ISTEA's stated transformative aims, federal and state policies still focus on raising dedicated revenues through gas taxes to fund new highways and major arterials and maintain existing ones. Although more funds are set aside for transit, walking, biking, and beautification, the investment paradigm has not changed. Further, planners and engineers have not adjusted the tools they use to determine which roads should be built, rebuilt, or widened and why. Despite having too much roadway, the United States is still operating in construction mode, using the same basic approach used to finance and build the Interstate System quickly. Contrary to Bush's claim on signing ISTEA, we have yet to create a surface transportation program that addresses present and future needs instead of past problems. The United States is still in desperate need of a national transportation policy that can help address traffic safety, climate change, accessibility, and new forms of economic development. Everyone has eaten. The kitchen is getting more and more expensive. But the restaurant keeps serving omelets.

Over the remaining ten chapters of *Overbuilt*, I explore the history and contemporary role of the federal government in justifying, promoting, and eventually building urban highways; examine the costs of overbuilding; and look at interrelated investment and regulatory approaches to move beyond the legacy of the Interstate Highway System and develop a more financially, environmentally, and socially sustainable transportation system.

In the early chapters, I draw in part on primary planning documents from highway agencies, interviews with highway planners from the Public Works Historical society, several histories of the Interstate System, and personal and ethnographic accounts of citizens interacting and fighting with state and federal highway builders over the siting and construction of urban highways. Whereas the great histories of the interstates, such as Tom Lewis's *Divided Highways* and Mark Rose and Raymond Mohl's *Interstate*, tend to conclude with or shortly after the completion of the Interstate System, *Overbuilt*'s emphasis is on federal policy since system completion. The institutions, policies, finance mechanisms, and evaluation metrics developed since the creation of the Federal Highway Administration's predecessor in 1893 continue to directly influence how, where, and how much states, cities, and towns invest in highways.

These chapters also position the Interstate Highway System more appropriately as a single but important component of the larger and broader system of highways and arterials subsidized and regulated by federal policy. For example, the Federal-Aid Highway Act of 1921, the first to mention a system of connected interstate highways, allocated 40 percent of funds and nearly 60 percent of mileage to secondary highways and arterials. Federal policy currently subsidizes the construction, reconstruction, and maintenance of a wide array of roadways and roadway types. These chapters show how the roughly 40,000 miles of interstate highway are historically, fiscally, and functionally related to the broader 160,000-mile National Highway System and four-million-mile Federal-Aid Highway System. The interstate highways may get the most attention, but they do not function without a much broader system of highways, arterials, and local roads.

In the middle chapters, I draw on contemporary scholarship focused on the costs and benefits of roadbuilding. Somewhere between a city with no roads and a city composed entirely of roadway lies a theoretically optimal amount of roadway for a given city. The field of economics provides a general framework for finding this theoretical optimal: the point at which the additional benefits of a new road investment are equal to the additional costs. If the costs of new investments tend to outweigh the benefits, there is too much roadway. If the benefits tend to outweigh the costs, there is probably not enough. Factoring in external costs, like pollution and traffic fatalities, would tend to move the overall equation in favor of producing less roadway.

In the final chapters, I focus on how changes in finance and transportation evaluation measures can help start to undo the decades of transportation policy that has focused primarily on increasing traffic speeds and roadway capacity. While state and local highway and land use policies will continue to vary from place to place, shifts in federal policy have the potential to reshape urban transportation systems in the coming decades. Unfortunately, there are no silver bullets, and reversing the effects of an overbuilt road system will take decades. Congestion pricing, gas-tax alternatives, vehicle automation, and new transit technologies have a role to play in future urban transportation systems but will do little to nothing to resolve the fundamental problem of an overbuilt transportation system whose expansion state and federal policy continues to subsidize and encourage.

Cars will continue to play the primary role in getting people to and from work, school, church, ball fields, restaurants, and residents' many other destinations throughout the United States. The goal of federal transportation policy should be to help make these trips safer, shorter, and less economically and environmentally damaging. Living without a car—whether due to preference, income, or disability—should not exclude residents from basic social, economic, and recreational activities. Moving slowly in these directions will require moving past the finance and evaluation mechanisms that built the Interstate System. These mechanisms are not just dated and unresponsive to the country's twenty-first-century transportation needs, they are moving the country in the wrong direction. Bush's call to focus on future needs instead of our past problems remains as salient today as it was in 1991. The originally planned Interstate System was completed decades ago. It is time to move on.

CHAPTER 2

Out of the Mud and into the Cities

The urge to have the highways was not matched by an urge to pay for them.
—Senator Daniel Patrick Moynihan, *Urban Roads and Chaos, 1960*

The federal government was slow to take on its role as the driving force in planning and financing a national highway system. Private interests and wealthy motoring enthusiasts did most of the heavy lifting to plan, finance, and build the United States' first cross-country highway, the Lincoln Highway, in the early twentieth century.[1] Early federal involvement focused on conducting research, setting standards, and promoting the benefits of improved roadways, such as helping farmers get goods to market. Between the first map of the system in 1922 and opening of the first official segment of the Interstate System, thirty-five years passed. Over a similar period, federal highway planning shifted focus from getting farmers out of the mud to getting urban motorists out of traffic jams. The estimated price tag of the highway system also increased substantially. Grade-separated limited-access superhighways were much more expensive to construct than two-lane rural highways. The costs of acquiring urban land to demolish buildings for urban highways were also prohibitive without substantial federal and state support.

Despite the tremendous cost and potential socioeconomic impacts, little in the way of economic or social analysis was ever conducted. The main analysis of what would become the core of the Interstate Highway System concluded in 1939 that motorists were unwilling to pay the high and, at the time, substantially underestimated costs of the system. Moreover, this analysis did not include the hundreds of thousands of miles of highways and arterials supported by the federal government but not a part of the proposed interstate highway system.[2]

Instead, highway planners developed an array of moral arguments, technical analyses, and maps to justify the tremendous financial costs and physical destruction that building a national highway system would entail. They argued that acquiring and demolishing urban homes and businesses—despite the protests of affected communities—was beneficial in and of itself. Highways could support slum clearance while also combating the traffic congestion strangling cities. Highway construction, they argued, would create jobs and stimulate the economy. Highways would support military movements and help evacuate cities in the event of a nuclear attack. Most importantly according to General Lucius Clay, the man President Dwight Eisenhower put in charge of developing interstate highway legislation, building a national highway system would support car travel and thus an "essential part of American family life."[3]

Out of the Mud

Federal highway planning started small and with an emphasis on rural roads. The Agricultural Appropriations Act of 1894 established the Federal Highway Administration's predecessor, the Office of Road Inquiry. The act "enable[d] the Secretary of Agriculture to make inquiries in regard to the systems of road management throughout the United States, to make investigation in regard to the best method of road-making, to prepare publications on this subject suitable for distribution, and to enable him to assist the agricultural college and experiment stations in disseminating information on this subject."[4] General Robert Stone was the first head of the federal highway agency.[5] At $10,000 (about $350,000 in 2024 dollars), this first federal highway appropriation was enough to hire a few staff members and begin cooperating with other organizations and state agencies promoting and developing improved roadway systems. Over the next three decades, the federal highway agency would change names and directors several times but remain located in the Department of Agriculture.

In these first decades, most early federal plans, projects, and partnerships focused on helping farmers get out of the mud and get goods to market. An early and widely distributed publication in the *Farmers' Bulletin* described best practices in the building and maintenance of earth roads.[6] Directors' annual reports to the Department of Agriculture generally contained requests for additional funds for staff and publications, descriptions of tests of building materials and construction methods, and accounts of dissemination activities, such as train tours and public lectures. Over time, the reports increasingly detailed activities in partnership with the National Good Roads Association and argued for more direct federal investment in road construction. In 1905, the newly appointed director of the renamed Office of Public Roads presented at major national and local Good Roads conventions in Florida, Oregon, New York, Illinois, and a "number of minor conventions in various parts of the country throughout the year."[7]

Federal funding and responsibilities increased slowly over time. The Agricultural Appropriations Acts of 1912 and 1913 provided the first dedicated revenues to finance and construct public roads, though the focus was on building and maintaining roads and trails in National

Forests.[8] At almost $7 million in 2024 dollars, the funds would barely cover the costs of reconstructing one or two of the country's 107,000 total lane miles of urban interstate.[9] At the time, it nearly doubled the total budget of the Office of Public Roads.

The Federal-Aid Road Act of 1916, the first federal highway law, expanded the federal mandate and funding further. The act provided $75 million of funding over five years to "aid the States in the construction of rural post roads, and for other purposes."[10] Post roads could be any road that carried or might one day carry mail, but the act remained expressly rural and forbade investments in any area with more than twenty-five hundred residents unless houses were more than two hundred feet apart on average. Although small by contemporary standards—around 0.8 percent of the Federal Highway Administration's annual highway spending in 2022—federal funding increased sixtyfold.

This first highway law also set forth two principles that would carry forward through the next century of federal highway policy. First, the federal government would plan and finance roads in partnership with state highway departments and in coordination with the American Association of State Highway Officials (AASHO). The law allowed for a one-to-one financial match up to a maximum $10,000 per mile, around a tenth of the inflation-adjusted cost of a contemporary rural highway on flat ground. Second, the legislation explicitly prohibited spending federal funds on toll roads.

Beyond these principles, little came from the first federal highway act. The United States declared war on Germany just nine months later. In Chicago for a meeting with AASHO's Executive Committee, the federal highway director Logan Page fell ill and died on December 9, 1918, less than a month after the Armistice of Compiègne and six months prior to the Treaty of Versailles.[11] When civil engineer Thomas MacDonald took over the renamed Bureau of Public Roads in 1919, only $500,000 had been spent and only a dozen miles of roadway constructed.[12]

Over MacDonald's thirty-four years in charge of the federal highway program, funding increased substantially, the military began to take a more active role in highway planning, and there was a slow shift away from emphasizing rural needs to emphasizing interstate commerce, national defense, and urban transportation needs. Uniform design standards, minimum road widths, signage, increased cooperation between federal and state highway officials, and rules of the road also began to fall into place.

The Federal-Aid Highway Act of 1921 first directed policy toward "the completion of an adequate and connected system of highways, interstate in character."[13] The law tasked the Bureau of Public Roads to develop an interstate highway map within two years and provided a series of formulae about how much funding individual states would receive, how many rural roads could be designated as interstate, and what share of funding could go to interstate highways relative to "intercounty" state roads. Total funding increased to $75 million in the first year, and the amount that could be spent on each mile of roadway doubled to $20,000.

Road construction rapidly increased, and by 1923, the Bureau of Public Roads and state highway planners had designated 6 percent of all public roads as a part of the federal-aid road system.[14] The overall focus remained rural, but the funding and road-systems designations now prioritized an interconnected national highway system within the larger Federal-Aid Highway System. In 1922, General John Pershing, at the request of director MacDonald, produced a map that designated two hundred thousand interconnected roads deemed critical for national defense. Although the Pershing map contained many of the routes that would eventually help form the much smaller Interstate Highway System, the plan generally avoided large urban areas.

Over the next decade, rapid growth in auto ownership and urban congestion contributed to a major shift in federal highway policy.

Writing in the County Road Association of Michigan's magazine in 1935, MacDonald exclaimed, "We have reached a point in our development where we can no longer ignore the needs of traffic flowing from the main highways into and through cities and from feeder roads to the main highways."[15] The next major amendment to US highway policy, the Federal-Aid Highway Act of 1944, provided specific funding allocations for urban highways and explicitly called for a highway system connecting all principal cities and metropolitan areas. The vision for urban highways started to move away from the relatively conservative and integrative plans of the 1930s to the massive and disruptive urban expressways that would soon cut through every major US city.[16]

Into the Cities

The City of Boston Planning Board's 1930 *Report on a Thoroughfare Plan for Boston* provides an early look at urban highway planning in the United States.[17] As in other large and economically productive cities, private automobiles had become popular and were creating substantial congestion, traffic fatalities, and disruption as they competed for space with pedestrians, buses, streetcars, cyclists, and other road users. In metropolitan Boston in 1927, there were already around two hundred registered cars per one thousand residents, and motorists drove an estimated 1.8 billion miles. These large cities were pioneers in building and planning for urban expressways.

Massachusetts was also a leader in highway planning, construction, and finance. In 1892, the commonwealth created one of the first state highway panels to oversee county highway construction and, shortly thereafter, provided funds to carry out construction, as well as the legal authority to charge counties for 25 percent of construction costs.[18] Although small by today's standards, the $300,000 Massachusetts state highway budget was thirty times larger than the Office of Road Inquiry's budget. Stone based the federal highway agency's first model road-building program on a similar program in Massachusetts.[19] The federal highway administration's third director, Logan Page, came from the Massachusetts State Highway Commission.[20]

Boston's 231-page highway plan contained elements that would be familiar to contemporary transportation planners and engineers: an analysis of existing traffic conditions, traffic forecasts, detailed origin-destination and travel-flow maps, reference images of best practices from other cities, cost estimates, travel-time savings estimates, a twenty-five-year construction and finance plan, and arguments for expanding road capacity or risk business stagnation and overwhelming congestion. The document also made the kinds of generic calls for increased state funding that remain pervasive today.

According to author Robert Whitten, planning consultant and president of the American City Planning Institute, the Boston highway plan "furnishes what is probably the most complete factual basis for the design of highway improvements that has ever been secured for any great city."[21] Whitten would have known. He had participated in highway and land use plans for large cities around the United States. And the Boston plan drew on and acknowledged the earlier work of Dr. Miller McClintock, a pioneer in traffic engineering, data collection, and traffic forecasting.[22]

Somewhat less familiar is that the plan contained elegant hand-drawn maps, diagrams, and street sections. Several figures presented renderings of the proposed Central Artery, a roadway that features prominently in the history of US urban highways: first as an example of the callous and casual destruction caused by early urban highway construction; later as a rallying point for the urban freeway revolt, an ambitious attempt to undo the harms of urban highway construction, an engineering marvel, and a symbol of government waste; and finally as a project that improved the city of Boston but consumed tremendous state and federal transportation resources.

At the street level, pedestrians, cars, trucks, and buses continued to have easy access to shop fronts and offices (figure 2-1). Unobtrusive entrance and exit ramps allowed easy access to and from the express lanes above, where traffic would move at an uninterrupted 25 to 30 miles per hour. In short, the roadway design was well integrated with its surrounding urban land uses and articulated the plan's desire for construction to "harmonize with the existing appropriate development" and "avoid injury to the historic interest or charm of the crooked streets of Old Boston."[23] The plan went to great lengths to demonstrate how physical interventions and design treatments—like wide, grassy medians and protected pedestrian crossings—would improve pedestrian safety. Photographs and renderings showed how urban highways could be carefully inserted into existing urban fabrics by trenches that ran below the largely untouched city life above.

When I teach about the history of urban transportation planning, I ask my students what they think about this early highway rendering. Most respond with comments about noise, shadows, vibration, pollution, and the general unpleasantness of living or working next to the elevated structure. They imagine a modern expressway with vehicles whizzing by at speed. Some have even lived in cities with double-decked freeways winding between large apartment and office buildings.

Bostonians would have seen something quite different, something more like the elevated trains running down Washington Street and Atlantic Avenue at the time, something not too dissimilar from the elevated trains still running down major avenues in Chicago, Philadelphia, New York, and other large cities. Whitten even took time to argue that the familiar elevated train infrastructure was wider, louder, and uglier than the proposed roadway.[24]

Although Boston's highway plan called for increased state highway funding, its analysis concluded that a six-cent toll for the express lanes would be sufficient to pay off any bonds used to acquire land and build

Figure 2-1. The planned Central Artery in Boston cuts through the urban fabric but integrates closely with surrounding land uses and allows access to new high-rises by foot, car, bus, and truck. (Whitten, "Report on a Thoroughfare Plan for Boston," figure 47.)

the roadway. According to Whitten, several investments that might have improved traffic had also been analyzed but were excluded because their benefits to motorists did not outweigh their financial costs.

The 1929 *Regional Plan of New York and Its Environs*, an early privately funded and produced metropolitan land use and transportation plan, presented a similarly fiscally and physically conservative view of urban highways. In addition to elevated expressways resembling Boston's proposed Central Artery, the New York plan included sections of highways with tree-lined central medians, wide sidewalks, cycle paths, and easy connections to surrounding buildings by transit, car, and delivery truck. These proposed major highways had more akin to the grand boulevards and parkways of cities like Boston, New York, Paris, Chicago, and Washington, DC, than anything a city dweller would consider a highway today. The plan even lamented that the hundreds of miles of highways under construction had harmed rather than improved surrounding land values and economic activity in and around New York.[25] The authors argued that "the highway system should be developed on lines that will promote the best economic use of land abutting upon it and thereby create new value in land and buildings as a result of the expenditures on highway improvements."[26] Whitten served as one of several dozen engineering, legal, and planning consultants to New York's 1929 regional plan. The emphasis on integration with existing land uses was consistent with plans for Los Angeles, Oakland, St. Louis, Chicago, San Diego, and other large cities at the time.[27] Coordination with mass transit also tended to feature prominently.

The plan even drew a direct lineage to Daniel Burnham's 1909 *Plan of Chicago*, an exemplar of the City Beautiful movement, and was dedicated to the memory of Charles Dyer Norton, the first chairman of the New York plan and a member of the Commercial Club in Chicago, a group whose membership included Burnham and directly shaped and sponsored the Chicago plan.

Boston and New York's early highway plans, however, also foreshadowed some of the carelessness and destruction that would characterize urban highway building after the National Interstate and Defense Highways Act. In the Boston plan, for example, a dozen images showed transparent lines where new roads would cut through existing shops, houses, and offices in the urban core and neighborhoods, like Roxbury, Dorchester, and Jamaica Plain (figure 2-2). Twenty-five years later, similar lines would partially determine which residents lost their homes and businesses in service of modernity and the modern expressway.

Although careful not to show any images of the downtown property the Central Artery would have consumed, the Boston plan hinted at substantial takings. Land acquisitions accounted for 80 percent of

Figure 2-2. Transparent lines on a bird's-eye view of Boston show where a new highway would have destroyed surrounding shops, houses, and businesses. (Whitten, "Report on a Thoroughfare Plan for Boston," figure 55.)

the project's total $28 million estimated cost, a share consistent with other highway projects of the time.[28] Whitten, recognizing the massive expenditure for a city with a similarly sized total annual budget, made three main arguments to justify the investments. The first was a moral argument. Congestion was an "organic defect," a "widely spread evil" threatening collapse and preventing Boston from reaching its economic potential.[29] Planners, engineers, and architects had a moral obligation to address and repair this growing urban disease.

The next two arguments were more technocratic but again foreshadowed a willingness to destroy substantial urban wealth for exaggerated savings for motorists. First, Whitten argued that although the price tag was high, it was "but 3.2 per cent of the assessed value of the central district," or 1.6 percent of the total city's value.[30] To put that number in perspective, the equivalent share of Boston's contemporary total tax-assessed value roughly equals the city's entire operating budget.[31] It is not and was not anything close to a trivial expenditure. Contemporary infrastructure projects of this magnitude are generally financed almost entirely by state and federal funds. Second, Whitten argued that the price tag was low relative to the $180 million that motorists spent annually on cars in Boston and its surrounding suburbs. The estimated benefits, however, appear to have been excessively optimistic. According to Whitten's calculations, people spent as much money on their 400,000 motor vehicles per year as the entire annualized value of the City of Boston, home to 781,000 residents and the lion's share of metropolitan jobs. Moreover, Whitten claimed that the 1.5-mile Central Artery, despite only carrying 2 percent of traffic, would conservatively create a 10 percent travel improvement for all 1.8 billion miles driven annually in the region. As with many of these types of projects, the costs may have also been substantially and willfully underestimated.[32]

Finally, although Boston's early thoroughfare plans did not appear to contain any overt or covert attempts to target or segregate specific ethnic or racial groups, Whitten's 1922 zoning plan for Atlanta showed the kind of men that would soon be given the power to erase neighborhoods with the stroke of a pen. Whitten's Atlanta plan established legally segregated residential zoning districts for White and Colored races.[33] People could occupy servant's quarters in any district regardless of race. While Whitten generally framed the racial zoning as a matter of reducing conflict and improving conditions for all races, he also presented the Atlanta City Council with a blunter and less idealized perspective: "Home neighborhoods had to be protected from any further damage to values resulting from inappropriate uses, including the encroachment of the colored race."[34] Soon state highway engineers, almost exclusively White,

Christian men, would begin to draw the thick black lines on maps that would disproportionately uproot, divide, and destroy communities of color in scores of US cities.[35]

Funding never materialized for Boston's first elevated expressway, and the plan collected dust. The Great Depression, the high price tag, and limited federal funding made the project unrealistic. The concept, however, would persist, and a starkly different-looking elevated Central Artery from the artful rendering would open to traffic two decades later.

Outside of the largest cities, highway plans generally remained rural. Texas, for example, was one of the last states to develop a highway department and start funding and building highways. Although Texas received the largest funding allocation of any state from the Federal-Aid Road Act of 1916, only one hundred miles of road had been paved by 1923.[36] After a corruption scandal slowed work and ended federal aid, a reorganized Texas Highway Department began building and planning the state highway system in earnest using revenues from vehicle registration fees, a gas tax, and county bonds.

The 1933 Federal-Aid Highway maps provided a starkly different view of urban highways in Dallas than the visions presented to city officials in Boston or New York. The plan showed ten designated highways converging on Dallas, the country's thirty-third largest city in 1930, but stopping at its borders. State Highway 360, where President George H. W. Bush would sign the 1991 highway act ushering in the end of the interstate era, did not appear in the plan, nor did any of the other major highways running north-south in between Fort Worth and Dallas. Multiple state highways and interstates now converge and connect along massive interchanges spanning more than six hundred feet in width. Together, these highways consume about a thousand acres of land area in downtown Dallas. Although Dallas has expanded and grown around highways over time, the 1930 city limits still contain 16 percent residents and 21 percent of jobs, particularly high-paying office jobs.

Envisioning the Modern Urban Expressway

Over the next decade, US highway policy became increasingly focused on the jobs created by building urban highways. With the Great Depression, Presidents Herbert Hoover and, to a greater extent, Franklin D. Roosevelt promoted and funded roadbuilding to stimulate the economy and provide employment. In 1930, Hoover nearly doubled annual federal road aid from $75 million to $125 million. Through the New Deal, Roosevelt's administration put an additional $1.8 billion into roadbuilding.[37] Marking this shift in federal priorities, the Bureau of Public Roads moved from the Department of Agriculture to the Federal Works Administration and became the Public Roads Administration in 1939. This focus on employment continues to pervade federal transportation laws and roadbuilding. As Bush described his signature transportation law a half century later, "Really it is summed up by three words: jobs, jobs, jobs. And that's the priority."[38] President Joseph Biden's 2021 federal transportation law's full name is the Infrastructure Investment and Jobs Act.

Many New Deal–era urban highways, such as Connecticut's Merritt Parkway, resemble most closely the images and renderings presented in Boston's *Thoroughfare Plan* and New York's *Regional Plan*. The parkway's two lanes of winding road, separated by a wide grassy median and passing below stone bridges, provided connections across the state and an alternative to the congested Boston Post Road. The parkway continues to serve around sixty thousand car trips per day and, when Interstate 95 is congested, is frequently part of the quickest path between Boston and New York.

The National Register of Historic Places describes the roadway as "the quintessential parkway," "an outgrowth of the City Beautiful Movement," and the culmination of "a generation of experiments in combining the talents of engineers, landscape architects, and architects to create parkways that served recreational purposes and gave aesthetic pleasure while providing safe transportation."[39] The document also sets the parkway in contrast with modern highways, with their focus on high-speed travel and historical connections to Germany's Autobahn. Federal government standards, however, would soon favor the construction of large limited-access urban highways with massive interchanges.

MacDonald and other highway officials visited the Autobahn and other European highway projects in 1936. MacDonald described the completed sections of the Autobahn, which opened the previous year, as "wonderful examples of the best modern road building."[40] He was particularly impressed by the limited access points and complete grade separation, which allowed for the smooth flow of substantial traffic volumes. Unlike in Germany, where the modern superhighway bypassed towns and cities, MacDonald saw the roadways as particularly applicable in and around the large cities and metropolitan areas where congestion was most substantial.

Whereas MacDonald, a technocratic roadbuilder, noted the German Autobahn being constructed in advance of the traffic that might eventually match its substantial capacity, others saw its military purposes. As Representative Wilburn Cartwright, chairman of the Committee on Roads in the House, put it to AASHO representatives in 1938:

> I was in Germany this summer and when I think of super-highways, I think of Germany, for, regardless of what we think of him as a man, we must give Fuehrer Hitler credit for building a system of super-highways in his country which are second to none in the world today. It is undoubtedly true that the construction of these highways was prompted by the same motives which are behind Germany's huge expenditures for armament and for the building up

> of her army to the limit of her manpower. The super-highways will become very important assets to that nation in the event of another war in Europe.[41]

Around the same time, a new vision of urban highways began to enter the popular imagination. Five million people visited the General Motors' *Futurama* exhibit at the 1939 New York World's Fair. Through models, images, and full-scale recreations of cities, neighborhoods, interchanges, and pedestrian walkways, *Futurama* showed an American landscape transformed by superhighways. According to its designer, Norman Bel Geddes, *Futurama* was the most popular attraction of any World's Fair.[42]

Bel Geddes drew closely on the most modern practices and arguments of contemporary highway engineers. The introduction to his book on the exhibit credited AASHO, state highway departments, the Institute of Traffic Engineers, the Public Roads Administration, and others. His renderings contained modern highway interchanges, cloverleafs, limited use zoning around highways, and reference materials from existing roadway projects. Bel Geddes also presented the naïve view that modern highways could "make automobile collisions impossible and … eliminate completely traffic congestion."[43] City planners and road designers needed only focus on supplying roadway. Demand was not an issue. He argued that parking fees and tolls were simply a tax and unrelated to congestion. Highway planners should predict demand for traffic and provide supply in the form of grade-separated highways.

Unlike the parkways and elevated highways presented in plans from a decade earlier, Bel Geddes's highways were not shaped by surrounding land uses or landscapes, but shaped them. He visualized "how a motorway system may be laid down over the entire country—across mountains, over rivers and lakes, through cities and past towns—never deviating from a direct course."[44] Pedestrians were no longer accommodated by separate crossing or parallel facilities, as in previous highway plans, but moved entirely to a segregated and elevated walkway system. Parking no longer hindered the smooth flow of vehicles but existed entirely in underground and segregated parking spaces. Massive new high-rise and midrise buildings grew around massive urban interchanges. completely replacing existing urban fabrics (figure 2-3). Single buildings accommodated entire communities. As Bel Geddes described, "The doctor will be there, and the butcher, the movie, the mayor, the grocer, the drug store, the per shop, bank, post office, employment agency."[45]

Unlike the 1930 renderings of the Central Artery, these images would have been alien to a typical World Fair visitor. The modern superhighways did not fit neatly into existing space, nor did the buildings that surrounded them. As if to articulate its realness, Bel Geddes projected his modern utopia onto the maps and forms of existing cities, towns, and landscapes twenty years into the future. Echoing Boston's 1930 plan and future interstate plans, lines drawn at a bird's-eye view eliminated and disconnected entire neighborhoods and commercial corridors.

Bel Geddes's visions also introduced a new moralistic argument beyond combatting the evils of congestion or ushering in the modern age. Highways did not just consume urban land to make space. Highways served to intentionally depopulate cities, populate the suburbs, flatten the difference in value between central and peripheral land, and enable development of unexploited and beautiful countryside. Urban highways would do no less than prevent the accumulated evils of the unplanned city and allow its continued existence as a civilized entity.[46] Bel Geddes concluded his exhibit book with hopes of avoiding US involvement in the war in Europe but acknowledged the importance of a national highway system for defense.

These moral arguments and *Futurama*'s urban renderings are almost entirely derivative, plagiarized even. Bel Geddes, a talented and well-regarded designer, would have almost certainly been exposed to Le

Figure 2-3. Futurama's wide and modern expressways divide a landscape of large modernist towers where residents live, eat, sleep, play, and park their vehicles. (Photo courtesy of General Motors 2025.)

Corbusier's influential writing and architectural drawings when working with Eva La Gallienne on a production of *Jeanne d'Arc* in Paris in the 1920s.[47] Le Corbusier's 1925 *Plan Voisin* proposed essentially eliminating the Marais district along the Seine and replacing it with a series of tower blocks running along major arterial highways.

Urbanisme, sometimes translated as *The City of Tomorrow and Its Planning*, presents Le Corbusier's vision and earlier proposals for a modern city.[48] He saw the poverty, desolation, and congestion of parts of Depression-era European cities as a direct result of their unplanned medieval roots. He believed that only a radical, strictly ordered physical and social restructuring could move Europe's cities past the destruction of the Great War and into a prosperous and fulfilling modernity and that city centers were terminally ill and needed to be demolished and rebuilt. Destruction and rebirth were essential underpinnings of *Futurama*'s popular vision for modern urban expressways.

Financing the Modern Urban Expressway

As the vision, scale, and scope of modern expressways expanded, so too did their price tag. At the same time, simply rebuilding and maintaining the existing Federal-Aid Highway System would cost substantially more than was being spent. Many highway planners began to argue for a substantially increased federal role. In a 1936 speech to AASHO representatives, MacDonald noted that the amount of new federal road construction, particularly on less-used roadways, had surpassed state highway departments' "ability properly to improve and maintain."[49] Bel Geddes, like Whitten and so many other highway builders, had argued that the price of inaction was higher than the cost of building the new highways. These costs, moreover, would only increase over time. The federal government took a more pragmatic view. Through the Federal-Aid Highway Act of 1938, Congress tasked the Bureau of Public Roads with developing a feasibility study for up to six toll-financed transcontinental superhighways. Roosevelt sketched the general locations for MacDonald, who spent the next year developing a plan.[50]

Toll Roads and Free Roads, delivered to Congress in April 1939, concluded that even under the most optimistic cost and revenue assumptions, tolls would only cover around 40 percent of the costs of the system.[51] Although MacDonald may have been unduly pessimistic about toll roads in general,[52] the report argued that only a few sections of highway would raise enough revenue to cover their annualized costs. In Indiana, the typical roadway carried just fifty-one vehicles daily, not even enough to cover half of average maintenance costs.[53] In short, the costs of the highway system outweighed drivers' willingness to pay to use them. Only in and around large cities did the traffic volumes economically justify wide, limited-access superhighways. MacDonald supported these conclusions with detailed charts, origin-destination studies, speed-flow diagrams, and available information on land acquisition and construction costs. While MacDonald's total estimated annual cost was substantially larger than the federal road budget of the time, it was an order of magnitude lower than what the federal government currently spends on highways each year.

Undeterred, MacDonald produced a recommendation for a federally funded highway system without tolls that was nearly double the length of the fourteen-thousand-mile tolled highway system that the Bureau of Public Roads had deemed financially infeasible. This proposed highway system, supported by the Department of War and state highway departments, would connect and enter all major US cities and metropolitan areas. MacDonald's report concluded that in large cities, nothing less than the creation of an elevated urban highway would suffice.[54] The recommended program would also finance the construction and improvement of secondary roads and feeder roads. MacDonald argued that these road improvements were essential to increasing traffic on the primary highway network.

The report emphasized urban highways and urban problems. Of note, the report highlighted the difficulty in acquiring sufficient land to build wide expressways in the urban areas with the most traffic. Land acquisition accounted for 90 percent of the total costs of building Woodward Avenue in Detroit and a similar share of the estimated costs of the Central Artery in Boston. Echoing Le Corbusier, MacDonald argued for using land takings for highways by eminent domain to clear blighted areas. In a letter to Roosevelt, MacDonald's boss, Secretary of Agriculture Henry A. Wallace, touted a major side benefit of highway construction as the "elimination of unsightly and unsanitary districts where land values are constantly depreciating."[55] Congestion was contributing to cities' slow moral and physical decay. Recognizing the tremendous cost of urban land takings, MacDonald recommended the creation of a Federal Land Authority that could purchase land and hold land for state highway departments.

Neither Roosevelt, nor Wallace, nor MacDonald, nor the many urban highway planners appears to have recognized the contradiction between land values being so high that they required federal support to acquire and land values being so low that clearing the land was valuable in and of itself. MacDonald even lamented that new urban developments "will block the logical projection of the needed new arteries into the city center."[56] The report argued that land should be taken to prevent blight but also to prevent new development that might hinder urban highway construction.

Plate 50 of *Toll Roads and Free Roads* presented one such "decadent area fringing a city business section," stating that "almost untenable, occupied by the humblest citizens, they fringe the business district, and form the city's slums—a blight near its very core!"[57] The image showed connected, primarily well-maintained, and occupied three-story brick row houses and a first-floor corner shop (figure 2-4). A few dozen residents, primarily Black and wearing suits and dress hats, went about their daily business. The built environment does not look dissimilar from many low-vacancy, low- to moderate-income neighborhoods in some cities, like Baltimore and Philadelphia.

While the report never mentioned race, the subtext is clear. Urban highways could be a powerful tool for Negro removal, a term James Baldwin popularized two decades later to describe the disproportionate, intentional, and forced removal of tens of thousands of Black residents in the name of urban renewal and freeway construction. Highway plans in the 1930s and 1940s frequently made explicit mention of slum removal. Some, such as Robert Moses's plans for Baltimore and Detroit, clearly and directly targeted Black neighborhoods.[58]

Figure 2-4. Federal highway planners' chosen image to articulate the moral and physical decay of urban areas to be cleared with highway investments. (Bureau of Public Roads, *Toll Roads and Free Roads*, plate 50.)

Roosevelt and MacDonald appear to have had somewhat differing views of the purpose of the proposed Federal Land Authority. In a letter introducing the report to Congress, Roosevelt emphasized how excess land takings might be used to finance the highway system. New highways would increase the property value of surrounding land, and the federal government would recuperate costs by selling or leasing the land. MacDonald, by contrast, presented the land authority as a mechanism for preserving rights-of-way for future highway widenings. The authority would draw on federal authority to purchase rather than sell land. The report even discussed the ways that urban freeways could reduce the value of adject properties. There are no detailed estimates of revenues raised through land sales, only the high and unresolved cost of acquiring urban land for highways.

With financing still unresolved, Roosevelt appointed MacDonald to head another committee studying the development of a cross-country highway system.[59] The committee's report, *Interregional Highways*, drew heavily on analysis and arguments from *Toll Roads and Free Roads* and presented a plan for a thirty-four-thousand-mile highway system that closely resembled the Interstate Highway System. The estimated annual costs would be $750 million over twenty years, a substantial increase in spending and about a fourth of contemporary federal highway spending after adjusting for inflation. Roosevelt also submitted a highway bill to fund the proposal. After nearly a year of negotiation in the House and Senate, Roosevelt signed the Federal-Aid Highway Act of 1944 on December 20.

The act provided $500 million per year—roughly $9 billion in 2024 dollars and about a fifth of contemporary annual highway spending—over three years for road construction with a one-to-one match from state highway departments.[60] Roughly half would go to the Federal-Aid Highway System, a fourth to secondary feeder roads, and another fourth to urban highways. Unlike construction costs, federal funds could only be used for up to a third of land acquisition costs. The act also prompted state highway departments to begin mapping and planning urban highway networks through major cities and metropolitan areas. These would form the basis of a yellow-covered 1955 report documenting how the interstate highways would move and connect through one hundred of the country's largest cities.

Although highway spending increased after 1944, so did the costs of roadbuilding. Rapid economic growth after World War II led to a substantial increase in the motor vehicle fleet and total vehicle travel. Mass homebuilding, commercial expansion, and European reconstruction contributed to material shortages and a rapid inflation in construction costs. President Harry Truman limited and even halted federal highway spending for two months in 1946 to reduce inflation pressures on homebuilding materials.[61] Unlike after World War I, the government explicitly chose not to repurpose wartime construction equipment for roadbuilding.[62]

The Federal-Aid Highway System continued progressing at a similar pace to the previous decade despite increasing traffic, construction costs, and maintenance costs. In a 1949 speech to AASHO, MacDonald lamented that "we are seriously losing in the battle with traffic."[63] With the Korean War straining the federal budget and putting additional inflationary pressures on raw materials, Truman capped highway spending.

As the recommended widths and size of interchanges increased to accommodate more traffic, paying for urban highways and a regional interstate system remained the major sticking point. The general aversion to toll roads continued beyond Eisenhower's sacking of MacDonald in 1953. Roosevelt's vision for land value taxes never progressed beyond the concept in his introductory letter to *Toll Roads and Free Roads*. State and federal gas taxes and vehicle registration fees did not always go to roadbuilding and were insufficient to the task of building and maintaining a national highway system. With little progress made on funding an interstate system, state governors and highway officials began to argue that the federal government should eliminate the federal gas tax and get out of the business of roadbuilding entirely.[64] Massachusetts issued bonds to start building parts of its 1948 metropolitan highway plan for Boston, including the Central Artery, without federal support.[65] Texas similarly began building urban highways, including a long-planned Central Expressway cutting through Dallas's segregated Freedman's Town to the north and into downtown.

In 1954, Eisenhower appointed a special committee headed by General Lucius D. Clay to work with state governors to develop a plan to fund and build an interstate system over ten years. Clay was a board member of General Motors and had been Eisenhower's deputy during World War II and, later, military governor of occupied West Germany. The Clay committee's report identified a $101 billion need to build, upgrade, and maintain the proposed national highway system. The report recommended continued funding of secondary highways and feeder roads but also recommended a substantial increase in the amount and share of federal funds used to build a 37,600-mile system of interstate highways. Using bonds paid by federal gas taxes, the federal government would pay $27 billion of the estimated $29 billion interstate costs. In addition to rejecting the use of tolls, the report recommended incorporating existing state toll roads into the proposed interstate system and reimbursing states for their construction. Urban highways represented 12 percent of the total interstate miles but were projected to carry half of all vehicle travel and account for half of the total program costs.[66]

In a statement to the Senate's Subcommittee on Public Roads, Clay offered four main justifications for the highway system: national defense, emergency evacuation of cities, economic growth, and, most importantly, because the automobile had "become a very essential part of American family life."[67] In an opening letter to the report, Eisenhower emphasized traffic fatalities, growing congestion, and the moral argument for returning fuel and vehicle taxes to road users in the form of new roadways. Gone were the detailed analyses of highway use or construction costs that were featured in *Toll Roads and Free Roads*.

After a year and a half of negotiations in the house and senate, Eisenhower signed the Federal-Aid Highway Act of 1956, known more commonly as the National Interstate and Defense Highways Act, into law. As with earlier highway laws, the federal government supported primary and secondary Federal-Aid Highways. The law now also allocated additional and substantially increased funding to develop the forty-thousand-mile Interstate Highway System. The federal government would cover 90 percent of highway construction and land acquisition. The law also explicitly empowered the secretary of commerce and the attorney general to acquire land for states in the interest of highway construction. A 50 percent increase in the federal gas tax and the creation of the dedicated Highway Trust Fund provided financing without increasing government debt. By funding the program so generously and capping the total length but not the width nor the cost of the Interstate Highway System, the law greatly encouraged and perhaps even ensured overbuilding.[68]

Over the next two decades, the newly created Federal Highway Administration would spend a half trillion inflation-adjusted dollars on interstate highways. In the process, a million residents would lose their homes. Cities, towns, and countryside would be transformed. Total vehicle travel would double. The trucking industry would boom. Traffic fatalities would increase. Congestion would persist. And spending would increase, even as the system neared completion.

CHAPTER 3

Building the Interstates

We have good reason to be anxious … that neither of these administrators had the slightest notion of what they were doing.—Lewis Mumford, Address to the Hartford Conference, 1957

Opposition to urban highways predated the National Interstate and Defense Highways Act. Although their pleas were initially ignored, residents of Chinatown managed to convince sympathetic public officials to sink a portion of Boston's Central Artery to reduce the harmful impacts of displacement and disconnection that were apparent in other neighborhoods through which the highway had already cut. By contrast, scant record exists of any public opposition to the Central Expressway tearing through Dallas's Freedman's Town. As with interstate construction, early highway building disproportionately harmed ethnic and racial minorities. While it took decades for widespread protests to slow highway building and eventually shift public policy, the roots of most major complaints were established well before interstate construction began in earnest. In addition to citizen protests, academics, planners, politicians, real estate developers, and a range of business elites criticized various aspects of the program from the beginning. Highway building was poorly coordinated with existing land uses and frequently created blight as it destroyed neighborhoods. Highway building encouraged sprawl and consumed parks, the natural environment, and countryside. Highway building consistently failed to reduce congestion and even exacerbated it in central cities. Interstate construction was extravagant and wasteful with uncertain benefits. Transit could do a better job of moving people in central cities. Put simply, public officials were blithely undertaking the largest experiment in social planning in US history with almost no understanding of the larger social, environmental, or economic impacts. The federal government's $9 to $1 match did not just solve the problem of the high cost of urban land and encourage overbuilding, it enabled state and federal highway planners to ignore and circumvent the many concerns about the program as they radically transformed US cities, suburbs, and towns.

The First Urban Expressways

The first modern urban expressways predated the National Interstate and Defense Highways Act. Early examples, like Boston's Central Artery and Dallas's Central Expressway, cut through neighborhoods and disproportionately burdened racial and ethnic minorities. Neither expressway did much to achieve the stated goals or meet the claims of the highway builders that promoted them. Neither project solved congestion. In fact, the congestion that followed construction was nearly immediate and endemic. Neither supported interstate travel or military movements. Neither saved lives. More likely, these expressways led to additional fatalities by encouraging more urban travel at faster speeds. By providing states and cities a $9 to $1 match, the National Interstate and Defense Highways Act ensured that these types of projects would continue despite their expense, failure to achieve stated aims, and disruption of neighborhoods and urban fabric. Fearful of losing federal funds, some state and city officials worked behind the scenes to limit the damage and reshape highway policy. Others seemed to relish the opportunity to clear urban neighborhoods in the name of progress. The highway engineers and planners, supported by maps and analysis produced by other highway engineers and planners, worked to deflect criticism and build highways.

The Central Artery

Constructing Boston's Central Artery destroyed approximately a thousand midrise apartment buildings and local businesses throughout the 1950s. In his book on transportation planning in Boston, MIT professor Ralph Gakenheimer referred to this early urban highway investment in a densely populated city "as a kind of landmark of urban disruption."[1] The Boston Public Library maintains a 225-photo online album of the destruction and construction of the elevated highway.[2] Most focus on the scale of changes: before, during, and after photos of urban blocks, their destruction, and the construction of mass interchanges, like those from the Futurama exhibit of 1939. A series of photographs from nearby buildings provides a sense of the scale of destruction of what would have otherwise been some of the most valuable real estate in the United States today (figure 3-1). Many photos feature construction workers, either in action or posed smiling in groups. Just one photo shows any of the thousands whose lives the project uprooted or disrupted (figure 3-2). An elderly shopkeeper stands in front of her shop with her hands by her hips. She wears and displays patterned dresses along her shop's front window and front entrance. Workers in front of her shop clear rubble and debris. Another shopkeeper, out of view, displays bananas for sale on empty crates and a wooden table.

Residents and business owners protested the taking and destruction of their commercial corridor and surrounding neighborhoods. Complaints went largely unrecorded and had little impact.[3] Representatives of the Massachusetts Department of Public Works (DPW) simply

Figure 3-1. Demolition of entire blocks of midrise buildings on some of the most valuable real estate in the United States made room for Boston's Central Artery. (Courtesy of the Boston Public Library, Leslie Jones Collection.)

responded that the project was consistent with the 1948 metropolitan highway plan and that the chosen route was best for traffic flow and downtown business.[4] The matter had already been decided. As Fred Salvucci, engineer, professor, and former state secretary of transportation, said of the era of Massachusetts's highway construction, "It's just people didn't matter, they were gonna get pushed out of the way, and that's the way it was in the highway program."[5] The 1948 highway plan's earlier recommendation that tenant relocation should be "an integral part of a highway project"[6] was simply not heeded. Residents were left to fend for themselves.

Several years into construction, the destruction was apparent. The new public works commissioner, John Volpe, set about burying the

Figure 3-2. Workers load or unload truck in front of business during Central Artery construction. (Courtesy of the Boston Public Library, Leslie Jones Collection.)

remaining sections of the Central Artery where possible.[7] Two decades later as US secretary of transportation, Volpe oversaw the then controversial decision to cancel the section of Interstate 310 that would have devastated New Orleans's French Quarter. Most other urban highways proposed in the metropolitan highway plan had to wait for additional federal finance. The political and financial costs of urban land acquisition were simply too high without external incentives.

Central Expressway

A plaque at the entrance to 3600 North Central Expressway, just off the expressway's three-hundred-foot-wide right-of-way, commemorates Dallas's first freedman's cemetery. Three miles and five to ten minutes away by highway, the African American Museum of Dallas houses a permanent exhibit paying tribute to the cemetery and the surrounding Freedman's Town, Dallas's most prominent historical Black neighborhood. The Central Expressway's construction "virtually eliminated all above-ground reminders of the cemetery,"[8] paved over parts of the cemetery, destroyed homes and businesses along the widened highway, and divided North Dallas in two. Future freeway construction further divided and uprooted the community.[9] "Freedman's Cemetery is one of the few historic and cultural resources remaining in the area where for more than 100 years existed the largest segregated African American community in Dallas and one of the largest in the country."[10]

As with Boston's Central Artery and many other early highway projects, plans for Dallas's Central Expressway predated construction by decades. The initial roadway, proposed by city planner George Kessler, would have converted a railway bed into an at-grade boulevard, like those presented in New York's Regional Plan. Freedman's Town, founded shortly after the end of the Civil War, grew rapidly along this railway corridor in the early twentieth century. Residents came from a range of socioeconomic positions and included doctors, workmen, blacksmiths, preachers, farmers, and engineers, according to early city directories and archaeological remains from burial sites.[11] Segregation and Jim Crow laws restricted Black residents from living or owning property in most other neighborhoods. This initial proposal for a one-hundred-foot corridor would have involved substantially fewer land takings and maintained pedestrian connections across the neighborhood and into central Dallas.

The destruction created by the Central Expressway in the late 1940s went largely unrecorded. White newspapers focused on difficulties acquiring the railway corridor and hopes that removing residents would not delay the project.[12] The Black-owned *Dallas Express* told the story of families losing homes they had lived in for generations with nowhere to move in the legally segregated city.[13] The city government provided no relocation assistance and severely restricted the neighborhoods where ousted residents could move. The Central Expressway dedication program explicitly thanks the Southern Pacific Railway Company for making the roadway possible and explains the challenges of acquiring rights-of-way from multiple railway companies.[14] There is no mention of Freedman's Town or any other private land takings. While the Massachusetts DPW largely dismissed residents' concerns about Central Artery, it is difficult to imagine state officials even bothering to listen to Freedman's Town residents in Jim Crow Dallas.

The cemetery remained largely erased for decades until the 1980s, when the Texas Department of Transportation (TxDOT) sought to rebuild and expand the Central Expressway.[15] TxDOT archaeologists and staff from the University of Texas Southwestern Medical Center staff exhumed, documented, and reburied the remains of 1,157 individuals over the course of three years. Documentations included 33,000 pages of analysis and 185,000 photographs of artifacts and remains.[16] The cemetery had been the primary burial grounds for Black residents of Dallas from 1869 to 1907. The TxDOT project also supported the creation of a memorial and exhibit documenting the history of the Freedman's Town's cemetery and residents.

Yet this history also remains largely ignored. The Texas State Library and Archives maintains an online exhibit on the Texas State Highway Department from 1917 to 1968 that includes before and after photos of the Central Expressway. The 1947 photo shows a series of shacks along a rail corridor, with a large puddle of water and an abandoned tire. The 1949 photograph of the six-lane expressway looks like it is from an entirely different location, the geographic and physical features erased. The caption reads: "This photograph shows the Central Expressway Project which was constructed in Dallas under the supervision of the State Highway Department of Texas. It is illustrative of the type of roadway which must be planned and constructed in order to handle the traffic needs of our great metropolitan areas in Texas."[17] There is no mention of Freedman's Town, the cemetery, or the residents who lost their homes.

Early Critiques

The backlash to urban highways and the interstate program was immediate. At a 1957 conference sponsored by the Connecticut General Life Insurance Company in Hartford, organizers framed the highway program as a substantial but largely unrealized opportunity to help improve metropolitan areas.[18] Attendees and speakers included academics, journalists, heads of automobile associations, bankers, real estate developers, consultants, manufacturers, planners, and state and federal highway officials.[19]

Speakers' prepared conference papers leveled several primary critiques. The program focused exclusively on highways while ignoring land use planning, mass transit, pedestrians, and other federal housing and urban renewal programs. New interstates were displacing nearly one hundred thousand families per year but providing no relocation support. New highways were also encouraging rapid suburban expansion and consuming rural land with little intention or planning. Highways were not solving congestion and, moreover, could not provide sufficient access to dense urban cores without replacing most of the urban core with freeways and parking.

Real estate developer and future congressman James Scheuer began his paper on the housing impacts of the highway program by saying, "It is a significant and disturbing commentary on the state of the nationwide movement to replan our metropolitan areas today, that the $100 billion Interstate highway program, perhaps the most potent urban planning tool of the 20th century, has been placed in the hands of highway engineers."[20] Speakers and attendees presented multiple recommendations. The critics' main conclusion was that urban interstate construction should be halted until adequate land use planning could be conducted.[21] Much of the planning had already been conducted but was entirely supplanted by state and federal highway engineers whose roadbuilding experiences were primarily rural.[22]

Federal Highway Administration director Bertram Tallamy took the criticism in stride and remained resolute as he closed the first day's events. He reiterated the importance of the highway system and hailed the interstate program as the chance of a century to eliminate urban blight and revive urban cores. He agreed that highway officials should plan carefully but cautioned against planning schemes that would slow highway construction and hinder progress. Improving vehicle flow in cities would reverse urban decline and provide cities with a bright future.[23]

Author and planning scholar Lewis Mumford gave the event's final speech, summarizing the weekend's critiques. After a meandering opening full of jokes and reflections on the event, Mumford took Tallamy and earlier speaker Albert Cole, administrator of the Housing and Home Finance Agency, to task. The federal agencies were not sufficiently coordinated, Mumford stated. Each held expertise in "their own narrow line of thinking and of acting," and neither understood the full reach or impact of the policies they enacted. He continued, "If they had really any notion of what they were doing, they would not appear as blithe and cocky over the way they were doing it as they actually appeared the other night as we listened to it." Mumford concluded that Americans' love of automobiles had allowed Congress to pass the Interstate and Defense Highways Act without sufficient study or consideration of the consequences. Highway planning was too important to be left to the highway planners, whose "one-dimensional thinking will be ruinous, no matter how expertly it is conceived and how carefully it is carried out."[24]

Three decades later, Federal Highway Administration director of highway policy and unofficial interstate historian Lee Mertz reflected: "The conference turned into a kind of 60 Minutes ambush interview.

The highway folks were completely unprepared for what they ran into. Mumford and the city planners really took the highway folks apart."[25] The conference made national news and painted an ugly picture of the highway program and federal highway builders.

Critiques continued throughout the interstate program's infancy. *Reader's Digest* published "Our Great Big Highway Bungle," an article that focused on waste, mismanagement, and outright corruption.[26] Future US senator Daniel Patrick Moynihan's 1960 article "New Roads and Urban Chaos" charged the interstate program with being extravagant, wasteful, regionally unfair, and poorly planned.[27] Citing a report from the General Accounting Office, Moynihan singled out a series of freeway interchanges that cost $384,000 (around $4 million in 2024 dollars) and served just eighty-nine cars per day. With the federal government covering 90 percent of costs, any project looked good from local policymakers' perspectives. Previous federal laws that covered up to 60 percent of costs had done little to spark highway construction. Mostly, however, Moynihan criticized interstate construction for destroying urban neighborhoods, cutting cities and towns from their waterfronts, consuming the countryside, and promoting urban sprawl. More roads meant more driving, and the interstate highway program represented an unprecedented venture into national metropolitan planning with scant consideration of the environmental, social, or physical consequences. "For good or ill, the location of the Interstate arterials would, more than any other factor, determine how growth would take place. Yet no planning provisions of any kind were included," he wrote.[28]

Critique of the highway program was not limited to academics, planners, and journalists. Multiple sources have recounted President Dwight Eisenhower's surprise and dismay at learning, stuck in traffic from interstate construction in 1959, that interstates would cut through instead of circumventing cities.[29] In a meeting a year later, Eisenhower indicated that running "Interstate routes through the congested parts of the cities was entirely against his original concept and wishes."[30] Costs had also spiraled, largely due to urban highways. In just two years, the estimated cost of the Interstate Highway System had increased from $27.5 billion to $39.9 billion.

Eisenhower appointed Major General John Bragdon to head a commission to investigate and make recommendations related to the interstate highway program. Bragdon, a decorated military engineer and former engineering instructor, was Eisenhower's West Point classmate and had served on his Council of Economic Advisors. The committee, which included former highway department heads, professors, other retired military officers, and a staff member from the Bureau of Public Roads, collected and compiled information on the interstate program over the next year and a half.[31]

The Bragdon Committee's first interim report echoed many critiques raised at the Hartford conference three years earlier.[32] Urban highways could not and would not solve urban transportation problems. As reported: "The use of the controlled access highway has been found not to solve the rush hour problem in Los Angeles";[33] road investments were "often self-defeating";[34] and "roads in themselves increase the demand for cars."[35] Accommodating all urban movement by cars would require repaving most of a city in highways and parking. Echoing Mumford's critique of narrow and one-dimensional thinking, the report continued: "An engineering estimate based on 'needs' predicated on estimated future vehicle miles, although useful as a tool for application to a highway route, becomes fallacious as an over-all measuring rod. The vehicle miles of the future can be as fantastic as the quantity of roads and available funds can make them."[36]

Instead, the Bragdon report argued that highway plans should be a part of holistic transportation plans, which in turn should be part of larger metropolitan plans. Transit, which could accommodate four to twenty times more passengers than highways in an equivalent space, should be given greater support and priority in urban areas. The report suggested that "the problem can be alleviated by the use of rapid transit, other forms of mass transit, and by new methods of control of traffic which are evolving. These are less expensive than structures that destroy existing physical assets including other transportation means."[37]

The Bragdon Committee also noted that urban highways were the major reason for increased program costs and ran counter to the Interstate System's stated military goals: "The Department of Defense has emphasized that outer bypass roads are more favored for purposes of defense."[38] The report recommended prioritizing outer ring roads, avoiding urban interstates in dense locations, reducing federal support to 50 percent for projects that accommodated local traffic, relying more actively on toll roads, and incorporating interstate construction into a larger comprehensive planning process. Ideally, the authors argued, the federal government should prioritize investments that promoted interstate commerce and defense.

The Highway Builders Respond

State and federal highway engineers generally dismissed these critiques and doubled down on their technical expertise, existing highway plans, and an unassailable conviction in the moral correctness of what they were doing. Highway builders believed that they had the interests of the public at heart and that opposition came from special interests. As one American Association of State Highway Officials (AASHO) official put it in 1958: "Try as we might, we have not been able to halt the outcry of the motel, restaurant, and service station people. Most of the public are on our side, but they make up the great silent majority.... We can only hope that as the Interstate program pushes ahead, in spite of this opposition, the benefits will come to be so gratifying that the tide will automatically turn in the right direction."[39]

In her social history of the bulldozer, planning historian and colleague

Francesca Ammon draws extensively from the Public Works Historical Society's interviews with engineers who helped build the Interstate System.[40] Throughout the interviews, engineers expressed a great faith in the work they were doing and belief that the benefits of the many motorists outweighed the harm to specific individuals or neighborhoods. It was the job of highway engineers to convince communities of the correctness of their plans. Alf Johnson, AASHO executive secretary, warned that highway builders should avoid agreeing to any roadway reallocations lest subsequent locations be entirely blocked by public and political pressure.[41] As environmental and social criticism continued, some highway officials reported feeling betrayed.[42]

In interviews in the late 1980s, Tallamy, first director of the Federal Highway Administration, expressed admiration and longing for the days when a small number of highway officials could determine where and how urban highways would go despite opposition. "You have got to some way control the welfare of the public, but a smaller number of people involved," he said.[43] He fondly recalled how he and several other highway officials decided after a brief conversation to widen Interstate 95 outside Washington, DC, with no analysis or public consultation. Environmental and social protections put in place in the 1960s and 1970s merely hindered the good work of highway engineers. Asked somewhat rhetorically whether he thought of himself as a dictator, Tallamy embraced and celebrated the term dictator and his power, responding: "I had the authority to build bridges across them, to move traffic from one side to another. I had authority to build the road anywhere I wanted to make it. I had authority to buy property and sell any. I myself could do it, or my signature on the whole thing, for 680 miles of highway."[44]

This belief in the unique skill of engineers to evaluate and improve the public good pervades the planning documents of the time. The 1948 metropolitan highway plan for Boston, for example, encouraged highway planners to overcome reluctance to land takings by eminent domain: "The natural reluctance on the part of highway officials to force people to vacate their homes in these times of housing shortages, while understandable, has nevertheless resulted in postponement of essential highway projects. On the one hand, the vigorous opposition of persons whose homes are involved is also easily understandable. Arguments that the few must suffer for the benefit of the many fail to impress the man who is told he will have to vacate his home to make way for a projected highway."[45] With the $9 to $1 match, hesitance to use eminent domain all but disappeared. Individuals losing homes and neighborhoods held little sway. As William Bugge, AASHO president and director of the Washington State Department of Highways, reflected: "In Seattle we didn't have any opposition. Oh, we had opposition, but I mean, nothing major.... Most of it was the fact that people were losing their homes and we were displacing a lot of people. You'd just buy them out and let them shift for themselves."[46]

Others' reflections were even more callous. Richard Zettel, a California highway builder, fondly recalled forcing a highway through an undesired section of Los Angeles County by threatening to dump the expressway onto a local street. He explained: "We just bring the freeway down to ground level and dump it on the street—on both sides of El Monte and see how they like them apples. They didn't like them apples. They wanted us to go around El Monte if I understand it."[47]

The highway builders dismissed Mumford, Moynihan, and the Hartford conference's main critiques. Decades later, Tallamy remained derisive of efforts to make highway investments conform to larger comprehensive plans. When asked who was pushing for such reforms, he responded: "I haven't the slightest idea. But whoever it is is a joker. When everybody wants—when anybody wants to stop anything from going ahead, 'Let's have a land-use plan,' or some other plan."[48] AASHO organized additional conferences on the highway program and made sure not to invite any of the critics from Hartford.[49] The highway builders would now do their best to interact only with other highway builders.

Dismissing Bragdon and the president's critiques would be more challenging. Tallamy and his staff made three main points in meetings and written exchanges with Bragdon. First, highway builders had already done the required analysis and mapping to justify and locate interstate highways. Second, urban highways had been on the books since 1944. And third, US representatives and senators had been provided with urban maps when they voted to fund and build the Interstate System. Tallamy recalled a critical meeting with Bragdon and Eisenhower:

> He [Bragdon] was given the responsibility of studying the actions that we were taking in regard to advancing city routes. And he was saying we were always not right in doing that. Well, we had a conference in the President's office. I was defending what we were doing, obviously, and Bragdon had an easel there with a lot of display charts and some young lawyer—no, some young—well, maybe a lawyer—some young officer there operating the charts for him. And he started the discussion and continued for quite—at length. And then I think the President interrupted him and said, "Well, I would like to hear what Mr. Tallamy has to say." … So I said, "Mr. President, I would like to show you this book which was on everybody's desk at the time the Interstate legislation was approved." … And then I leafed through and showed a couple of charts showing the cities and said, "These are the routes in them." He said, "Are you sure? This was on everybody's desk?" I said, "Well I'm pretty sure. I wasn't there at the time, but I am as certain as can be that that was the case." I'm not sure of this, but pretty sure, he turned and asked General Bragdon if that was his recollection too, and I am quite sure he said it was. Well then, I think the President said "I

> didn't realize that that was the case"—something to that effect. Then he said, "The meeting's over gentlemen, I'll let you know what I decide." This is the way it ended.[50]

The book in question—known as the Yellow Book for its yellow cover and officially titled *General Location of National System of Interstate Highways: Including All Additional Routes at Urban Areas Designated in September 1955*—provided the official designation for where the urban Interstate System would go. Prepared in just three months, the Yellow Book contained 101 highway maps, no analysis, and just three bureaucratic sentences:

> General locations of routes of the National System of Interstate Highways, including additional routes into, through, and around urban areas, submitted by several State highway departments, as adjusted, and approved by the Commissioner of Public Roads, September 15, 1955, supplementing the National System of Interstate Highways approved by the Administrator, Federal Works Agency, August 2, 1947. Approved routes, including additions, are shown on the maps herein, one for each urban area. All urban areas on the National System of Interstate Highways not shown in this folio are served by the Interstate routes previously approved passing throughout or around these urban areas.[51]

Some urban maps built on and matched earlier state highway plans. Boston's proposed highways, for example, had already been sited and mapped for the 1948 metropolitan highway plan. That map contains clearly designated geographic and political boundaries. Others, like that of Tucson, Arizona, appear hastily drawn and crudely defined. Some states, like Arizona, Wyoming, and Mississippi, were poorly prepared for the interstate program and were only completing five miles of interstate per year in the program's first five years.[52] Urban boundaries are pixelated and abstract. Major geographic features are excluded. All one hundred urban maps contain thick black lines that indicate the general highway locations. Each black line, drawn from a bird's-eye view, would require the destruction of hundreds and even thousands of homes and businesses. The maps provided the highway builders a singular focus and vision, a road map, as it were, for construction and the moral and technical justification for any financial or social excess. Congress may or may not have had copies of the Yellow Book but had certainly approved the urban interstates.

The Bragdon Committee's report died a quiet death. After a year and half of inquiry and back-and-forth letters and meetings with Tallamy and other officials, Bragdon left the committee to join Eisenhower's Civil Aeronautics Board. His successor Floyd Peterson submitted the Bragdon Committee's final report three days before Eisenhower's last day in office. While the inquiry had shaken up the highway builders with concerns that urban portions of the Interstate System might be abandoned, Tallamy and the Bureau of Public Roads successfully fended off the challenge to the highway builders' authority to designate and build the urban interstates.[53]

Revolt, Refusal, and Incremental Change

Challenges to the highway builders' power and plans would continue for decades. Many challenges would reshape highway locations and lead to gradual reforms to highway construction and federal policy more general. Many others, particularly from Black communities, would go unheeded but bear testament to the disproportionate impacts that highways placed on communities of color: "White Roads through Black Bedrooms," as the *New York Times* headline summarized protests against federal highways.[54] As Ohio engineer Weese reflected, "Most urban areas, where the Interstate has been shoved through, were socially disadvantaged."[55]

In 1959, the San Francisco Board of Supervisors, responding to citizens protests, narrowly voted to oppose planned interstate construction through San Francisco. Although the local government did not control finance, rights-of-way, or construction, California law required municipal approval to shut down roads for demolition and construction.[56] Without such approval, highway construction could not advance. According to California highway builder Zettel, Californian engineers and politicians were happy enough to remove San Francisco's highways from the list and build new ones in Riverside.[57]

A similar law slowed freeway construction in Baltimore, though with less organized intention. Local politicians struggled to agree on where highways should go.[58] After mocking a decades-long back-and-forth highway planning process, the *Baltimore Sun* concluded in 1968:

> If expressway planning is a mess in Baltimore, at least the city has been spared the greater mess of those other cities which already have built their expressways. The nation has been learning what not to do, and presumably Baltimore will be a beneficiary, if ever there comes agreement on what is the right course to follow. A city without much in the way of expressways is not a total loss. It may even have a distinct advantage if national policy some day shifts to funding rapid mass transit systems as the longer-range answer to urban transportation.[59]

New York City's leaders, like those in many other cities, took a quieter and more centralized approach for fear of losing federal highway dollars. Federal funding had given life to Robert Moses's long-standing proposal to build elevated highways cutting across Manhattan. New York City officials, however, did not want the highways, and construction had not begun. Mertz, who "went up to solve New York!"[60] with other Bureau of Public Roads officials, recalled:

> All across the country, the Interstate got realigned where there were pressures. The whole New York City Interstate got realigned along with what the city wanted. For example, the two stalemates were the Cross-Midtown Expressway and the Lower Manhattan Expressway. The Midtown was to connect the Lincoln Tunnel with the Queens Midtown Tunnel, right across Manhattan. The lower Manhattan was to connect the Holland Tunnel to the Williamsburg Bridge. The city was flat-out opposed to those all the time I was there. I remember a night meeting that we had there with the head of the New York Highway Department and Mayor Lindsay and [Governor] Rockefeller's representative … where Burch McMorran, the head of the New York Highway Department, said, "Okay, inside this room I will say to you that I won't build those projects, but I can't say that outside this room because here is what will happen. If I announce that I am not going to build those, the Bureau of Public Roads must, according to the rules set up by the Congress, remove those from the cost estimate. That means next year's apportionment, that the State of New York gets will be so many million dollars less. Every project that we are building in the State of New York will suffer. Right away, next year, that much money will fly away so I can't say that. I will lose it."[61]

Throughout the United States, determined citizen activists and local politicians fought to delay, reroute, downgrade, or entirely prevent urban freeways. In New Orleans, well-connected young activists successfully prevented Interstate 310 from cutting through the French Quarter and separating much of the city from its riverfront. To keep a state highway out of San Antonio's Brackenridge Park, Ralph Yarborough, senator from Texas, inserted a provision in federal law preventing the taking of parklands for highways if other feasible routes existed. The law went all the way to the US Supreme Court in a case related to the siting of Interstate 40 through a park in Memphis, Tennessee.[62] TxDOT responded to Yarborough's law by removing the San Antonio highway from the Federal-Aid Highway System and built it anyway. Former Philadelphia mayor and Pennsylvania senator Joseph Clark accused, on the Senate floor, the highway builders of being uncivilized barbarians for their indifference to historic sites and neighborhoods.[63]

In Boston, a coalition of activists, academics, and neighborhood groups convinced the governor, Frank Sargent, to suspend highway construction until a comprehensive review of highway and transit plans could be conducted. Sargent had taken over as governor when Volpe left Massachusetts to become President Richard Nixon's secretary of transportation.[64] Both men had come up through the DPW, the agency in charge of building the state's highways. Sargent put Alan Altshuler, Harvard professor and future Massachusetts secretary of transportation, in charge of the review, which Altshuler summarized as follows:

> Several months later, rather to our surprise, we came to the conclusion that the Interstate program for the Boston area didn't make any sense at all. That it was going to be devastating in environmental impact terms, that it had never been seriously analyzed in terms of its economic and accessibility consequences, let alone these other adverse side-effect consequences. When one asked the transportation planners, the Department of Public Works officials why it was going through, they basically had no answer except to say that every place in the country was doing it. We should be doing it too.[65]

On February 11, 1970, Sargent announced on statewide television the cancelation of most major highway construction within Boston's first ring road: "Four years ago, I was the commissioner of the Department of Public Works—our road building agency. Then, nearly everyone was sure highways were the only answer to transportation problems for years to come. We were wrong.... Are we really meeting our transportation needs by spending most of our money building roads? The answer is no."[66] One project that remained was a proposal to bury the Central Artery, Boston's original urban highway sin. Volpe, although privately frustrated with Sargent's decision, financed the original study and worked with Tip O'Neill, Ted Kennedy, and other sympathetic politicians in Washington to make sure that cities and states that turned down highways were not also turning down their share of federal highway funds.[67] As Altshuler put it, "It was clear that that if Sargent permanently stopped the highways, the major criticism was not going to be on transportation grounds. It was going to be that he had lost $600 million that was coming to the state of Massachusetts."[68]

Although there were some notable successes, Black communities tended to fare more poorly in efforts to reroute or stop highways, particularly in the Jim Crow South. In Nashville, Tennessee, White highway builders and business leaders pushed Interstate 40 through Black neighborhoods in North Nashville.[69] Despite halting the freeway through the French Quarter, Louisiana's highway builders destroyed much of New Orleans's Black community in Tremé, North Claiborne.[70] Opposition to interstates and letters to President John F. Kennedy did little to spare Black communities in Montgomery and Birmingham, Alabama. Alabama's state highway director Samuel Engelhardt, a White supremacist who would later lead efforts to defy federal antisegregation laws, appears to have intentionally targeted Black communities with highway construction.[71] In Miami, Interstate 95 along with other urban renewal programs helped destroy Overtown, Miami's largest Black community.[72] As in Dallas, segregationist zoning laws made the lack of housing relocation assistance even more onerous for Black families and households.

Federal highway law changed slowly over time in response to the many outrages, protests, and quiet circumventions of federal highway policy. Larger national environmental and social movements also contributed to legislation that would deeply influence the ability of highway builders to build highways. The Federal-Aid Highway Act of 1962 addressed several of the interstate program's early criticisms.[73] First, the new law required states to provide limited relocation assistance for families, businesses, and individuals affected by highway construction. Second, the law required state highway builders to work with local governments in cities of more than fifty thousand to ensure that highways were developed as part of a continuing, comprehensive, and cooperative urban transportation planning process. The law even declared that embracing various modes of transportation besides highways was of national interest. Finally, the law required public meetings and consultation with affected communities.

Change also came to the federal highway builders. Highway administrator Rex Whitton took a starkly less antagonist and arrogant view to planning processes and local communities than his predecessor, Bertram Tallamy. As the 1962 act's provisions came into effect in 1965, Whitton counseled the American Society of Civil Engineers: "The social implications of our actions must be weighed in every step of a highway project, from the location phase through the actual construction. Every conceivable effort must be made to minimize any adverse impact of a new road."[74]

President Lyndon Johnson signed the Urban Mass Transportation Act of 1964 ,which provided federal financial assistance for capital transit investments and created the Federal Transit Administration's predecessor. Further acts continued to provide funds and supported the buyout of bankrupt private transit agencies around the country. Two years later, Johnson created the Department of Transportation, which absorbed the Federal Highway Administration (renamed from the Bureau of Public Roads) and other federal transportation agencies. Alan Boyd, the first secretary of transportation, was a lawyer by training and had never served in the Bureau of Public Roads.

The Federal-Aid Highway Act of 1973, the "culmination of the Freeway Revolt,"[75] allowed cities and metropolitan areas to use federal highway funds for transit as well as highways. This change allowed local politicians to reject unwanted urban highways without fear of losing hundreds of millions of dollars in federal subsidies. No longer would New York politicians keep Manhattan interstates that they had no intention of constructing on the books.

Other laws, like the 1969 National Environmental Protection Act (NEPA), the Clean Air Act of 1970, and 1970 amendments to the Clean Water Act, also affected highway construction. NEPA would have a lasting affect by requiring environmental review for large federal transportation projects. Thenceforth, highway builders would have to explain what they were building and why. Moreover, they would have to consider alternatives through a formalized public process and provide mitigation for large environmental and social impacts. While the racist legacy of the Interstate System is frequently acknowledged, far less has been done to address its disproportionate impacts on Black communities and individuals.

Though a number of interstate projects—including a project to sink Boston's Central Artery—remained incomplete, the last major section connecting the originally planned Interstate Highway System opened in Colorado on October 14, 1992.[76] Eisenhower had signed the Interstate and Defense Highways Act thirty-six and a half years earlier.

Effects of the Interstate

The Interstate Highway System is the largest public works project undertaken in US history. Its construction corresponded with a sustained period of rapid economic growth after World War II, mass suburbanization, and a dramatic increase in the ownership and use of private cars. Was the interstate program worth it? This type of question almost certainly provokes knee-jerk reactions from supporters and critics alike. The question is also largely unanswerable. If you were to compare the system against a country without highways, it would likely pass any reasonable cost-benefit analysis with flying colors. If, by contrast, you were to compare it against a more modest system that did not tear through as much urban fabric or destroy as much of the natural environment, the record would look substantially less attractive.

Examining the areas near planned highways that were never built against highways that were built, economist Nathaniel Baum-Snow estimated that without the interstate program, central cities would have grown by 8 percent instead of decreasing by 17 percent from 1950 to 1990.[77] Baum-Snow estimated that each additional urban highway reduced central city population by 18 percent on average. Similarly, Jeffrey Brinkman and Jeffrey Lin from the Philadelphia Federal Reserve Bank estimated that urban freeways reduced total urban income by around 5 percent. This loss in income and population was, at least to some degree, offset by increases in suburban population and income. Moreover, as the Central Artery and Central Expressway show, cities and states built disruptive urban highways prior to the passage of the National Interstate and Defense Highways Act.

What might have been built in the absence of the act is difficult to deduce. It almost certainly would have been smaller and less disruptive. While many highway engineers seemed to view the Interstate System as inherently good, others took a more nuanced view. Three Ohio highway engineers, for example, agreed that engineers should have "done the obvious—be more sensitive to the people that we are serving and recognize … the economic good isn't necessarily a straight line.… It's a hard lesson. It goes all outside the training that you have as engineers."[78] As an engineer who helped build Interstate 10 through New Orleans reflected, "If we had to do it again, we wouldn't."[79] Mertz linked many of the Interstate System's problems to the $9 to $1 match from the federal government, a match that encouraged states to build ever more and wider infrastructure.[80]

Though disdainful of communities that turned down highways, California highway builder Zettel would have preferred that states run and fund the highway program entirely. He dismissed San Francisco as a "tiny … idiotic place" that highway builders should write off.[81] His main critique, however, was that the federal highway program wasted billions of dollars substantially overbuilding the rural sections of the Interstate System. He explained: "There's stuff out there that has no business being out there. Overpasses that have probably two cars a day. Four lanes.… In Wyoming, Montana, parts of Colorado—they're there. Great planning! Inter-regional! Defense-oriented! Jack rabbits running across the overpasses!"[82] That highway builders seriously considered detonating twenty-two nuclear bombs to clear a path through the Mojave Desert gives a good sense of the willingness to spend resources in unpopulated parts of the country. Fortunately, uncertainty about the fallout duration convinced the California Highway Department to abandon the idea for more expensive conventional blasting.[83]

Examining whether the interstate program was worth it also gives the false impression that the program has concluded. The Interstate and Defense Highways Act of 1956 increased the gas tax from 2 cents to 3 cents per gallon but also announced that the tax would be reduced to 1.5 cents in 1972 when the Interstate System was completed. Five years later, President Kennedy made a temporary 4-cent gas tax permanent. In 1990, just as the last few sections of the originally planned Interstate System were being completed, President George H. W. Bush increased the federal gas tax by 5 cents to 14 cents per gallon. Though the gas tax has not increased since 1993, federal spending continues unabated. Of the total $2.5 trillion inflation-adjusted dollars spent on highways from the Highway Trust Fund since its inception in 1956, about 60 percent has been spent since completion of the Interstate System.[84] In the next two chapters, I examine how, where, and why these public dollars have been spent.

CHAPTER 4

Sipping the ISTEA

We've got to take full advantage of our present opportunity to create a surface transportation program that will meet our present and future needs, not our past problems.—President George H. W. Bush, Remarks to the American Association of State Highway and Transportation Officials, Washington, DC, 1991

On December 18, 1991, President George H. W. Bush signed the Intermodal Surface Transportation Efficiency Act (ISTEA) at a highway construction site on Texas State Highway 360. The $155 billion bipartisan law heralded the biggest shift in federal transportation priorities since President Dwight Eisenhower's 1956 National Interstate and Defense Highways Act. ISTEA (pronounced like the beverage) emphasized environmental soundness, energy efficiency, traffic safety, financial accountability, fiscal responsibility, and the mobility needs of the poor, elderly, and physically disabled. The act prioritized multiple transportation modes, including walking, biking, and transit. ISTEA opened:

> It is the policy of the United States to develop a National Intermodal Transportation System that is economically efficient and environmentally sound, provides the foundation for the Nation to

> compete in the global economy, and will move people and goods in an energy efficient manner. The National Intermodal Transportation System shall consist of all forms of transportation in a unified, interconnected manner, including the transportation systems of the future, to reduce energy consumption and air pollution while promoting economic development and supporting the Nation's preeminent position in international commerce.

Senator Daniel Patrick Moynihan stood to the side as Bush, surrounded by construction workers and policymakers, signed ISTEA. Moynihan, a New York Democrat and chairman of the Water Resources, Transportation, and Infrastructure Subcommittee, had championed the law through the House and Senate.

He had also been an early and vocal critic of the original interstate highway program, calling it extravagant, wasteful, regionally unfair, and poorly planned.[1] Promoting ISTEA thirty years later, Moynihan presented the damage done by the interstate program as largely irreversible: "Now it's done and I think cannot be undone.... Too bad; we have made a mistake."[2] ISTEA would not reverse the negative effects of the highway program but represented a break from past policies and the opportunity to reshape the federal government's role and objectives in financing transportation infrastructure.

The need for a substantial shift in federal transportation policy was apparent. The originally planned Interstate System was nearly complete. The same year as ISTEA's passage, highway officials published a historical report documenting the planning, construction, and development of the Interstate System.[3] The report's conclusion and many of the more than a hundred interviews with highway builders discussed the impending closure of the interstate program. Since the 1970s, a decreasing share of federal highway funds had been going to interstate construction. Instead, federal funds were financing other high-capacity roadways—such as Texas State Highway 360—and the maintenance, repair, and reconstruction of interstate highways. As the national highway system has expanded and aged, the annual costs of repaving, repairing, and rebuilding roads, bridges, and interchanges have increased. The original interstate program had never envisioned these kinds of ongoing costs or shifting priorities. Instead, the law stated that upon completion of the Interstate System, the federal government was to revert its gas tax to pre–Interstate and Defense Highways Act levels. States were to have taken care of maintenance and repairs.

Politicians from both political parties hailed ISTEA as a landmark legislation, a paradigm shift in federal transportation policy. Bush praised the law as "the most important transportation bill since President Eisenhower started the Interstate System 35 years ago."[4] Secretary of transportation Sam Skinner called it a "a landmark piece of legislation that will carry the Nation into the post-Interstate era."[5] Moynihan presented the timing of the transportation act as "a once-in-a-generation opportunity to redefine federal transportation policy."[6] He stated, "We are about to enter a new, post-Interstate era that will emphasize system performance rather than system building."[7] The *New York Times* claimed that ISTEA "dramatically, and for the most part sensibly, refocuses national transportation policy."[8] The law passed by an eight-to-one margin in the House and a ten-to-one margin in the Senate. A couple of years after passage, President Bill Clinton's associate deputy secretary of transportation Robert F. Martinez hailed ISTEA as "the most revolutionary approach to thinking about transportation systems since the creation of the Interstate Highway System." He continued, "It offers a holistic approach to transportation problems that breaks with all precedent."[9]

ISTEA in Action

Despite the bipartisan hype, ISTEA largely failed to meet Bush's goal of a surface transportation program to meet present and future needs instead

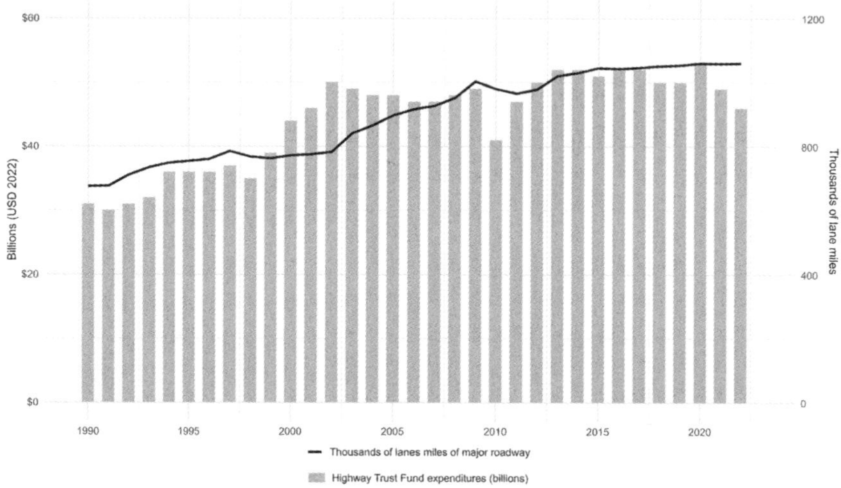

Figure 4-1. Inflation-adjusted highway expenditures (in 2022 dollars) from the Highway Trust Fund and total lane miles of highways, arterials, and major collectors. (Source: Federal Highway Administration, "Highway Statistics.")

of past problems. Annual inflation-adjusted highway expenditures from the Highway Trust Fund—excluding the roughly $10 billion per year currently spent on transit—are $15 billion to $20 billion higher than they were during peak interstate construction (figure 4-1). Although the system was declared complete, the number of lane miles of urban interstate increased 73 percent, from 63,000 in 1991 to 108,000 in 2022.[10]

Reconstruction also frequently widens lanes, shoulders, and rights-of-way without increasing the number of lane miles. Minimum design standards for lane widths, shoulders, and other highway features have increased in the range of 175 percent to 400 percent since the Interstate and Defense Highways Act.[11] The Interstate System is also part of a much larger system of highways, arterials, and major collectors that federal highway laws also help to fund. Between the 1990 and 2020 US Censuses, the lane miles of major urban roadways and highways grew 75 percent faster than the US population.[12] In total, federal, state, and local governments spend more than $200 billion annually on building, rebuilding, widening, and repaving highways and other roads.[13]

ISTEA allowed for increased local influence on design and locations but did not change the fundamental paradigm of national highway policy.[14] States and the federal government raise dedicated revenues through the gas tax. These funds are primarily spent to build, widen, upgrade, and maintain major highways and arterials. In the words of transportation historian Thomas Karnes, ISTEA "did not change methods of financing much but focused more on the contribution of states and counties to design and location."[15] Given the importance of finance in determining highway design and location,[16] it is hardly surprising that, as interstate historians Mark Rose and Raymond Mohl put it, "ISTEA produced few startling results."[17]

The Big Dig

Boston's Central Artery/Tunnel project, popularly known as the Big Dig, is somewhere between an emblem and a bloated caricature of interstate highway building since ISTEA. Of the $7.6 billion out of $151 billion allocated for interstate construction by ISTEA, essentially all of it went to Boston's Big Dig, a massive three-in-one investment to bury the Central Artery, connect northbound and southbound rail tracks under the city, and build a tunnel to Logan Airport in East Boston.[18] Throughout ISTEA, Massachusetts received $2.80 in federal funds for every $1.00 in federal gas taxes collected, more than any other state. Half went to the Big Dig.[19] ISTEA even included a special provision on how funds would be allocated differently to Massachusetts than other states.

In many ways, the Big Dig was a first attempt at undoing some of the damage of the interstate era. Almost as soon as the Central Artery opened in the early 1950s, planners and engineers began looking at ways to bury the elevated sections, like Massachusetts Department of Public Works commissioner John Volpe had done with later sections through Chinatown. The highway cut off sections of the city, had become almost immediately congested, and developed a reputation for being dangerous.[20] Initially conceived by engineer Bill Reynolds, the plan to bury the Central Artery found a champion in Fred Salvucci, at the time a transportation advisor to Boston mayor Kevin White.[21] Along with the tunnel connection to Logan Airport, burying the Central Artery was one of two highway projects Governor Frank Sargent and his staff proposed to construct in 1972 after declaring a moratorium on new highway construction in the city in 1969. Over the next three decades that it took to plan, finance, and build the Big Dig, the estimated costs of the project increased from $2.3 billion to $14.6 billion.[22] In addition to a bloated example of near universal increases in the costs of building highways,[23] the Big Dig is representative of three main aspects of highway policy since ISTEA.

First, ISTEA continued and formalized the trend of growing local control over the design, location, and content of federally funded transportation projects. The federal government was generally opposed to the Big Dig. With the original proposal adding no capacity and replacing a fifteen-year-old project, Sargent found the project attractive but unlikely to move forward.[24] By 1974, however, Governor Michael Dukakis and his then secretary of transportation Salvucci made burying the Central Artery a top priority.[25] Despite general federal opposition, Salvucci managed to enlist the support of powerful local politicians, like Representative Tip O'Neill, and get the project onto a list of projects eligible for interstate funding at a deeply underestimated cost of $360 million.[26] By adding lanes to the proposal and combining the project with tunnels to reach the airport and connect railways underground, Salvucci garnered additional local support and filed an environmental impact statement in time for a 1983 deadline for remaining interstate highway segments.[27] In 1985, federal highway officials estimated that the overall project had benefit-to-cost ratio of just 0.4 to 0.5, roughly half to a fourth of Massachusetts officials' estimates. Since burying the Central Artery looked no worse a project than building a tunnel to the airport, however, federal officials included the project on the list of eligible projects, and the Big Dig was included in the Surface Transportation and Uniform Relocation Assistance Act of 1987.[28] President Ronald Reagan singled out the Big Dig as an example of wasteful spending as he vetoed the bill, calling it "a textbook example of special-interest, pork-barrel politics at work."[29] Congress and the Senate overrode the veto within a week.

Second and strongly related to local control, the Big Dig helps articulate the increased emphasis on mitigating the harmful effects of highway building that continued with ISTEA. Planners and engineers went out of their way to avoid taking any houses for the Big Dig. State officials estimated that there were more than fifteen hundred mitigation agreements from more than twenty permitting processes.[30] In addition to adding the north/south rail connector and airport tunnel to the Central Artery depression, Salvucci, through mitigation, committed the state to fourteen major transit extensions.[31] In total, mitigation agreements added nearly $5 billion—equivalent to the Big Dig's total estimated cost in 1991—to the final price tag of $15 billion to $20 billion.[32] This accounting corresponds well to economists Leah Brooks and Zachary Liscow's finding that the greatest contributor to the tripling in the cost of interstate construction per mile between 1960 and 1980 was citizen participation and mitigation.[33]

Third and most importantly, the Big Dig shows how ISTEA fundamentally continued federal highway policy's focus on increasing roadway capacity regardless of the emphasis on local control and mitigation. The original plan to bury the Central Artery did not increase capacity. However, adding lanes to the proposal and combining it with the tunnel to the airport increased the project's political appeal and attractiveness to federal highway planners. The official record to justify the project states that the main purpose was to improve traffic on the Central Artery:

"Unless improvements are made to increase the capacity of the Artery and revise ramp connections and the surface arterial in the downtown area, Artery congestion will continue and worsen, severely affecting the operation of Boston's regional network in the core area."[34] Despite the substantial political shifts, the justification for the Big Dig thus hardly differs from the 1930 or the 1948 highway plans: congestion bad; highways good.[35] In addition to the new tunnel to the airport, the Big Dig widened and added two to four expressway lanes underground and a multilane surface arterial, "a fancy median strip flanked by four-lane boulevards."[36]

Meanwhile in Dallas

If the Big Dig is a caricature of highway policy since ISTEA, the Dallas region's highway building is far more representative of national shifts in highway building. In 1993, the North Central Texas Council of Governments—the Dallas region's federally mandated regional planning authority—updated its long-range transportation plan to comply with ISTEA's new rules and emphases.[37] The plan and its update help articulate the way that ongoing shifts in federal policy played out at the local level. Of note, the new law required regional plans to identify funding sources for all proposed projects. Other shifts in policy often reflected ongoing trends, such as a continued emphasis on funding public transit, or business as usual. Three main trends are particularly relevant to the federal government's contemporary role in highway building.

First, ISTEA accelerated an ongoing shift in spending more federal highway dollars on state highways and other major roadways instead of interstate highways. ISTEA's two largest highway allocations went to the 160,000-mile National Highway System, which is primarily comprised of state highways and arterials, and the Surface Transportation Program, a flexible program that could be used on a broad range of projects. Both the Interstate System and the National Highway System are historically, fiscally, and functionally connected to a much larger four million miles of Federal-Aid Highways that the federal government has long played a role in funding. The Federal-Aid Highway Act of 1921, the first to mention an interstate highway system, allocated 40 percent of funds and nearly 60 percent of mileage to secondary highways and arterials. Interstate highways may get the most attention, but they do not function without a much broader system of highways, arterials, and local roads. The federal emphasis on building the Interstate System was a relatively short-lived endeavor. Even during peak interstate construction, state highway planners used federal funds to build new state highways, like Texas State Highway 360.[38] Only a small fraction of ISTEA's allocations went to interstate construction, mostly for the Big Dig in Boston. A more substantial 15 percent of funds went to repairing and rebuilding interstate highways. These funds, however, could also be used to widen interchanges, acquire land, and add new high-occupancy or auxiliary lanes. Moreover, reconstruction often widens roadways to meet increased recommended standard lane and shoulder widths.

In the Dallas region, the 1993 regional plan update identified $15.2 billion ($35 billion in 2024 dollars) in transportation investments over the next two decades. In 2024 dollars, that would be around $25,000 per household in greater Dallas. Nearly 60 percent would go to new highways and arterials, 14 percent to transit, 12 percent to maintenance and safety, 8 percent to high-occupancy vehicle lanes, and the remainder to congestion management, nonmotorized investments, and other transportation enhancements. ISTEA helped fund the widening of the Central Expressway, State Highway 360, and a broad range of other highways and arterials. Outside of the list of projects, the plan made no distinction between state roads or interstates and no distinction between federal dollars and state dollars. The planners and engineers instead matched projects to allowable sources of dollars for a wide range of projects and summed them up to present the fiscally constrained metropolitan transportation investments of the next twenty years.

Second, ISTEA continued the trend of requiring additional mitigation. Most notably, ISTEA required that regional plans result in compliance with air quality requirements. In addition to fiscally constrained investments, the Dallas regional plan update focused on how the region would comply with the Clean Air Act Amendment of 1990. At the time, the greater Dallas region produced twice the allowable amount of smog-producing volatile organic compounds. Without a plan to reduce emissions, the region risked losing federal transportation funds. Regional forecasters predicted that the investment plan would cut emissions to a third of 1990 levels, thanks in part to travel demand management, high-occupancy lanes, and other congestion-mitigation strategies. To meet ISTEA's new requirements, the Dallas regional plan also increased investments in pedestrian and bicycle infrastructure and developed a billion-dollar congestion management system. Many of these features already existed in the original plan but were updated with a focus on compliance with new guidelines and adherence to the new sources of funding.

Third and most notably, the Dallas region's plan shows how federal policy continued to raise funds through the gas tax and spend those funds to build and widen highways and arterials. Even the air quality and congestion management reduction strategies were primarily capacity increases. Two-thirds of congestion management funds went to upgrade traffic signals and improve the throughput of vehicles by increasing vehicle flow at intersections and highway interchanges. The high-occupancy vehicle lanes were fundamentally road-widening projects. Despite substantially increasing roadway capacity, regional planners predicted that the plan would result in decreased vehicle travel and 6.1 percent reduction in volatile organic compounds relative to doing nothing.[39] Given the billions of dollars spent to reduce travel time by car, it is difficult to come to any conclusion other than state highway planners were disingenuous, woefully ignorant of their craft, or blinded by a desire to see new highways built.

Congestion and vehicle travel have since increased substantially. Between 1990 and 2010, the number of hours that drivers lost in traffic increased from 78,000 to 175,000.[40] Improvements in fuel efficiency, the gradual retirement of cars without catalytic converters, and better engines helped Dallas and other regions meet air quality standards. Investments in additional roadway capacity did not.

A cynic might argue that even the much-touted fiscally constrained planning environment was largely meaningless. The original 1991 plan advertised a need for $15.8 billion in investments to solve most of the Dallas region' congestion problems. Just four years later, the plan claimed $18.5 billion in needed investments, which had to be constrained to $15.2 billion in available funding.

Surface Transportation Policy since ISTEA

Federal transportation laws have generally followed ISTEA's model. The 1998 Transportation Equity Act for the 21st Century (TEA-21) made direct reference to ISTEA through its acronym as well as its commitment to maintain and expand ISTEA's funding program. Despite the emphasis on a conservative system and the much-heralded completion of the Interstate System, TEA-21 represented a 40 percent increase in spending over ISTEA (table 4-1). As with subsequent federal transportation laws, the main emphasis of TEA-21 was to spend money raised from the gas tax to build, widen, rebuild, and maintain roadways. As the system has aged and expanded, more and more gets spent on reconstruction and maintenance. But new construction has continued apace. Each additional lane mile of highway and arterial commits federal and state planners and engineers to spend even more to future maintenance and reconstruction.

As the largest federal transportation act ever passed, not only in terms of headline numbers but inflation-adjusted annual spending, the 2021 Infrastructure Investment and Jobs Act (IIJA) included substantial

Table 4-1. US Federal Transportation Acts in the Post–Interstate Highway System Era

Federal Transportation Act	*Enactment*	*Period of performance*	*Dollars per year (2021 billions)*	*Federal share spent on expansion*[1]	*New urban lane miles*[2]	
					Highways	*Arterials*
Intermodal Surface Transportation Efficiency Act of 1991 (ISTEA)	1991	1992–1997	44	0.82	15,875	100,131
Transportation Equity Act for the 21st Century (TEA-21)	1998	1998–2003	61	0.59	11,799	53,312
Safe, Accountable, Flexible, Efficient Transportation Equity Act: A Legacy for Users (SAFETEA-LU)	2005	2005–2009	68	0.27	14,451	127,813
Moving Ahead for Progress in the 21st Century Act (MAP-21)	2012	2013–2014	62	0.29	9,915	48,183
Fixing America's Surface Transportation (FAST) Act	2015	2016–2020	70	0.22	3,503	14,225
Infrastructure Investment and Jobs Act (IIJA)	2021	2022–2026	115	—	—	—

1. Adam Millard-Ball and Erick Guerra, "Should Environmentalists Support the Gasoline Tax?," *Journal of the American Planning Association*, September 24, 2024, 1–4, https://doi.org/10.1080/01944363.2024.2394058.

2. Federal Highway Administration, "Highway Statistics."

language on sustainability, equity, and multimodality. The law also contained unique provisions focused on the economic and social harm of previous highway building. As with previous acts, however, the IIJA will put hundreds of billions of dollars into building, rebuilding, widening, and maintaining an already overbuilt roadway system. Fewer than one in five hundred transportation dollars will go to a much-touted program to reconnect communities divided by urban highways. As former federal deputy assistant secretary for transportation policy Beth Osborne put it, "The infrastructure bill is supercharged status quo."[41] The United States remains in need of a national transportation policy that is focused on present and future needs, not past problems.

CHAPTER 5

How, Where, and Why Do We Build Roads?

It is clear that without these proposed facilities there will be a complete breakdown in the city's highway system.—Robert Whitten, *Report on a Thoroughfare Plan for Boston, 1930*

Occasionally, a roadway investment is so bad that the project makes national news. For many, Boston's Big Dig was such a project due to its extraordinary cost and alarming fraud and waste. The construction oversight was so poor that faulty adhesive led to a panel falling and crushing Boston resident Milena del Valle to death and injuring her husband. Others, however, have portrayed it as an expensive correction—even a resounding success—to mistakes of the past.[1] Fred Salvucci, state secretary of transportation, argued that the $5 billion in mitigation costs reduced social costs while increasing government costs: "You're cleaning up after yourself; you're not dumping these problems on others."[2] And, for what it is worth, the North End and downtown Boston are substantially nicer without the Central Artery cutting through them. And the Leonard P. Zakim Bunker Hill Memorial Bridge is a triumph of elegant, functional engineering and monument to the city.

Few, however, have much to say in support of Alaska's Gravina Island Bridge, which made national news as a symbol of pork-barrel politics and extravagant waste during the 2008 presidential election campaign. "The Bridge to Nowhere," as politicians and journalists dubbed it, would have connected Ketchikan, Alaska, a town of eight thousand, to its airport on Gravina Island at an estimated cost of $400 million, replacing an existing ferry service. While funding for the bridge was a casualty of the election cycle's news, the Gravina Island Bridge shows how nearly any project can move through federal evaluation processes. The proposed bridge, being a bridge, easily met the stated purpose of its required environmental impact statement: "The purpose of the Gravina Access Project is to improve surface transportation between Revillagigedo Island and Gravina Island."[3] This type of circular logic is common for large transportation projects. The purpose of a roadway expansion, even one like the Big Dig,[4] is nearly always to increase capacity. There are no federal requirements for stated purposes to pass any evaluation or even make much sense. Few bother to read an environmental impact statement, which can run in the thousands of pages and cost millions of dollars to produce.

Outrageous projects like the Gravina Island Bridge are not a new phenomenon. Five decades earlier, Senator Daniel Patrick Moynihan of New York had singled out a series of freeway interchanges that cost $384,000 (around $4 million in 2024 dollars) and served just eighty-nine cars per day.[5] They are also not an isolated phenomenon. The US Public Interest Research Group maintains a list of what it calls highway boondoggles. The seventy-three highway projects listed are estimated to cost nearly $200 billion while providing limited benefits to the cities and towns where they are being built.[6] More importantly, these projects are just the tip of the iceberg. For every outrageous investment, there are scores of investments, both small and large, that should not have been built but receive little scrutiny. The Alaskan government, for example, spent $28 million to build an access road to the empty beach where the proposed bridge would have attached Gravina Island to Ketchikan.[7] There is almost certainly a distribution of projects that range somewhere on the spectrum from good to bad. Unfortunately, the costs of an average project almost certainly exceed the benefits, especially when considering the external costs of pollution, global warming, and traffic safety (more on these topics in the following chapter).

In this chapter, I shed light on the technocratic process that structures horse-trading between state departments of transportation and local municipalities to determine what road projects get funded and why. These mechanisms, largely obscure to the general population, add a technocratic legitimacy to a process that largely exists to construct more roadways in service of more traffic. There are no real mechanisms for determining whether project benefits outweigh costs nor stopping rules for when there is too much infrastructure. There are no bad projects outside the rare boondoggles that make national news, only a list of projects to be prioritized and negotiated due to funding constraints.

Desire Lines

The first *Highway Capacity Manuals* are refreshingly up-front about the purpose of building roads: "to serve traffic."[8] Even though Highway Capacity Manuals have become the primary guidebooks for how, where, and what types of roads to build in the United States, urban planners and traffic engineers—men like Harland Bartholomew and Dr. Miller McClintock—had begun developing the tools and metrics to serve traffic decades before the publication of the first manual in 1950. These techniques were refined over time and applied to hundreds of cities, but the basic premise was the same. Planners and engineers collected data on land uses, traffic flow, car ownership, population, the economy, and road networks. They mapped traffic flows onto city streets and then projected future traffic based on projected growth in vehicle ownership, population, land use, and the economy. The desired connections between different origins and destinations produced desire lines showing where people would travel decades out into the future. The planners and engineers then recommended expanding and adding roadways with enough capacity to handle the estimated increase in traffic.

Bartholomew, considered one of the most important traffic planners of his time, began his career developing traffic plans as a civil engineering consultant in Newark, New Jersey, where he oversaw the collection and analysis of data on population, traffic, and transportation networks.[9] This position led to his appointment as the "first full-time, public-sector city planner in America," where he completed Newark's 1915 comprehensive plan, and his recruitment to the city of St. Louis, where he worked and employed his analytical techniques from 1915 to 1950.[10] His 1917 traffic plan for St. Louis and experiences in Newark served as a model for hundreds of traffic studies and plans over a half-century career, during which he published frequently and taught courses on urban planning and urban design.[11] The St. Louis plan contained detailed descriptions of existing traffic patterns and recommendations for widening streets throughout the city, with detailed cost estimates and recommended funding sources.[12] Estimates of predicted future traffic flows and dire warnings of the tremendous costs of inaction would come with later traffic plans. Early on, Bartholomew argued that the reason for the road widenings should be obvious: "It will permit of a traffic capacity many times that of today."[13]

McClintock—as professor and researcher at both Harvard University and what is now the University of California, Los Angeles—further popularized and legitimized traffic planning and forecasting techniques through his writing, teaching, and consulting.[14] In his 233-page book, *Street Traffic Control*, McClintock covered a wide range of transportation issues: the sources and causes of congestion; methods of documenting and forecasting traffic demand; traffic controls, regulations, and enforcement; street capacity estimation; traffic safety; and a range of methods to increase street capacity through management and regulation.[15] The importance of increasing street capacity to meet future demand was the book's fundamental driving argument. In addition to better management and enforcement, McClintock recommended several now-common approaches: taking abutting property to carve out new streets or widen existing ones, narrowing sidewalks, using land use regulations to provide more space for new streets, moving sidewalks entirely onto property lines, double-decking roadways, building tunnels, reducing turning angles, building pedestrian bridges, and erecting fences to prevent pedestrians from crossing the roadway.[16] As a practitioner, McClintock promoted his work as a smashing success. For example, he celebrated that Chicago's new highways moved substantially more vehicles than the roads they replaced.[17]

McClintock's ideas and methods also featured prominently in the development of the original plan for Boston's Central Artery. Whitten thanked McClintock for advice, recommendations, and the 1928 Mayor's Traffic Survey, which formed the empirical basis of Whitten's traffic plan.[18] The report's second and third images provide an apt summary of the traffic planning process at the time. One image (figure 5-1a) superimposed a diagram of 1927 traffic volumes over existing streets, whereas another (figure 5-1b) projected the doubled 1965 traffic volumes onto the city's existing and proposed new streets. The original caption for these images concluded that "it is clear that without these proposed facilities there will be a complete breakdown in the city's highway system."[19]

Bartholomew, McClintock, and the work of other transportation forecasters also profoundly impacted federal highway plans and regulations. In *Toll Roads and Free Roads*, Bureau of Public Roads chief Thomas MacDonald took the approach even further. Gone were the city planners' and engineers' recommendations for transit investments, pedestrian facilities, and integrated land use. The Bureau of Public Roads'

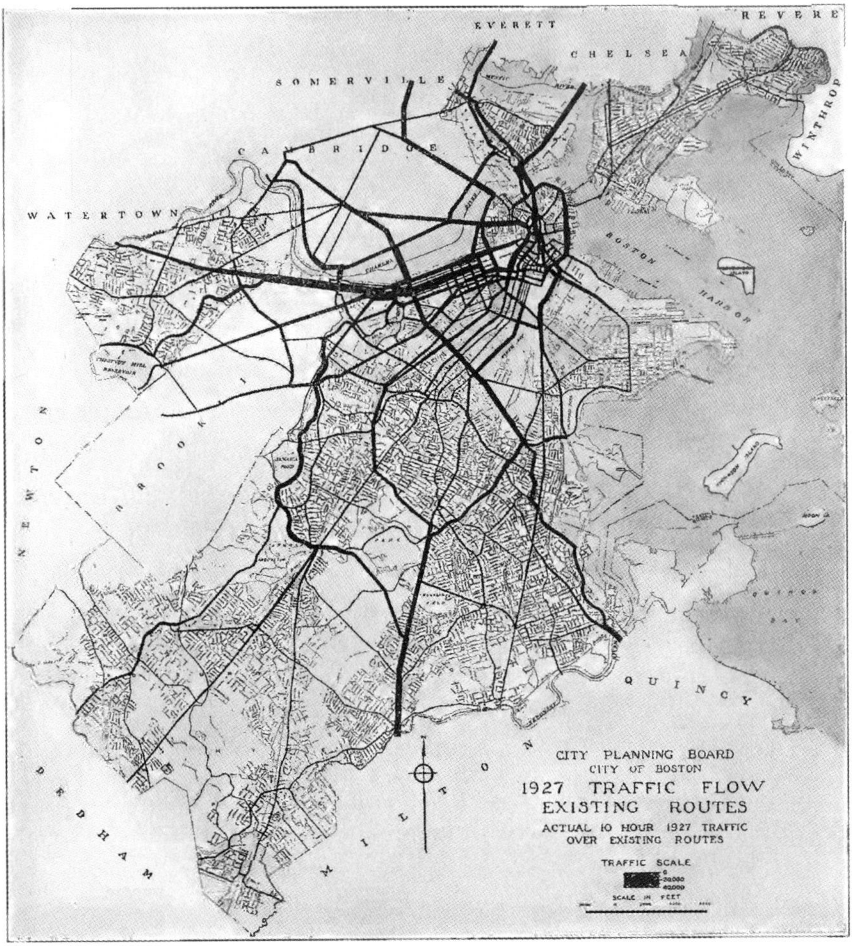

Figure 5-1. Highway planners map the estimated (above) current and (opposite page) predicted future traffic onto city streets in a process that remains largely unchanged since the early 1900s. (Whitten, "Report on a Thoroughfare Plan for Boston," figure 1 and figure 3.)

focus was to build as much high-capacity roadway as cheaply as possible.[20] Highway capacity should be expanded to meet demand on the peak days and peak hours of vehicle travel.[21] As stated in *Toll Roads and Free Roads,* "In large cities, nothing less than the creation of an elevated urban highway would suffice."[22]

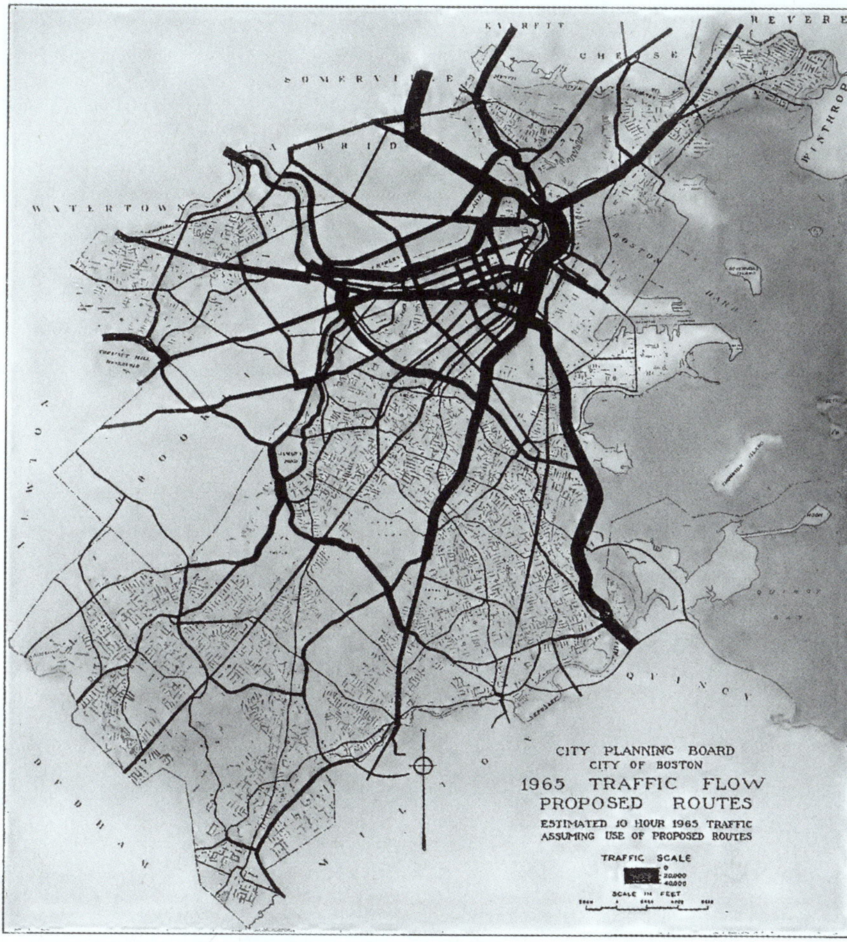

Although more deferential to cities and urban planning, the National Interregional Highway Committee, on which Bartholomew served as a key member and author, put an equally strong emphasis on serving peak traffic volumes into the future.[23] The first state highway guidelines recommended meeting the thirtieth highest projected hour of traffic over twenty years.[24] No justification was given for the figure, but it corresponds to 99.98th percentile busiest hour of traffic and remains the American Association of State Highway and Transportation Officials' contemporary recommended design guideline for new roads. The goal was and remains not just to serve traffic, but traffic at close to the peak of peak demand, a clear recipe for overbuilding.

While the language surrounding the stated purpose of roadways has evolved to focus on congestion, traffic safety, economic competitiveness, and more abstract concepts, the basic highway planning tools have hardly changed. Traffic engineers and planners examine origin and destination patterns, predict how traffic will grow, and for the most part recommend building roadways that are large enough and wide enough to accommodate that predicted growth. As a shortcut, they frequently simply assume that traffic will increase by 3 percent each year, nearly doubling every twenty years.[25]

Looking at the Dallas regional transportation plans discussed in chapter 4, the analytical exercises, takeaways, and recommendations bear a striking resemblance to Bartholomew's and McClintock's work from nearly a century earlier. A series of exhibits mapped travel demand and congestion with and without proposed highway and arterial additions and widenings. The biggest difference is that the quality and detail shown in plans like the 1930 highway plan for Boston have degraded substantially. Thick black and colored lines and shaded areas of congestion—rather than the elegant hand-drawn maps in figure 5-1—showed where and how new roadway investments would solve Dallas's congestion problems. Perhaps most disingenuously, one map showed how the desired investments would reduce congestion below 1986 levels.[26] The language also shifted somewhat from doomsday scenarios about what would happen without roadway investments to much more confident justifications of investment. According to the Dallas plan, scaling back investment plans "would clearly result in significant increases in congestion and resultant costs which are not acceptable solutions."[27] Unlike Bartholomew and McClintock, regional highway planners in Dallas knew that their plans would be funded. In many ways, the planning exercise was more about justifying expenditures than planning a sound transportation system. The overarching goal was to build ever-wider highways and arterials to move even more vehicles as quickly as possible.

Road-Building Alphabet Soup

Which transportation projects get funded and how? Local politicians, planners, and engineers work to get their projects prioritized and built while state and metropolitan transportation bureaucrats manage the analytical and logistical processes that determine which projects move forward. An alphabet soup of acronyms manages, governs, and adds a technocratic legitimacy to these processes.

The Texas Department of Transportation (TxDOT) provides a dense one-page summary explaining how to bring "a transportation project from concept to concrete."[28] The single page contains eleven acronyms, only some of which are defined, used dozens of times. First, a proposed project needs to get on a list of desired projects on state and metropolitan long-range transportation plans, like the Dallas 2010 plan. These plans go out a minimum of twenty years and need to be coordinated with federal regulations and entities as well as local counties, municipalities, and transit agencies. Since the passage of the 1991 Intermodal Surface Transportation Efficiency Act, these projects also need to be constrained to reasonable expectations of funding and in compliance with environmental regulations. As seen in Dallas, however, neither reduced funding nor reasonable assumptions about how new investments will affect pollution are required. Although plans are projected twenty years in the future, new plans are required every six to ten years.

So how does a project get onto a long-range planning document? It varies a bit by investment type, but there are two main ways for building or widening roadways. The first is based on the process of projecting traffic into the future and assigning it to existing roadways at different times of day. These assignments will then result in different levels of service (LOS) based on how much and how quickly traffic moves through freeways and intersections. Roadways with worse LOS scores are prioritized for transportation investments.

Although design manuals are careful to state that the scores ranging from A to F are not associated with qualitative judgments, any American schoolchild knows that is false. Oh, and F is bad, very bad. It is the point at which congestion becomes notable and you could have more people moving through a roadway system by limiting the number of vehicles on the road. Somewhat strangely, the F designation includes roadways operating at a complete standstill of bumper-to-bumper traffic as well as roadways that are operating at close to maximum operational capacity. It is something like a highway moving densely packed vehicles through space at 40 miles per hour as opposed to a less crowded highway moving the same number of people through space per hour but at maybe 50 or 60 miles per hour. Oh, and moving from C to D, D to E, or E to F is bad, very bad.

LOS A and LOS B really don't matter at all. They are empty rural freeways or urban freeways operating with little traffic late at night. Differences between A and B are described in terms of driver comfort and freedom to maneuver. These roads are widely underused, and there is no congestion. By LOS C, drivers experience less "comfort and convenience" (terms undefined) but can move basically just as quickly as at LOS A and LOS B. By LOS D and LOS E, highways are moving the most vehicles possible, but with less "comfort and convenience" and at lower speeds. More importantly, breakdowns or traffic collisions are much more likely to move the highway to the dreaded LOS F. Urban highways in large urban areas spend a fair amount of time at LOS F during the morning and evening rush hours.

The second way that road investments make it onto long-range planning documents follows a process more akin to that of the Big Dig or the Gravina Island Bridge. A local engineer, planner, or politician identifies a project, develops a coalition of support for that project, and shepherds it through the official planning process. Projects with an expected influence on LOS through capacity increases are much likelier to go the distance than those without such a trait. At the end of the day, capacity increases are still primarily judged on their ability to serve traffic. The addition of highway lanes under the old Central Artery and the tunnel to Boston's Logan Airport got funded and built. The bridge to the Ketchikan International Airport did not.

Next, a project needs to make its way onto state and metropolitan (or rural) lists of projects to be funded over the next four years. In metropolitan areas, local towns and counties negotiate which projects make it onto the list. Metropolitan Planning Organizations (MPOs) and state Departments of Transportation (DOTs) manage the process and negotiations. In some, the MPOs play a strong role in selecting projects. In others, they generally just rubber-stamp DOT plans and ensure that they comply with federal legislation. In large urban areas, MPOs may have hundreds of staff. In smaller areas, the MPO may have a single engineer on staff. Regardless of the local dynamics, urban projects need to move from state and metropolitan long-range plans to state and metropolitan transportation improvement programs (TIPs). Improvements! Such a loaded term clearly announces traffic planners' and engineers' underlying belief that all transportation investments are good investments. To be clear, it is not just widenings or new interchanges that qualify as improvements. Spending money to remove a travel lane or install traffic calming devices is also an improvement. All transportation investments are improvements.

My first TIP meeting helped instill a general skepticism in US transportation planning processes decades ago. (A decade of teaching bright-eyed graduate students the history of US transportation policy reinforced this skepticism and ultimately led to this book.) Representatives from the largest city in the metropolitan area skipped the meeting. The rest of the cities and towns could not exclude the largest city or allocate projects without setting any aside for it. What really bothered me, however, were the horse trading over projects and the cynical use of models and allocations to select projects. One engineer from a suburban town argued to use funds set aside for air quality improvements to widen a congested main street. He argued, correctly, that the models showed that doing so would improve air quality, but he knew, correctly, that it would not. That was the available funding for the scale of project, however, and that project was his main concern. In other places, highway engineers still boldly claim that their models show that increasing highway capacity will reduce pollution and greenhouse gas emissions.

Once a project makes it onto a long-range transportation plan, it can become exceedingly difficult to remove. A project may consistently fail to make the TIP because it does too little to improve LOS or is too expensive for its projected accomplishments. Local planners and engineers, however, will continue putting the project up, again and again. They will trade support for one bad project for support for their own. Eventually, an influx of investment dollars from something like the 2021 Infrastructure Investment and Jobs Act or the exhaustion of the rest of the region will help get the project onto the TIP and eventually built. Even using problematic metrics, like LOS, evaluated by people who are overly fond of building roads, we build more roads than we should. And there are thousands of other even worse projects, just waiting for an influx of cash or lax planning environment to get onto the long-range plan.

Stealth Widenings

A declining share of federal transportation dollars go to building and widening roadways (see table 4-1). An increasing share goes to maintaining and rebuilding existing roads. Although different climates and materials require different standards, the United States should be repaving approximately 30,000 lane miles of highway every year. Almost a third need complete structural resurfacing each year. Bridges and elevated structures need to be carefully maintained and rebuilt as well. In 2020, state and federal agencies spent more than five times as many public dollars on resurfacing, restoring, and rehabilitating highways as they did on building new ones.[29] They also spent nine times more dollars reconstructing and rebuilding highways than they did building new ones. Of these allocated dollars, roughly half went to projects that explicitly added new capacity. However, even projects that do not explicitly add road capacity often grow wider and allow for higher vehicle volumes. I call them stealth widening projects because they tend to receive less scrutiny than projects that add new lanes and they do not enter official records as capacity increases. If spending, rather than rhetoric, reflects policy goals, the main purpose of US transportation policy is to continue to rebuild an ever-widening and growing highway network.

Pulitzer Prize–winning journalist Inga Saffron became interested in highway reconstruction in Philadelphia a decade or so ago after examining and conducting interviews for a story about Pennsylvania DOT (PennDOT) plans to reconstruct Interstate 95 in North Philadelphia.[30] The plans promised a sensitive approach and new amenities around the highway, including sound barriers and rain gardens. She never wrote the story. She said that she felt she lacked the tools to understand whether the project was good or bad and whether it should be criticized or touted as a new day in urban highway planning. Once the project was built, her answer was apparent, and she regretted not running the initial story. The right-of-way was widened by ten to twenty feet. A massive new interchange that dominates a neighborhood is far more impactful than presented or than what PennDOT engineers had anticipated.[31] There is more highway and less city. These kinds of increased footprints are common. The minimum requirements for shoulder widths and curve freeway curve radii increased by 25 percent to 400 percent between 1955 and 1985.[32] As Saffron summarized, "Rain gardens don't make up for it."[33]

PennDOT put forward preliminary designs to rebuild additional sections of Interstate 95 in South Philadelphia toward the end of 2023.[34] Despite proposing new lanes, wider lanes, wider shoulders, and new interchanges, the engineer in charge of the project has insisted that it is not a capacity-adding project.[35] Official PennDOT documentation makes the opposite claim. The stated purpose of the project, like nearly all highway projects, is to manage growing congestion by increasing capacity. This time, Saffron and local residents better understood the nature of the project. Yes, there are proposals for new bike lanes and even a highway capping just down the street from the nation's first post office and Benjamin Franklin's former home. No, it is almost certainly not a good project for the city. The title of her article makes her position clear: "I-95 Reconstruction Is Really a Widening Project That Will Hurt Philly Neighborhoods."[36] Most stealth widenings throughout the United States, however, will go unchallenged. By their nature, they often go unnoticed.

Old-School Widenings

There is little stealth to the highway widenings happening in many other parts of the country. Since ISTEA, TxDOT has added enough highway lane miles to cross the width of the United States two and a half times over. The Katy Freeway (Interstate 10) famously cuts across Houston with two dozen separate lanes. Its interchanges consume entire city blocks. Highway widenings continue to demolish homes and businesses, often in predominantly Black communities. As Harris County judge Lina Hidalgo put it when filing a case against TxDOT for violating Title VI of the 1964 Civil Rights Act with its expansion of Interstate 45 in Houston, "For too long, transportation policy in our region has been stuck in the fifties."[37]

In her book *City Limits*, journalist Megan Kimble documents an ongoing movement pushing back against three major highway widenings in

Dallas, Austin, and Houston. Although there have been victories—such as the Federal Highway Administration (FHWA) temporarily halting the Interstate 45 widening in Houston to evaluate the unfair burdens placed on minority households—widenings have continued apace often despite substantial opposition, including from city mayors. Like in the past, highway engineers fall back on their model predictions—what one highway engineer likened to brain surgery—doomsday congestion scenarios, and arguments about the need for modernization. Though her book ends on an optimistic note with reference to progress made in other states and an optimistic resident joining the fight, all three of the proposed widenings get approved. Little by little, Texas's great cities are losing more and more homes, daycare centers, restaurants, soccer fields, and schools to highways. TxDOT estimated that the Interstate 45 widening alone would destroy more than a thousand homes, two schools, four places of worship, and three hundred businesses employing thirty thousand people. TxDOT, moreover, concluded that the widening "would cause disproportionate high and adverse impacts to minority or low-income populations."[38] The planners and engineers justified these impacts with the circular logic that widening was essential but that any widening would have disproportionate, high, and adverse impacts on low-income minority residents.

Politics and Road Investments

Political power plays a critical role in which roads get built or blocked. As discussed in chapter 3, highways were and continue to be particularly likely to get routed through poor and minority communities. Bartholomew, McClintock, Whitten, and other early highway planners tended to support downtown business interests, racial segregation, and slum clearance.[39] For all the focus on highway planning as a technocratic science, Bartholomew recommended ignoring traffic flow data to focus on downtown revival in St. Louis.[40] Explaining why he wrote his

1,246-page biography on New York City's master road builder Robert Moses, Robert Caro opined on his experience taking a land use and urban planning class at Harvard in 1965: "They were talking one day about highways and where they got built, and here were these mathematical formulas about traffic density and population density and so on, and all of a sudden, I said to myself: 'This is completely wrong. This isn't why highways get built. Highways get built because Robert Moses wants them built there. If you don't find out and explain to people where Robert Moses gets his power, then everything else you do is going to be dishonest."[41]

Yet the equations and formulas did and do matter, especially when backed by dollars. As Brian Taylor, Eric Morris, and Jeffrey Brown argue in their book on the fiscal politics of highways, the Interstate and Defense Highways Act of 1956 put technocratic state and federal highway engineers largely in charge of what got built and where.[42] The rerouting of highways to serve the politically connected did not change the overall approach to designing an urban highway system to meet peak demand far into the future and building it as quickly and inexpensively as possible. Moses, through his position collecting toll revenues, had a uniquely powerful and somewhat unusual position in the history of US urban highway construction. According to one Bureau of Public Roads official, Moses even remained aloof from federal highway planners and treated them with disdain and disinterest.[43]

Serving Traffic

Serving traffic has done a tremendous job of serving traffic. As noted by early observers such as Moynihan and Lewis Mumford, increased traffic was generally the largest and most substantial effect of new highway investments.[44] Throughout the 1930s and 1940s, local and regional planners in New York, San Francisco, and throughout the United States fretted that new highways would fail to solve congestion and create even more traffic in downtowns.[45] As early as 1929, even regional planners eager to widen streets and build new highways had already observed that "widening streets does not in itself, except for very short periods, lessen congestion. It is apparent that doubling the width of a street, or double decking it for the same width, will not lessen congestion if the traffic use is doubled soon after the increased capacity is provided."[46]

Several decades of more recent empirical studies have confirmed these early observations. Looking at twenty-two years of highway investments across thirty-four urban counties in California, Berkeley planning and engineering professors Robert Cervero and Mark Hansen found that increased investments in highway lane miles corresponded with a proportional increase in vehicle travel within just a few years.[47] Estimating simultaneous models of vehicle travel and highway lane miles, they concluded that increasing lane miles by 10 percent led to an 8 percent increase in vehicle travel within a few years. Moreover, increased vehicle travel spurred highway planners and engineers to add more new land miles. Cervero, also my dissertation advisor and mentor, often compares building highways to reduce congestion to the somewhat hopeless and poorly conceived notion of buying a bigger belt to lose weight—a reference to a similar analogy made by Mumford in the 1950s.[48]

More recently, economists Gilles Duranton and Matt Turner examined the role that highway investments played in increasing vehicle travel across the United States from 1983 to 2003. Comparing interstate highways to locations that were most likely to have received interstate highways but did not, they concluded that urban interstate highway investments led to proportional increases in vehicle travel not just in the large, congested metropolitan areas but throughout the country. They found similar but slightly smaller effects for smaller highway types and no evidence that increased highway travel diverted travel from smaller arterials or local roads. Of note for future chapters on public policy responses to an overbuilt roadway system, transit investments did not reduce vehicle travel either.

Why do new roads generate traffic and fail to stem congestion? The short answer is that new roads reduce the most important cost of travel—the time we spend traveling. Shorter travel time means more trips, longer trips, and a higher share of trips by car. In this respect, travel is like other typical goods, such as the size of housing, food at the grocery store, and clothes. As the cost goes down, people consume more.

Travel also exhibits some unique attributes related to congestion and even, perhaps, humans' underlying evolutionary biology. Congestion exists in time and space. In his books *Stuck in Traffic* and *Still Stuck in Traffic*, economist Anthony Downs built on thirty years of work to argue that three main factors prevent new highways and highway widenings from making a dent on congestion.[49] First, and probably less importantly today than in 1962 when Downs published his seminal article "The Law of Peak-Hour Expressway Congestion" and workers were about four times more likely to commute by transit, people shift modes.[50] Instead of taking the train or perhaps telecommuting, people will take advantage of new space on a highway to drive instead. Second and third, and more importantly, shifts occur in time and space. If you previously left at 6:30 a.m. to avoid traffic on your way to work, now maybe you leave at 7 a.m. instead. If you previously left your house at 10 a.m. to visit a friend, maybe now you leave at 9:30 a.m. instead since the morning rush hour traffic has dissipated. The peak hours of travel may become compressed, but everyone is still dealing with the same level of congestion on average.

In terms of space, you may now choose to take the highway instead of local roads. Doing so not only leads to congestion on the highway, but often much longer trips as well. If I had left work at the University of Pennsylvania at 5 p.m. to pick up my infant son at his great-grandmother's house in North Philadelphia, it likely would have taken me thirty to thirty-five minutes to drive 6.4 miles on local roads. If I worked late or left before 2 p.m., I might have saved a few minutes by taking the highway, but I would have driven another 3.4 miles, consuming 53 percent more roadway capacity on the way. The highway only really saved me time at the least congested times.

People also almost certainly take more trips to farther-away places and adjust daily routines to involve longer distance trips. For example, if a new freeway cuts the drive time to a relative, store, or favorite restaurant, people become more likely to make that trip more often and at more congested times of day. Over time, people also adjust where they are willing to live, go to school, work, attend religious services, or spend time on a typical day.

There are likely even fundamental biological or sociological components to how much and how far people travel. Building on the concept of travel-time and travel-money budgets—the time and money that people can allocate to moving around—Italian physicist Cesare Marchetti argued that much of human travel and subsequent city form stem more from social and evolutionary imperatives than the economic theories that underpin most theories of travel behavior. This universal travel-time budget—sometimes called Marchetti's constant after his paper "Anthropological Invariants in Travel Behavior"—posits that people tend to travel a little more than an hour per day on average, regardless of how much money they earn, how they get around, or even where they live. Tanzanian villagers, Parisians, São Paulistas, Dutch, Japanese, and US residents all spend about 1.1 hours traveling per day on average across places and over time.[51] That's not to say that all people or types of people are the same. For example, children and the elderly travel less than that on average. Residents of the world's largest cities also tend to travel more than anyone else on average. However, almost universally, faster travel results in more travel—over time and across towns and cities. If a series of highway investments resulted in a city moving about 10 percent faster, its residents would travel about 10 percent longer distances.

Many highway builders reject these assertions. First, they argue that serving traffic is fundamentally about serving people. For many, as shown in the previous chapters, serving traffic is entirely synonymous with serving people. Others reject the idea that widening highways creates more traffic. In an interview reflecting on his career, Lee Mertz, longtime FHWA employee, FHWA chief of the Urban Planning Division (1969 to 1973), and later unofficial historian of the interstates, complained that "highways don't generate traffic.... I have a deep resentment about that traffic generation because I've been beaten up on subject so many times in a public forum. That hopeless idea—that defeatist idea—that you build a highway and brand new traffic from nowhere springs up to fill it, as though that traffic demand didn't exist before. Well, that's a lot of nonsense."[52]

Despite this kind of reluctance, the recognition that serving traffic creates more traffic has begun to make it to the top of some state and federal highway planning agencies. Referencing the head of Colorado's Department of Transportation's comments on responses to congestion on Interstate 70 in Denver, secretary of transportation Pete Buttigieg stated in 2022, "Now, there's a relationship between supply and demand, and as the director of CDOT has said, you can't always build your way out of congestion."[53] Even more importantly, the recognition has begun trickling down into the state and regional planning practices that largely determine what gets built and where. In her book, *Shifting Gears*, planning professor Susan Handy documents recent experiences with incorporating estimates of how much traffic new highway investments are likely to generate into state and federal transportation modeling and evaluation processes.[54] In 1997, the Sierra Club sued the US Department of Transportation for its failure to consider how new transportation investments influenced vehicle travel into its modeling. The court agreed, and the Environmental Protection Agency published a 2002 guidebook describing how transportation agencies fail to account for the feedback effects of new highways on travel and recommending steps to account for it. States like California and Colorado have begun incorporating highway feedback effects into modeling and evaluation processes.

Progress, however, has been slow. Even in California, most highway projects ignore feedback effects altogether. When they do not ignore them, estimated effect sizes are much smaller than what would be expected based on empirical studies.[55] In Pennsylvania, Texas, and other states, curbing congestion remains the number one stated priority for highway widenings, whether the stealth widenings in Philadelphia or the aggressive and seemingly anachronistic widenings in Houston. Acknowledging feedback effects makes highway projects look worse, and most highway engineers' primary objective remains to justify and build new highway capacity. Somewhat ironically, Handy shows that the Bureau of Public Roads and even the leading traffic engineering textbook the year President Dwight Eisenhower signed the Interstate and Defense Highways Act both acknowledged that highways generated new and additional vehicle travel.[56] Somewhat encouragingly, nearly three-fourths of contemporary transportation engineering students understand that highways create new traffic.[57] The general public, however, does not. And even well-informed experts tend to discount the evidence when it comes to the specific project that they favor.[58]

Just because highways generate additional traffic does not mean that they are not beneficial. Handy, Duranton, and Cervero all drive. So do I. We are not opposed to highways, nor do we avoid using them. Making it easier for people to drive to the same places at the same times has important social and economic benefits. We do, however, share a concern that the stated benefits are often substantially lower than the actual ones—sometimes so much lower that the whole process feels disingenuous. We also worry that the benefits are often small compared to the costs, especially when considering environmental and social costs or the opportunity costs of using more land for transportation instead of parks, houses, shops, offices, and other uses. Given the methods used to decide where and how to build and widen roadways, it is hardly surprising that the roadway system is overbuilt. The process considers all investment decisions as good investment decisions—transportation improvements. There just is not always enough money to go around. Try to imagine any kind of business that could succeed or even stay afloat for a short period with that kind of investment strategy. It is a recipe for overinvesting, for overbuilding. As the next chapters will show, the costs and consequences of overbuilding are substantial.

CHAPTER 6

The Economic Costs of Overbuilding

For years, we have deferred tough decisions, and today, our aging system of highways and byways, air routes and rail lines hinder our economic growth. Today, the average American household is forced to spend more on transportation each year than food. Our roads, clogged with traffic, cost us $80 billion a year in lost productivity and wasted fuel.—President Barack Obama, Remarks by the President on Rebuilding America's Infrastructure, 2010

Roadways are the negative space that define the shape and form of cities and towns. As a thought experiment, consider a city composed only of roadways and a city with no roads at all. Neither would have much value. In the former, there is nowhere to go. In the latter, there is no way to get to where you are going. There is a balance between the form of the spaces taken by houses, offices, parks, and shops and the in-between spaces that connect and bind them. And yes, spaces like China's Kowloon Walled City—an amalgamation of buildings in a space with no streets and at absurdly high densities that housed more than thirty thousand residents on a single megablock—can exist and do have value.[1] They are, however, extreme outliers.

The balance between negative and positive space—the background and the foreground—varies by place. The dull, fuzzy negative space isolating Leonardo da Vinci's *Mona Lisa* would not suit the dynamic spaces giving action and vibrancy to Michelangelo's Sistine Chapel fresco paintings. Similarly, Philadelphia's narrow residential streets and long, narrow blocks suit its neighborhood row houses but are poorly suited to Chicago's downtown high-rises. And while urban form and layout are intrinsically linked, a particular layout cannot on its own cause a particular outcome. You cannot, for example, pave Manhattan's grid over a cornfield and expect Manhattan to appear. Otherwise, developers would have long ago bought up all the cornfields, paved streets, and sold off the parcels to fund the increasingly expensive next cornfield purchase.

Although the balance will inherently vary by city and within cities over time, somewhere between a place with no roads and a place comprised only of roads lies an ideal, an optimum. The costs and benefits of new roadway investments will almost certainly vary depending on how far away a city, town, or nation happens to be from that ideal. To make the thought experiment a bit easier, imagine a city that is comprised entirely of narrow, unpaved roads giving limited and slow access to each building. The effects of the first major road investment—say a paved boulevard—would be apparent. Shops and multifamily homes would soon line the street, which now has better access to the rest of the city than anywhere else. Perhaps the benefits of a second roadway investment would be even higher. The accessibility benefits of the second major roadway might have network effects that grant even greater access and increase values along both roadways substantially. Similarly, the first major highway would generate value by allowing the city to expand and perhaps better connect to surrounding cities and towns. Eventually, however, the benefits of new roadways would decrease. Instead of generating new value, investments might simply shuffle land value from one place to another. The costs could also increase. New roadways may require more urban land with already high accessibility and high land value. The easiest, cheapest, and best places to build have already likely been converted to roadway. At a certain point, the costs of building more roads will begin to outweigh the benefits. Taking the thought experiment one step forward, traffic safety, congestion, pollution, and aesthetics—not just accessibility and costs—will play a role in defining this optimum. At a certain point, the next roadway investment's costs outweigh the accessibility benefits. The previous roadway investment, however, was net beneficial. That is the theoretical optimal amount of roadway.

Accepting this reality is the first major step on the path to accepting the fundamental argument of this book that the United States has overbuilt its roadway infrastructure. It also leads inevitably to questioning whether all transportation investments can possibly be improvements and whether building roads to serve traffic could ever possibly be the best way to arrive at optimal levels of road investments. It might also eventually lead to questioning whether the agencies and individuals who benefit the most from more highways and more driving should really have so much control over what gets built and where—and whether it makes any sense to continue to use the same evaluation tools and financing mechanisms that were developed to build the initial Interstate System.

The next steps, however, are to accept that the point where costs exceed benefits is measurable and then to attempt to measure it. These steps may require ignoring a century of rhetoric on doomsday congestion, crumbling infrastructure, economic competitiveness, and even household preferences. Yes, these factors matter, but they can be measured, at least roughly, and held to some account. They do not uniformly justify all roadway investments as highway promoters and politicians sometimes appear to believe. Just like the rhetoric around evacuating cities from a nuclear attack that Lewis Mumford rightly mocked in the 1950s, the contemporary rhetoric about the need for massive new transportation investments should be met with a healthy dose of skepticism. Highway planners—no longer as focused on moral arguments about national defense, connecting the country, or clearing slums (chapters 2 and 3)—tend to emphasize the congestion and the economic benefits of new highway investments. The evidence supporting either benefit is weak.

An Accounting

One approach to understanding whether the roadway system is overbuilt it is to examine whether the benefits of a typical new investment outweigh the costs, including social costs, like traffic pollution and traffic fatalities. Since highway costs have been increasing and benefits decreasing since completing the Interstate Highway System, more recent investments almost certainly perform worse than older investments.[2] So how much do highways cost, and what are their benefits?

The sums are staggering. When adjusted for inflation, the US federal government alone has spent more than $2 trillion on highways since 1956. Collectively, federal, state, and local governments spend another $1 trillion every five years or so building, expanding, rebuilding, and maintaining roads.[3] For the most part, these figures do not even include the tremendous value of the land that roadways sit on. The United States does not keep records on how much space is taken up by roads. Filling this gap in knowledge, my colleagues at the Wharton Business School and I generated predictive models of how much space roads took up in 2016 and matched them to data on land values.[4] Urban roadways take up more than one-fifth of all urban land, land that is worth more than $5 trillion and covers an area as large as West Virginia. In total, the US surface transportation system also claims around forty thousand lives per year and injures millions more. Depending on how quality of life issues were treated, the total economic costs of traffic collisions ranged from $340 billion to $1.4 trillion in 2019, the safest travel year since 2015.[5] Each year, cars and trucks emit more than a billion tons of carbon-equivalent greenhouse gas emissions into the atmosphere, with a federally estimated economic cost of more than $250 billion. Academic estimates put the cost between $75 billion and $1 trillion.[6] In its annual report on congestion, the Texas A&M Transportation Institute estimated that Americans spent around $200 billion per year in fuel and time costs due to congestion in 2019.[7]

Highways also have enormous benefits. They allow more people to travel more quickly to more places at similar times of day. They make it easier for firms to attract workers and send and receive goods and materials. New highways can also unlock land for new productive uses like houses, offices, and shopping centers. By lowering the cost of movement, they can increase productivity and enable more and more people and businesses to interact. Reflecting those benefits, households spend nearly $1.5 trillion per year on cars, fuel, maintenance, and repairs. Using a common heuristic of valuing time at half the wage rate, drivers and their passengers spend another $1.4 trillion worth of time in cars. The trucking industry also spends more than $325 billion per year on drivers, fuel, insurance, vehicle maintenance, and other variable costs.[8]

These sums are so large that they are difficult to digest, let alone compare. It is that difficulty digesting and comparing that makes the $80 billion referenced by President Barack Obama at the start of this chapter—and countless other billions referenced by other presidents when promoting or signing federal transportation laws—feel so staggering. To help facilitate understanding and accounting, table 6-1 compares the sums per household per year in 2024 inflation-adjusted dollars. These figures are for comparative purposes only. There is double counting. The estimated costs of congestion, for example, are also included in household fuel expenditures and travel-time expenditures. There is also not a linear relationship between roadway and driving or costs. For example, removing all roadways would destroy land value, not unlock $3,000 to $5,000 in wealth per household. The table also excludes numerous costs

Table 6-1. Per Household and Total Values of Major Costs of Roadway Transportation System

	Per household	Total (billions)
Government spending on roads[1]	$1,939	$244
Consumer spending on vehicle purchases[2]	$4,797	$622
Consumer spending on motor fuel[3]	$2,520	$327
Consumer spending on other vehicle expenses[4]	$3,807	$493
Time costs (urban households)[5]	$14,554	$1,419
Variable costs of urban freight trucking[6]	$3,328	$325
Land value of urban roads[7]	$2,856–$5,141	$272–$488
Cost of collisions[8]	$3,305–$13,319	$425–$1,713
Greenhouse gas emissions[9]	$603–$7,914	$77–$1,018
Congestion (494 urban areas)[10]	$2,471	$238

Note: The estimated costs of congestion compare free-flow travel to congested travel and though commonly referenced almost certainly exaggerate the costs of congestion.

1. Federal Highway Administration, "Highway Statistics"; US Census Bureau, "Annual Survey of State and Local Government Finances"; US Census Bureau, "Census of Governments."

2. US Bureau of Labor Statistics, "Consumer Expenditures (Annual) News Release," August 29, 2017, https://www.bls.gov/news.release/archives/cesan_08292017.htm; US Bureau of Labor Statistics, "Real Average Hourly Earnings up 1.4 Percent for the Year Ending March 2016," *Economics Daily*, April 19, 2016, https://www.bls.gov/opub/ted/2016/real-average-hourly-earnings-up-1-4-percent-for-the-year-ending-march-2016.htm.

3. US Bureau of Labor Statistics, "Consumer Expenditures (Annual) News Release"; US Bureau of Labor Statistics, "Real Average Hourly Earnings up 1.4 Percent for the Year Ending March 2016."

4. US Bureau of Labor Statistics, "Consumer Expenditures (Annual) News Release"; US Bureau of Labor Statistics, "Real Average Hourly Earnings up 1.4 Percent for the Year Ending March 2016."

5. US Bureau of Labor Statistics, "Consumer Expenditures (Annual) News Release"; US Bureau of Labor Statistics, "Real Average Hourly Earnings up 1.4 Percent for the Year Ending March 2016"; U.S. Department of Transportation, "National Household Travel Survey," 2017, http://nhts.ornl.gov/.

6. American Transportation Research Institute, "An Analysis of Operational Costs of Trucking: 2020 Update," 2020, https://truckingresearch.org/wp-content/uploads/2020/11/ATRI-Operational-Costs-of-Trucking-2020.pdf; US Department of Transportation, "National Transportation Statistics: Truck Profile," 2019, https://doi.org/10.21949/1503663.

7. Guerra, Duranton, and Ma, "Urban Roadway in America."

8. Blincoe et al., "The Economic and Societal Impact of Motor Vehicle Crashes, 2019 (Revised)."

9. Tol, "Social Cost of Carbon Estimates Have Increased over Time"; Environmental Protection Agency, "Inventory of U.S. Greenhouse Gas Emissions and Sinks."

10. Texas A&M Transportation Institute, "Congestion Data for Your City—Mobility Division," Urban Mobility Report 2021, August 27, 2020, https://mobility.tamu.edu/umr/congestion-data/.

of surface transportation, such as the costs of parking—which may be worth more than the entire vehicle fleet—local pollution, and heat-island and flooding effects from impervious surfaces. The main point is that there are many large costs and benefits associated with the roadway system. For all the discussion of congestion, congestion costs are lower than land costs, collisions costs, and the average estimates of the carbon costs of the cars and trucks on the road. The amount of time that people spend on the road, however, remains the highest estimated cost of the transportation system. Understandably, reducing those costs could produce substantial economic benefits and inspires much of the interest in improving the transportation system.

While it is difficult to guess how a massive change to the roadway network would affect costs and benefits, existing data and research provide a relatively straightforward view of the effects of a small change—and thus a decent accounting of whether the road network is overbuilt. Expanding on work with Gilles Duranton and Xinyu Ma at the Wharton School of Business, I present a back-of-the-envelope estimate of the likely effects of a 10 percent increase in roadway capacity. A 10 percent increase is large enough to have meaningful impacts but also small enough to be historically appropriate and achievable through plausible and common lane widenings, new road investments, and reconstruction to bring older highways and arterials up to contemporary standards. For context, the United States has added 13 percent to 29 percent more lane miles of urban streets and highways each decade since 1990.[9] Similarly, a 10 percent increase or reduction in roadway capacity is small enough to achieve without having major impacts on the access or amenity values of surrounding parcels. Going back to the amount of urban lane miles of 2010, for example, will not bring the United States anywhere close to the zero land values associated with having cities without roads. Within these bounds, accessibility can be measured in terms of the effects on increased or reduced travel speeds.

From there, my basic approach is to compare the expected value of time savings to drivers and cost savings to the trucking industry from a 10 percent increase in roadway capacity to the costs of government spending, the value of the land used, and the expected external costs associated with increased driving from the road investments (table 6-2). Due to data limitations, I exclude investment costs borne by private developers, benefits to bus users, and external costs other than greenhouse gas emissions, local pollution, oil dependency, congestion, and traffic collisions. In general, I choose conservative estimates that are more likely than not to be favorable to the positive effects of roadway investments. For example, I assume that a 10 percent increase in urban roadways would result in a 1 percent increase in speed and travel times savings. This assumption is on the high end of existing estimates, even assuming that the increased roadway infrastructure comes entirely from additional highway miles or converting local roads and arterials to highways.[10] Increasing urban travel speeds by 1 percent would save travelers approximately $14 billion worth of time ($146 per urban household) and the trucking industry $850 million in cities. That is about 15 percent lower than the estimated construction and maintenance costs of the new roadway (see table 6-2).

In general, I also apply conservative estimates of costs. For example, I assume a linear increase in lost land and construction costs. Building new highways, however, is more likely to be more expensive than the average cost of building new highways and other streets. Similarly, the land used for new highways is more likely to be from more central and valuable parts of cities and towns where highways are often constructed than from outside the city. Moreover, I apply a lower bound estimate of the annualized value of land used for urban roadway.[11] I also assume no effects on the amenity value of parcels from the 10 percent increase in roadways. These effects can be substantial in central locations. Federal reserve economists Jeffrey Brinkman and Jeffrey Lin, for example,

Table 6-2. Estimated Costs and Benefits per Urban Household of a 10 Percent Increase in Urban Roadway Capacity

Benefits	
Time savings	$145.54
Freight trucking	$33.28
Costs	
Government spending	$209.82
Land value	$285.67
Externalities	$279.03
Benefit-cost ratios	
Without land or externalities	0.85
Without land	0.36
Total	**0.23**

estimate that Chicago's census tracts near freeways have 17.5 percent lower amenity values than they would have had without freeways. In total, they estimated that Chicago had 5 percent less overall income and 8 percent fewer residents on account of the negative effects of highways. Regardless, including the value of land that could otherwise be used for houses, shops, and businesses, the conservatively estimated costs of a roadway expansion exceed the benefits by a factor of nearly three.

Finally, I assume that a 10 percent increase in major roadways corresponds to a 7 percent increase in vehicle travel and associated external costs. As discussed in chapter 5, this 7 percent increase is on the lower end of expectations about increased travel on major highways.[12] I also apply older, more conservative estimates of the external costs of vehicle travel.[13] For perspective, these estimates put the cost of greenhouse gas emissions five to seventy times lower than the figures presented in table 6-1. The estimated costs of collisions are three to twelve times lower. Despite using conservative estimates, the external costs of the additional vehicle travel from a 10 percent increase in roadways exceed the benefits to drivers and the trucking industry by around 60 percent.

In sum, the construction and maintenance costs of building new highways are modestly higher than the benefits. When accounting for the external costs of car travel and the opportunity costs of valuable urban land that could be used for houses, shops, and offices, the costs of new highways outweigh their benefits by a factor of four to five (a benefit-to-cost ratio of just 0.23). The lost land, in particular, is extremely valuable. Recall that the major challenge of the shift from building rural highways to building urban highways in the first half of the twentieth century was the land acquisition costs. The United States would be wealthier and healthier if less of that land had been converted to highways.

The finding that building more roadways is bad economic policy is robust to major changes in assumptions about the value of time, external costs of travel, or the value of trucking. Beyond the high costs of construction, land, and car travel, the main problem is that new highways simply do not save people very much time.

That finding is hardly novel. Two recent studies have put the estimated construction costs of interstate highways at around twice the benefits on average—a substantially worse performance than the conservative estimates shown in table 6-2.[14] In 1963, just a few years into interstate construction, Nobel Prize–winning economist William Vickrey estimated that motor vehicle taxes only covered about one-third of the costs of the roadway system.[15] As early as 1978, economist William Wheaton concluded that the urban Interstate System might already have been overbuilt.[16] He also showed that earlier, more rosy estimates of the Interstate System had been based on substantial underestimates of costs and an assumption that average travel speeds would double from around 25 miles per hour to 50 miles per hour. Summarizing the academic literature on highway investments in 1997, public policy professor Marlon Boarnet concluded that "recent evidence suggests that, at the margin, highway infrastructure contributes little to state or national productivity."[17]

That's not to say that all roadway construction projects are bad construction projects. There may even be certain types of investments, like removing certain types of bottlenecks, that are generally high performing. Given the increasing costs and decreasing benefits of highway construction over time, however, most new road widenings are unlikely to produce benefits that outweigh costs at the margin. Moreover, the places where new road investments are likely to produce the highest benefits are also likely the places where the construction and land costs are highest. It is also not to say that simply not investing in roadway will fix the problem. Even if the costs of a highway or bridge substantially outweigh the benefits, simply allowing the highway or bridge to deteriorate or fail structurally over time will not solve that problem. However, most new capacity increases are problematic and make an already overbuilt system even more overbuilt. I will return to these issues in the final chapters of this book, but for now, the main takeaway is that most new highways and highway widenings make the United States poorer and worse off. They are not a good investment in the future and likely have not been for decades.

Cost-Benefit Analysis in Practice

It is tempting to call it a day, conclude my book here, and recommend that all transportation investments go through a cost-benefit analysis. If some projects are likely beneficial but most are not, it makes apparent sense to require cost-benefit analyses. Without some external oversight or some of the stricter guidelines (see chapter 10), this approach is unlikely to do much, however. The evaluation and modeling tools used by traffic engineers and planners were developed to support and justify highway investments. The fundamental paradigm underpinning traffic forecasting has not changed substantially in the years since Harland Bartholomew and Miller McClintock first began projecting traffic growth and drawing ever thicker lines on maps (chapter 5). The purpose is not to model traffic or economic effects. The purpose is to justify massive road investments.

Even a not-so-close look at how transportation models get used shows this true purpose. Somehow, after throwing a few toll lanes and transit investments into their plan, serious planners and traffic engineers with impressive degrees and professional licenses spent substantial time, money, and computing power to predict that spending billions of dollars to add more than a thousand miles of highway lanes (a 45 percent increase) to the Dallas region would reduce the amount that people drive.[18] This calculation allowed for the prediction of an absurd benefit-to-cost ratio of 4.6 based on a 40 percent reduction in congestion.

These types of projections are neither uncommon nor a thing of the past. In 2017, the Texas Department of Transportation (TxDOT) published its 323-page environmental impact statement supporting adding four lanes, additional frontage lanes, and wider shoulders to one of Houston's already famously wide highways. Despite adding to highway capacity, the planners and engineers concluded that the project would reduce greenhouse gas emissions and dependency on fossil fuels by reducing how much time people spent on the road.[19] That the models are clearly wrong is irrelevant. This type of forecasting is an elaborate and costly ritual to justify highway investments. In his book *Confessions of Recovering Engineer*, Charles Marohn Jr. does not mince words: "All of this institutionalized fraud and elaborate self-deception is being done for the sole purpose of securing transportation funding."[20] Megan Kimble mocks the absurdity of TxDOT's conclusion that commuters would spend 3.7 hours driving across Austin on Interstate 35 by 2045 without widening the freeway.[21] The model results may defy reality and any reasonable notion of human travel behavior, but they nevertheless form part of the technical and legal justification for destroying thousands of homes and businesses.

Despite lacking the incentive to secure funding, federal accounting is not much better. The Federal Highway Administration maintains a model examining the effects of different levels of highway maintenance, reconstruction, and expansion.[22] The Highway Economic Requirements System (HERS) predicts higher benefit-to-cost ratios at lower levels of expenditures but unsurprisingly finds benefits to be higher than costs across all scenarios. On average, the benefits outweigh costs by 1.81 to 2.35 times. Even at the highest level of spending, benefits are equal to costs. Identifying better performing expenditure levels, however, is not the purpose of the model. Rather, the model is designed to identify the highest level of spending possible where the average benefits each year are equal to the average costs (the model's authors mistakenly refer to them as the marginal costs and benefits). Ignoring that this model implies that roughly half of all projects have costs that exceed benefits each year, the authors then make the convoluted claim that "achieving a minimum [benefit-to-cost-ratio] of 1.0 is estimated to require $1.465 trillion over the 20-year analysis period."[23] In fact, the model finds the opposite: it would be substantially easier to achieve a higher ratio by spending less. Moreover, since the average year of spending will always look better than the worst year of spending, the model cannot, by design, find spending packages where benefits do not exceed costs.

Looking under the hood, HERS contains many of the same problematic assumptions that go into state and local transportation models. The projected time and cost savings are excessive. Somehow, spending an extra $20 billion per year on highways saves drivers and truckers an extra $44 billion per year on average. The safety effects are counterintuitive. Somehow building more and wider arterials reduces traffic collisions and fatalities. Finally, the model completely ignores the opportunity costs of land and the environmental and social costs associated with driving. It is a model built by highway planners and engineers, for highway planners and engineers. Its main purpose is to justify higher levels of spending.

Improving these practices will be challenging. The technical tools and analytical models are so embedded in the transportation profession that it is likely difficult to step back from them. Moreover, decision-making about transportation investments has devolved firmly into the hands of state, regional, and local authorities. These authorities have every incentive to get their projects funded and supported by federal and state agencies. Even those who accept and mitigate problems associated with modeling are likely to see projects that they have come to support through rosy lenses. This type of optimism bias is pervasive in transportation modeling and evaluation.

Before examining approaches to stopping and reversing the trend of overbuilding, however, I want to look more closely at two important costs of overbuilding that remain inadequately examined. The first is traffic safety. The federal and many state departments of transportation frequently make the claim that safety is their number one priority. Moreover, federal and state planners and engineers typically claim that their highway investments will save lives. The TxDOT plans and federal HERS referenced earlier predict economic benefits from reduced collisions and fatalities, yet the United States has among the worst traffic fatality outcomes of any wealthy country (see chapter 7). Something has gone horribly wrong with US traffic safety, and the billions invested in highways in the name of safety do not appear to be helping.

Next, I look at the social costs of the US transportation system, particularly on more vulnerable households with lower income. Cost-benefit analyses tend to do a poor job of analyzing these kinds of social effects. The amount that households spend on cars (see table 6-1) shows the value placed on automobility. However, it fails to show how difficult the system can be for those who cannot afford a reliable vehicle or who scrape by after car payments and filling up their tanks with gas. It also fails to reveal the costs of parents shuffling kids from activity to activity until their kids are old enough to get behind the wheel of yet another household expense. The high willingness to pay for automobility reflects the value of automobility. But it also reflects the poor quality of the next best options. Outside of a few major cities, living without access to a car—whether due to income, age, disability, or preference—means living with a serious curtailment of economic, social, and recreational opportunities. These costs are neither trivial nor diminishing. They are a primary consequence of an overbuilt and still expanding roadway system.

CHAPTER 7

Roadkill

Although certainly as we pointed out, [the Interstate] is probably the safest system that we have, certainly in the Country, if not the world, we are still losing 43,000, 44,000 Americans every year on our highways.—Richard Capka, Administrator of the Federal Highway Administration (2006–2008), Remarks to Congress, 2006

If you are an adult who grew up in the United States, chances are that you have lost one or more friends, colleagues, or family members to a traffic collision. Maybe you are one of the unlucky who has lost a parent, sibling, spouse, or child. Maybe you or a loved one has suffered one of the millions of life-altering traffic injuries and survived. For an American family of four, there is about a one-in-thirty chance that a family member will lose their life to a traffic collision. Traffic collisions are a top killer of American kids, teenagers, and all but the youngest and oldest age groups. Since most top killers, like cancer and heart disease, disproportionately affect older residents, traffic collisions account for more years of lost life than any individual disease or injury. US transportation officials correctly put an emphasis on traffic safety, which is the top stated priority of the federal and many state departments of transportation. Improving safety was also one of the stated original goals of the Interstate and Defense Highways Act.

Alas, US transportation officials and traffic engineers are either disingenuous or incompetent. The United States has the highest traffic fatality rate of its wealthy democratic peers (figure 7-1).[1] Moreover, the US traffic safety record has improved less quickly than any of its peers. In 2000, the US traffic fatality was 1.2 times higher than the average of other high-income democracies. By 2022, Americans died at nearly three times the rate of residents of peer countries. The next most dangerous country, New Zealand, has about half the traffic fatalities per capita. The US traffic fatality rate has also worsened substantially—and substantially more than in most peer countries—since the COVID-19 pandemic. Despite some of the world's best emergency care, the United States appears to be the only wealthy democracy demonstrably losing the traffic safety battle. This chapter explores what has gone so wrong with US safety policy and how highway builders claim safety not only as a priority but as a success.

Why Is Driving in the United States So Dangerous?

Traffic safety—like other public health concerns—is a function of exposure, risk, and injury probability. For convenience, I am going to combine risk and injury probability into a single factor of risk of injury. It is true that there are instances in which the risk of a traffic collision goes up, but the probability of injury goes down substantially (such as in parking lots or garages). However, most state and national databases only collect data on collisions that are severe enough to result in injury or serious damage to a vehicle, so it is easier to discuss risk and the probability of injury combined. Exposure is the amount of time that people spend in risky situations, whether that's driving in a car, walking across a street, or riding a bike. One reason that the US transportation system is so much more dangerous than that of peer countries is because people

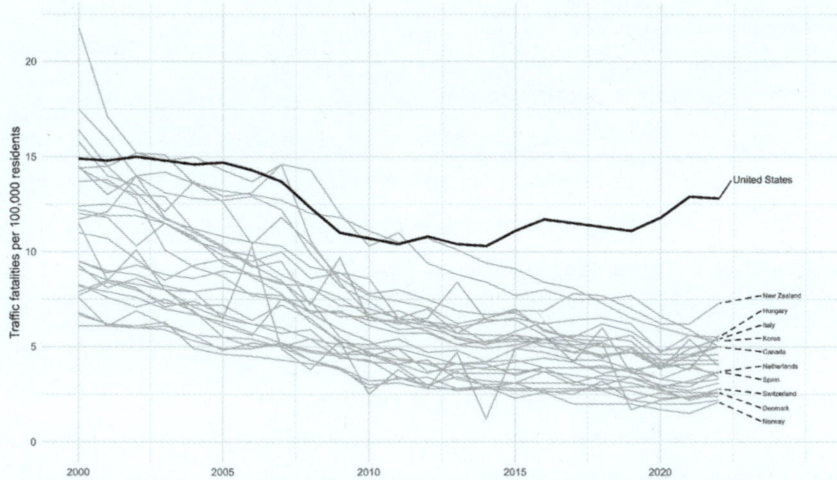

Figure 7-1. Road traffic fatalities per 100,000 residents in upper-income democracies. (Source: International Transport Forum "Transport Statistics.")

drive so much more, increasing their exposure. Residents of the United States, for example, travel more than twice as far in cars as residents of the United Kingdom on average.[2] Risk is the probability of an injurious or fatal collision occurring for each unit of exposure.

As shown in the previous chapters, building more highways leads to more driving and thus more exposure. Despite the stated focus on safety, early highway investments did not make traveling by car safer. In his opening letter attached to the 1955 Clay committee's report supporting the interstate program, President Dwight Eisenhower lamented the thirty-six thousand traffic fatalities that occurred each year.[3] By 1970, that figure had climbed to more than fifty-two thousand. By 1980, with nearly two hundred thousand lane miles of interstate completed, the traffic fatality rate per capita was just slightly above the 1955 rate at 22.5 deaths per hundred thousand residents. Highway builders, like Richard Capka, can credibly claim that the system is substantially safer per mile of travel. From 1955 to 1980, the fatality rate per vehicle mile had halved. To put it succinctly, Americans were driving nearly twice as much, thanks to wider and higher-capacity highways, and killing about the same number of people after adjusting for population growth.

Highway promoters like to compare these fatality rates across roadway types as a sign of how safe highways are. For example, Capka celebrated the Interstate System by favorably comparing fatalities per vehicle mile of travel on highways to the fatalities per vehicle mile on all roads.[4] Today, there are about half as many fatalities per mile driven on highways as on the system as whole.[5] The implication is that building more highways diverted a fixed amount of vehicle travel to safter highways and saved lives. More than an implication, it is also one of the primary assumptions underlying the claims made by federal and state departments of transportation that highway investments will save lives. There are, however, several major problems with the assumption.

First, it ignores that building more roadways causes more driving that offsets any safety benefits. A public health analogy would be something akin to looking at the effects of reducing the cost of cigarettes on lung cancer while controlling for the number of cigarettes smoked. Driving has substantially more benefits than smoking, of course, and improving safety by keeping everyone indoors is hardly good policy. Still, great care should be taken in examining the effects of any kind of public health policy that affects both exposure and risk.

Second, the focus on safety rates on highways ignores that highways are part of a transportation system. By their nature, highways have limited access. People need to get on to arterials and local roads to get to houses, shops, and business. The major arterials that connect towns and cities to the highway network are particularly dangerous. Without them, however, the highway network would be completely disconnected. They were built up and expanded as part of the modern highway program. There is no highway rate of exposure without also considering exposure on arterials and local roads.

Third, focusing on fatalities per vehicle mile of travel ignores that most people die when traffic is lighter and vehicle travel is lower.[6] Congestion, that longtime enemy of US highway builders, plays a major role in keeping Americans safer by reducing speeds and the overall risk of travel. The COVID-19 pandemic highlighted this effect: driving plummeted, fatalities increased, and fatalities per mile of travel skyrocketed. Nearly every other public health statistic is primarily reported on a per capita basis. Transportation officials focus on fatality rates per mile of travel because it makes them look better.

Looking better, however, is not necessarily looking good. Americans are about 60 percent more likely to die for every mile spent in cars than those living in peer countries.[7] Going back to the UK comparison, residents of the United States drive twice as much as residents of the United Kingdom but are about five times more likely to die in a car collision. Traveling in the United States is much riskier than it is in the United Kingdom. As with fatalities per capita, the United States also has the worst improvement record over time compared to its peers. Fatalities per mile of travel may have decreased by 28 percent from 2000 to 2021, but this rate of improvement was half the average of the fifteen wealthy democracies that reported statistics in 2000 and 2021. The next slowest improver, Australia, has about 60 percent of US fatalities per mile of travel and 33 percent of the fatalities per capita.

The claims that building more highways has saved lives starts to look even more absurd when considering the improvements in cars since 1955. Imagine what the US traffic fatality rate would look like if people were still driving the same cars as in 1955. Forget safety glass, modern trauma facilities, ambulances, or even high-quality brakes. As a thought exercise, just imagine away the seat belts and airbags. According to one federal study, seat belts and airbags reduce the probability of a traffic fatality by 61 percent in frontal collisions.[8] Airbags and seat belts do not do much for pedestrians or motorcyclists, but frontal collisions account for almost half of in-vehicle fatalities.[9] Traffic safety has improved despite building more highways, not because of it.

Professionally Embedded Incompetence and Disingenuity

In his book *Killed by a Traffic Engineer*, civil engineering professor Wes Marshall likens modern traffic engineering to the early days of medicine, a time before major scientific discoveries when doctors were as likely to kill a patient as to save them.[10] Similar to a doctor prescribing bloodletting, the science behind engineering safety standards is often shabby at best and nonexistent or even contradictory at worst. Tracing the evolution of the field through thousands of publications in its top traffic engineering journals and textbooks over the past hundred years, Marshall shows how early traffic engineers recognized how little they knew about safety or the effects of their interventions on safety. Yet, over time, in a bid to feel more scientific, engineers began presenting their safety guidelines and standards as cold, hard fact. In Marshall's words, "I should start by making it clear that traffic engineers—as far as I know—are *not* out there trying to cause deliberate harm to anyone. What traffic engineers are guilty of is creating a transportation system whose designs remain largely based on plausible, but unproven conjecture."[11]

Worse, a disproportionate share of these unproven conjectures support interventions that increase roadway capacity and traffic speeds. For example, it sounds plausible to say that wider lanes make roadways safer by giving motorists more room to maneuver. It is therefore difficult for citizens, politicians, and business owners to argue against bringing a highway up to modern safety standards. However, wider lanes allow for faster travel and are almost certainly more dangerous than narrower ones.[12] At the very least, the assertion that wider lanes making things safer is contested.

When affected residents in South Philadelphia examined the data and questioned whether regional travel forecasts by the Delaware Valley

Regional Planning Commission (DVRPC) justified widening Interstate 95, consultants from the Pennsylvania Department of Transportation (PennDOT) responded that it was actually a safety project: "We agree, the traffic data from DVRPC does not support adding thru lanes to increase capacity on Mainline I-95. The available DVPRC traffic data at this time has already been provided. The only road-widening that is being proposed is based on meeting safety standards for the traveling public. This includes the continuation of the northbound fourth lane approaching South Street, and providing adequate lanes for merging and shoulders for emergency pull-offs."[13] Despite this pronouncement and a similar claim made by another PennDOT engineer to journalist Inga Saffron (see chapter 5), the official engineering documents claim future congestion and capacity needs as primary justifications for the project. Several months later, a citizen's public information request revealed that PennDOT had been reporting misleading information about nearby residents' project preferences.[14] Instead of reporting that most survey respondents did not respond and likely wanted none of the options presented, PennDOT focused on a minority of respondents so it could claim that the majority of the public most wanted a specific highway option. Only twenty people in total indicated this choice as their preferred option. Six people in total indicated that they were in favor of one of the two other design alternatives.

Charles Marohn Jr. opens his book *Confessions of a Recovering Engineer* with a conversation between himself and a resident living next to a road proposed for widening. He describes the conversation as a "composite of many conversations I participated in during my years working as a civil engineer and urban planner for cities across Minnesota."[15] The affected resident keeps asking how things like adding lanes, removing trees, and widening the roadway will improve safety. Marohn dismisses each question with a reference to safety standards and design manuals, saying, "I'm sorry. But the traffic projections require a four-lane street for safety reasons. We must follow the standard."[16] Both Marohn and Marshall show how, despite claims of putting safety first, engineering standards focus first on increasing traffic volumes and traffic speeds. Safety comes third at best. Worse, it has become a cudgel to bully people into accepting projects that will almost certainly make them and their communities less safe. In this light, it is almost irrelevant whether US traffic engineers are incompetent or disingenuous. As Marohn confesses about his career as traffic engineer, they are "utterly and shamefully wrong."[17] By Marshall's account, the typical traffic engineer today is not so much malicious or indifferent as a not-so-innocent bystander who ought to know better but is stuck in the status quo of existing design manuals, safety standards, and funding practices.

Error Prone

A common way that US traffic engineers let themselves off the hook from building safer systems is to focus on human error. There is a very good chance you have heard the statistic that human error causes more than 90 percent of traffic collisions. The statistic has featured in hundreds, if not thousands, of speeches and newspaper articles on self-driving cars. Maybe you have even seen a tech enthusiast multiply the world's 1.35 million annual traffic fatalities by 0.94 to give an estimate of how many lives self-driving cars are going to save. In the wake of rapid increases in fatalities per mile driven after COVID-19, you may have also read or heard pleas from transportation officials to slow down, put away phones, and avoid impaired driving. This approach to traffic safety is consistent with findings from the National Motor Vehicle Crash Causation Survey, the origin of the much-quoted more than 90 percent statistic.

The National Motor Vehicle Crash Causation Survey was developed from data collected at the scene of 6,950 collisions from 2005 to 2007.[18] Researchers focused on the events leading up to a collision with an emphasis on what they refer to as the critical reason that the collision occurred. Table 7-1 presents the number of collisions with a reported critical cause as well as the two most common causes in each category and subcategory. Removing collisions with unknown critical causes, human error accounted for 95.5 percent of collisions after weighting the sample to be nationally representative. The researchers reported roadway design as the primary cause in just three collisions in their sample. According to the researchers, heart attacks and falling asleep at the wheel led to substantially more collisions than roadway design. So did "sleep, actually sleep." If people would just pay attention and stop speeding, goes the argument, the nearly perfectly designed and perfectly safe system would be nearly perfectly safe.

This type of view about what causes traffic collisions permeates the way transportation officials talk about safety, collect traffic safety data, and propose improvements to the system. Although the National Motor Vehicle Crash Causation Survey treats impairment as something that leads to a final causal behavioral error, like inattention or speeding, much national safety data, reporting, and enforcement priorities emphasize alcohol and drugs. According to the National Fatality Analysis Reporting System, approximately one third of traffic fatalities in 2022 involved a driver with blood-alcohol levels above the legal limit.[19]

The response to what has been dubbed the world's first fatal collision involving an automated vehicle provides insight into the collective national viewpoint about human error and poor behavior. Captured by the automated vehicle's many cameras, videos of the incident also provide unusual insight into an all-too-common occurrence.

A little before 10 p.m. on Sunday, March 18, 2018, Elaine Herzberg began to push her bicycle across Mill Avenue, a four-lane arterial, in Tempe, Arizona. She did not make it across to the other side. One of Uber's self-driving Volvo XC90s, traveling just under the posted 45 miles per hour speed limit, struck and ultimately killed her. The video of the incident is alarming. Before I show it to my students, I get their

Table 7-1. Estimated Percent of Critical Reasons Attributed to US Vehicular Collisions

Driver error	**95.4%**
Recognition error	***38.7%***
Internal distraction	19.4%
External distraction	10.2%
Other	9.1%
Decision error	***32.5%***
Too fast for conditions	8.0%
Too fast for curve	4.7%
Other	19.8%
Performance error	***9.8%***
Overcompensation	4.7%
Poor directional control	0.4%
Other	4.7%
Nonperformance error	***6.8%***
Sleep, actually sleep	3.0%
Heart attack or other physical impairment	2.3%
Other	1.5%
Other/unknown driver error	***7.6%***
Vehicle error	**2.1%**
Tires failed or degraded/wheels failed	0.9%
Brakes failed/degraded	0.5%
Other	0.7%
Roadway conditions	**1.9%**
Slick roads (ice, loose debris, etc.)	1.2%
View obstructions	0.3%
Other	0.3%
Atmospheric conditions	**0.6%**
Glare	0.4%
Fog/rain/snow	0.1%
Other	0.1%

consent and then give them a moment to prepare themselves. The driver's-eye view shows how quickly a person can seem to appear out of nowhere and how little hope a driver might have of stopping in time. The interior-facing camera shows a view of safety driver Rafaela Vasquez during the moments before the collision. Her eyes drift from the road to her lap as the automated system maneuvers the vehicle. The moment of impact shows her shocked and horrified reaction.

As with most of these incidents, the police quickly found no driver fault. In an interview the next day with the *San Francisco Chronicle*, Tempe police chief Sylvia Moir reported that "it's very clear it would have been difficult to avoid this collision in any kind of mode (autonomous or human-driven) based on how she came from the shadows right into the roadway." Going on to critique the recently deceased Herzberg, the chief continued, "It is dangerous to cross roadways in the evening hour when well-illuminated, managed crosswalks are available." Likely believing the collision to have occurred in a 35 miles per hour zone, Moir also reported the vehicle to have been traveling about 10 miles per hour slower than it was actually traveling.[20]

Due to the collision involving a self-driving car, the National Transportation Safety Board launched an investigation into the collision and published its findings in a seventy-eight-page report. Consistent with data from the National Motor Vehicle Crash Causation Survey, the report concluded that an attentive driver should have been able to stop the vehicle prior to impact.[21] Vasquez later took a guilty plea to one count of endangerment in exchange for three years of supervised probation.[22] It remains contested whether she was looking down to monitor the vehicle or to watch an episode of *The Voice*. Without the investigation and camera footage, there would have been no report of driver distraction. The report also indicated that Herzberg had indeed crossed the arterial illegally and had traces of amphetamines, methamphetamines, and THC in her bloodstream. However, it also criticized Uber for having a lax safety culture and indicated that the self-driving system had identified Herzberg with ample time to stop.[23] The vehicle simply was not properly programmed to stop.

Nowhere does the report criticize how planners and engineers have built Tempe's streets and surrounding offices, parks, and homes. According to the police report, Herzberg should have simply walked an extra two hundred to three hundred yards to cross a four-lane road. Never mind that traffic engineers sometimes remove crosswalk markings if there are too many collisions. As Marshall notes, the engineers do not want to encourage unsafe crossings or be held responsible for creating dangerous environments.[24] There has also been almost no focus on the issue of the Uber vehicle accelerating ten seconds before the collision in response to a shift in speed limit from 35 miles per hour to 45 miles per hour. The probability of a pedestrian dying in a traffic collision begins to increase substantially at speeds above 30 miles per hour.[25]

A confluence of human and programmer errors allowed the fatal collision to occur. Removing any one of these errors would have avoided the collision. From this perspective, it seems logical that human errors cause nearly all collisions and fatalities. If you included a failure to properly maintain vehicles or avoid inclement weather, the figure would jump even higher. This conclusion also begs the question of whether people in Tempe, Arizona, where the collision occurred, are really two to three times more error prone than people in Washington, DC, where the National Transportation Safety Board published its report. That is the difference in fatalities per capita in the two cities. Are Americans really dying in collisions at a rate five times higher than the British because we are such bumbling, distracted, error-prone, alcoholic, anger-fueled speed freaks? Every single fatal collision has a story of one or more failures of judgment, health, behavior, or technology in the moments before impact. Some places just seem to have an awful lot more of them.

Where Is US Driving Most Dangerous?

Within the United States, there is quite a bit of variety in traffic safety outcomes (figure 7-2).[26] States in the Northeast tend to have the lowest numbers of fatalities per person and mile of travel, though the rates are still generally higher than in other wealthy democracies. States in the Southeast are particularly deadly, with traffic fatality rates per capita as high as those seen throughout Africa and more dangerous parts of Latin America and Asia. States in the Midwest generally fall somewhere

Figure 7-2. Road traffic fatalities per 100,000 residents and 100 million vehicle miles of travel by state in 2022. (Sources: National Highway Traffic Safety Administration, "Fatality Analysis Reporting System"; and Federal Highway Administration, "Highway Statistics.")

between, while the West has the widest range, with Washington among the safest states but Wyoming, New Mexico, and Montana among the deadliest. More rural states and more rural counties within states tend to be most dangerous, but most traffic collisions and most fatalities occur in urban areas. These overall trends have been generally consistent over time, with most states following the national trend of decreasing slowly over time but starting to increase sometime between 2010 and 2020 (figure 7-3).

Despite highway builders taking great credit for traffic safety, the places that have the most highways have substantially worse traffic safety records. Moving from a less highway-dependent place, like greater Boston or New York City, to a more highway-dependent place, like greater Dallas or Phoenix, nearly triples the chances of dying in a traffic collision. This relationship is consistent throughout urban counties. The

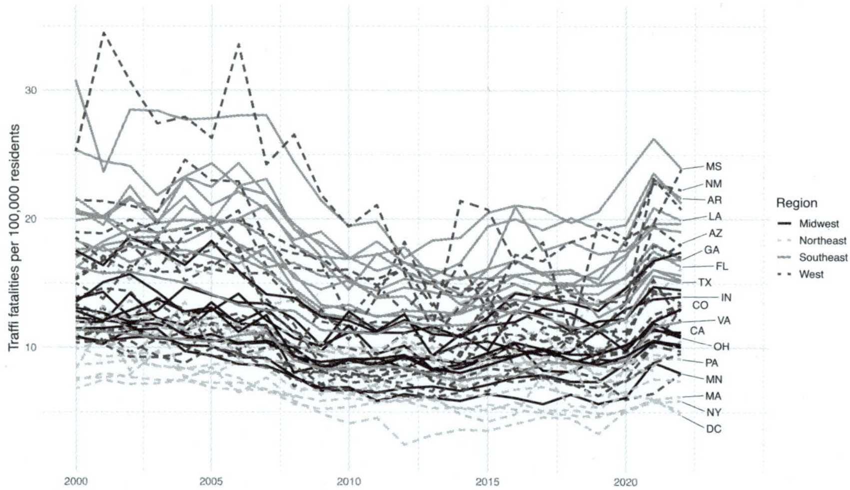

Figure 7-3. Road traffic fatalities per 100,000 residents by state (2000–2022). (Source: National Highway Traffic Safety Administration, "Fatality Analysis Reporting System.")

places with the most highways have the most arterials, the most local roads, the most driving, and the most traffic fatalities. Across urban counties, each 10 percent increase in roadway per capita corresponds with about a 4 percent increase in traffic fatalities per capita. Including state-level statistical controls makes the relationship even stronger and explains about 70 percent of the variance in urban counties' traffic fatalities per capita.[27] While highways may have a comparatively good safety record per mile of travel relative to nearby roads in the United States, they have a poor record when considered holistically as part of an overall urban transportation system.

As discussed in chapter 6, roads also replace and spread out houses, shops, offices, and other urban land uses. By economist Nathaniel Baum-Snow's estimates, central cities would have grown by 8 percent instead of losing 17 percent of their population if it weren't for the urban highways built between 1950 and 1990.[28] Across urban counties today, each 10 percent decrease in population density corresponds with about a 6 percent increase in traffic fatality rates.[29]

So why are denser places with fewer roads safer? The easy answer is that, for whatever reason, there is less exposure and less risk of injury per unit of exposure in those places. Beyond that, things get quite a bit more complicated, especially since denser places tend to have a lot more people walking and biking around, creating exposure for particularly vulnerable road users. Less driving does not always correspond with less exposure or even less risk. And to be perfectly honest, the academic and professional research around the relationship between the built environment and traffic safety is a bit of a mess, with poorly theorized ad hoc models that often fail to provide much insight into the causal mechanisms that make denser places with less roadway so much safer.[30]

One thing that researchers do know for certain is that more cars on the road moving at higher speeds leads to more traffic fatalities. Despite claims of putting safety first, US transportation finance, modeling, and evaluation have two clear principal goals: to increase capacity and to increase speeds. The best that could be said about safety is that traffic engineering has made it an important goal as long as it does not impede on speed and capacity. But it is certainly not the first goal. And it is hardly a success story.

There is also a lot more to traffic safety than just the way that cities, towns, and roadways are laid out. Utah, for example, is so much safer than its peers in the Mountain West. The uniquely low blood-alcohol limits to legally drive in Utah may play a role. More likely, the cultural differences that led to that legal decision result in a very different driving culture. I am surprised by how pleasant it is to walk across Salt Lake City's wide arterial roadways. Wide arterials are often among the most dangerous type of roads, and I can barely imagine the carnage that would result from laying Salt Lake City's road network over Philadelphia. Salt Lake City and Philadelphia generally have similar annual traffic fatality rates, being quite a bit higher than Boston, DC, or New York, but substantially lower than Dallas, Tempe, or pretty much any urban county in Florida. I do not wish to deny the importance of behavior or what the traffic engineers like to call human factors, but influencing human factors is not something that highway builders or highway policies have ever done much of or done particularly well. Little progress has been made since suggestions in the 1950s that religious leaders might do a better job of improving driving behavior than traffic engineers.[31] Driver error and human factors have simply become an excuse for why the national road-building experiment has failed so badly when it comes to traffic safety.

CHAPTER 8

The High Costs of Carlessness

Our central mission is to redress the social inequities thrown up by widespread auto use, and our central task is to invent ways of extending the benefits of auto-like transportation to those who are presently carless.—Mel Webber, "The Joys of Automobility," 1992

In the final exam of my graduate-level introduction to transportation planning class, I often ask my students to write a policy memo to a public official about whether to support a federal policy to help low-income households purchase cars. Most students recognize the high environmental, economic, and public health costs discussed in previous chapters and worry about policies that encourage greater automobile ownership and use. Most also recognize that, outside a handful of the largest cities, US land use and transportation systems have become so car-dependent that having a private car is a prerequisite to participating in basic everyday economic, social, and recreational activities. People from poor households without access to cars often live as second-class citizens. Many others make great personal and financial sacrifices to purchase a car. I want my students to have to wrestle with the internal conflicts they have between wanting the transportation system to be more environmentally and economically sustainable but also wanting it to be fairer, particularly in the short run.

The best answers discuss how the policy might vary by geography or subsidize transit or other transportation expenditures as well. Some students even suggest cash subsidies more generally—through something like a minimum basic income—so that households might choose how best to spend their money. Why subsidize a car instead of groceries, rent, or other household needs? The best student responses might even point out that helping purchase cars does little to support the millions of US residents who cannot physically or legally drive due to age, ability, or legal status. Some might make some back-of-the-envelope calculations using figures in table 6-1 to show how much the policy might cost. Assuming a $10,000 annual subsidy (a bit less than average annual car expenditures) for the households of the thirty million to forty million Americans living in poverty, the policy would cost about $150 billion, roughly three times total federal highway expenditures. A one-time subsidy or smaller amounts could substantially reduce costs, but any subsidy that makes a dent in the problem would also represent a large increase in federal expenditures.

Weaker answers might suggest funding transit instead of cars (more on that subject follows) or simply dismiss the importance of fairness in the face of issues like global warming. In the end, there is no right answer—only trade-offs and the acknowledgment that the problems of overbuilding highways disproportionately affect the poorest and most vulnerable households. This chapter explores these disproportionate impacts as well as some of the subtler social costs of living in a car-dependent society that are unlikely to feature in a cost-benefit analysis or in the ways that transportation planners and engineers evaluate highway investments.

First, an aside on transit. Although my claim that transit investments would do a lot less than car subsidies to make the US transportation system fairer is unlikely to raise the eyebrow of any US academic studying transportation justice or poverty, I know that it is likely to provoke a reaction from many of my students and likely readers. Transit has become so embedded in discussions about transportation justice that it can be easy to forget just how poorly transit works for most Americans, regardless of income, race, gender, physical ability, or other factors.

Of Transit Dependents and Choice Riders

Ideas around poverty, race, and car ownership have featured in discussions about transit for at least as long as federal and state governments have been funding bus and rail services. Prior to World War II, a combination of private for-profit companies and city agencies provided transit services throughout the United States. Although vehicle registrations were already rapidly increasing in the early twentieth century, the combination of increased automobility, major highway investments, and suburbanization in the postwar era contributed to a substantial reduction in transit ridership, the closure of multiple transit lines, the public takeover of many private transit companies, and an increasing need for public subsidies to maintain remaining transit services. In greater Philadelphia, for example, the city of Philadelphia and the Commonwealth of Pennsylvania began to subsidize transit services as early as 1960.[1] In 1963, the commonwealth formed the Southeastern Pennsylvania Transportation Authority, or SEPTA, which took over transit operations from the patchwork of transit companies throughout the region. In 1964, the federal government created the Urban Mass Transportation Administration (now the Federal Transit Administration) and began to pass a series of laws to support and subsidize urban transit systems throughout the United States.[2]

As public agencies continued to take over and subsidize transit operations in the 1960s and 1970s, terms like *choice* and *captive riders* made their way into technical transportation planning documents to describe categories of transit users.[3] For example, the 1961 Pittsburgh Area Transportation Study described a decline in captive ridership as more households acquired cars.[4] While many of these early transit planning documents provided circular definitions—a choice rider was someone who could choose to use transit—several key words frequently coincided with each term. Choice riders had cars, licenses, and suburban homes in wealthy neighborhoods. They were White, male, white-collar workers who took trains to downtown jobs. Captive riders were poor, racial minorities, housewives, the old, the young, the carless, and the differently abled. They relied on urban bus services to accomplish their daily tasks regardless of service quality.

The differentiation between choice and captive riders had implicit and explicit connections to the economic and environmental justifications for subsidizing transit. One common line of argument was that "the captive rider has no choice but to wait, regardless of the headway between buses or trains, but the choice rider can get back in his car and drive."[5] The captive rider market "will always exist," but the choice rider market "will exist only as long as transit service is attractive."[6] If transit ridership was to increase or draw passengers away from cars and thus reduce associated pollution and congestion, transit agencies needed to ignore captive riders and focus on choice riders.

After six decades, the definitions, uses, and implications of the terms choice and *captive rider* have persisted—though the term *dependent rider* has largely replaced *captive rider*.[7] There is just one problem. The terms do a terrible job of describing who uses transit, where, why, or how. Just 18 percent of US households earning below $25,000 per year do not have a car. Moreover, adults in these low-income carless households, rely on cars to get around more frequently than they rely on transit.[8] Instead of owning cars, they borrow, rent, or carpool.[9] Lacking a car, moreover, is also generally a temporary situation for low-income households without cars, not a permanent one.[10]

To better understand the distinction between choice and dependent riders, I conducted a study using household travel diaries and data on the transportation network to develop probabilistic models of transit use for trips in the Philadelphia region.[11] The Philadelphia region has one of the largest transit providers in the United States and a wide range of services, including commuter rail into wealthy suburban communities and bus services into low-income urban communities with low car-ownership rates in Philadelphia and nearby Camden, New Jersey. Service quality was the key determinant for whether people chose transit regardless of their income, background, or other factors. More generally, the lowest- and highest-income residents generally only chose transit when service quality was high and transit was cost- and time-competitive with the car; lacking a car, living in poverty, and other attributes assumed to be associated with transit dependency were far less important. In fact, so-called dependent riders were much more likely to be on the cusp of choosing between transit and cars to get around the region.

If that's the case, why am I so skeptical about simply investing more in transit? Shouldn't improving transit benefit poor and wealthy households alike? The problem is that transit does not come close to being competitive with private cars for most US trips. Most residents live and travel in areas where transit is simply not a reasonable option. Even in a transit-friendly region like Philadelphia, cars saved an average of 34 minutes per trip over transit in my study.[12] For the half of all regional trips where I estimated people to have less than a 1 percent probability of taking transit, taking a car saved about an hour relative to taking transit. Comparing that difference to the difference in cost between transit and driving, people would have to value their time at less than $1 per hour to choose transit. That is simply not a realistic trade-off.

The scale of highway investments since the Interstate and Defense Highways Act have helped make US urban form so car-dependent that even massive investments into bus and rail are unlikely to shift travel behavior much outside the more central parts of large urban areas, like Philadelphia, where transit is already somewhat competitive. Outside the core city and a handful of older town centers, origins and destinations have disbursed over time along the trillions of dollars invested in urban highway networks. Even for the poor families without cars, it is simply not that relevant if a car saves 40 minutes per trip instead of 60 minutes.

The High Costs of Carlessness

Meanwhile, not having access to a car has become more and more challenging over time. Planning professor David King and his colleagues looked at fifty years of data on car ownership and household expenditures and found that although the US poverty rate fell nearly in half between 1960 and 2014, it increased slightly for households without cars. This relationship holds in Los Angeles, but not in New York City, where incomes have risen substantially for carless households. It also holds in transit-rich Manhattan, but not in the more suburban Staten Island.[13] The city's older, denser built environments have been far less touched by highways and provide substantial opportunities for those with and without cars. Most of the US built environment has become so car-oriented that, outside of older, denser urban centers, poor households need a private vehicle to participate in basic daily activities. Gaining access to a car is associated with finding better-paying work within a year, and programs to subsidize car ownership frequently improve people's ability to find and retain work.[14] Carless individuals only tend to see economic improvements over time that rival those with access to cars in the central parts of older cities with the best existing transit services.

These places are uncommon. Table 8-1 summarizes the average number of jobs accessible by car and by transit for twenty-four metropolitan areas with data available from the University of Minnesota's Accessibility Observatory in 2018.[15] Across metropolitan areas, neighborhoods

Table 8-1. Estimated Average Number of Jobs Reachable in 30 Minutes across Neighborhoods by Car and by Transit

Metropolitan area	*Car*	*Transit*	*Difference*	*Ratio*
Baltimore-Towson, MD	627,632	32,277	595,355	19
Boston-Cambridge-Quincy, MA-NH	626,606	50,829	575,777	12
Charlotte-Gastonia-Rock Hill, NC-SC	462,709	10,448	452,261	44
Chicago-Joliet-Naperville, IL-IN-WI	816,506	53,205	763,301	15
Jacksonville, FL	348,483	6,150	342,333	57
Los Angeles-Long Beach-Santa Ana, CA	1,289,675	43,137	1,246,537	30
Memphis, TN-MS-AR	431,859	7,131	424,728	61
Miami-Fort Lauderdale-Pompano Beach, FL	597,269	19,967	577,302	30
Minneapolis-St. Paul-Bloomington, MN-WI	1,040,787	24,947	1,015,840	42
Nashville-Davidson-Murfreesboro-Franklin, TN	358,603	8,673	349,929	41
Orlando-Kissimmee-Sanford, FL	533,306	9,602	523,705	56
Philadelphia-Camden-Wilmington, PA-NJ-DE-MD	698,192	55,346	642,846	13
Pittsburgh, PA	350,391	18,669	331,722	19
Raleigh-Cary, NC	493,922	6,649	487,274	74
Richmond, VA	401,041	8,388	392,653	48
Riverside-San Bernardino-Ontario, CA	443,102	5,737	437,365	77
Sacramento-Arden-Arcade-Roseville, CA	500,139	11,852	488,288	42
San Diego-Carlsbad-San Marcos, CA	646,981	6,461	640,519	100
San Francisco-Oakland-Fremont, CA	661,689	78,968	582,721	8
San Jose-Sunnyvale-Santa Clara, CA	823,941	20,623	803,318	40
Seattle-Tacoma-Bellevue, WA	516,329	27,299	489,030	19
Tampa-St. Petersburg-Clearwater, FL	453,897	9,289	444,607	49
Virginia Beach-Norfolk-Newport News, VA-NC	354,392	5,886	348,506	60
Washington-Arlington-Alexandria, DC-VA-MD-WV	623,795	41,609	582,187	15
Average	**593,832**	**24,235**	**569,597**	**39**

Note: Data aggregated and averaged by block group as a proxy for neighborhood.

had 593,832 jobs accessible by car within thirty minutes compared to 24,235 accessible by transit. At night, when congestion is low and transit service infrequent, job accessibility by car looks even better compared to transit. Even in the most transit-accessible places, like Boston and San Francisco, a resident in an average neighborhood can reach approximately ten times more jobs by car than by transit.

Within the most transit accessible places, relative accessibility also varies tremendously. Figure 8-1 plots car accessibility against transit across neighborhoods in metropolitan Boston, Massachusetts, and Riverside, California—two metropolitan areas with similar population sizes and very different levels of transit accessibility. While Boston's transit accessibility is clearly and substantially higher, even the most transit-accessible neighborhoods have two to three times more jobs within 30 minutes by car than by transit. Additionally, much of the region looks like Riverside, where car accessibility varies but transit accessibility is consistently poor.

At the same time, the costs of car ownership have risen. Today, households spend nearly as much of their income on transportation expenses as they did in the 1950s. The burden is particularly pronounced for low-income households. Not only do low-income households spend substantially higher shares of their wages on the cars that they own, the share spent per mile driven has also increased with fuel prices, insurance, and other expenses.[16] Stagnant wages and longer-distance trips have been particularly burdensome for poor households. Despite these high costs, planning professors Michael Smart and Nick Klein find that the increased wages attributable to gaining access to a car likely outweigh the increased expenses in all but the most transit-friendly places in the United States.[17]

Given these benefits, it is unsurprising how many poor households choose to purchase cars despite the high financial costs. Moreover, carlessness tends to fluctuate substantially, with nearly half of poor households acquiring or losing a car at least once over a twelve-year period, according to one study.[18] Just one in twenty US families is consistently carless. To maintain access to a car, many will try to reduce expenses by, for example, driving without collision insurance, reducing travel, borrowing from friends, or reducing nontransportation spending.[19] Another recent trend has been to turn to crowdfunding to help replace a car lost to unexpected circumstances.[20] The national media, for example, picked

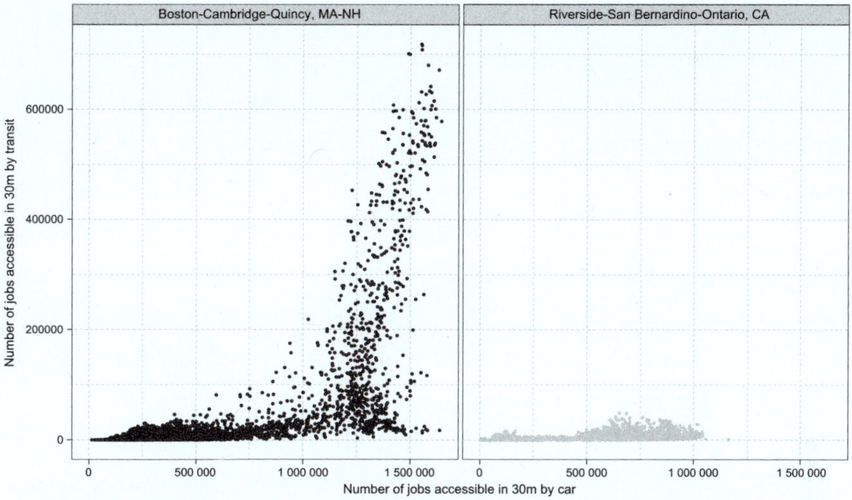

Figure 8-1. Jobs accessible by car and by transit within thirty minutes by neighborhood in the Boston, Massachusetts, and Riverside, California, metropolitan areas (Source: University of Minnesota Accessibility Observatory.)

up one such campaign and helped Detroit resident James Robinson raise more than $300,000 from thousands of donors across the United States. Robinson's campaign described walking more than twenty miles to and from work since his car had broken down ten years earlier. Although these campaigns have tended to only raise about a tenth of the $2,000 typically requested, they highlight and articulate one of the great costs of overbuilding: residents' basic levels of access to work, food, and recreation frequently depend on access to private and expensive automobiles. Losing access due to a collision, pay cut, or mechanical failure is deeply costly and viewed as socially problematic enough that people are willing to plead their case and beg for support online.

In a deliberately provocatively titled 1992 book chapter "The Joys of Automobility," noted University of California, Berkeley planning theorist Mel Webber posited that the central problem of the mass proliferation of cars was its exclusion of those too poor or physically unable to rely on cars. As a result, he argued that the central challenge of transportation planning was to extend carlike services to those who were excluded.[21] While I agree with the overall sentiment of extending accessibility to the poor, I disagree with the overall framing that gives cars so much agency over what has happened in US cities since the 1940s and 1950s. Widespread auto use did not cause the social inequities. Massive overbuilding did. The high costs of carlessness are a direct result of public policies that have made walking, biking, and transit such poor options in so many areas. This unfair system that makes poverty even more burdensome did not simply occur because cars are great. Cars are great and useful everywhere, not just in the United States. Federal and state transportation agencies governments have spent trillions of public dollars on a near singular vision of moving more vehicles at higher speeds on ever-wider highways and arterials. This system has social and economic benefits. It also has tremendous and unevenly distributed costs. Being carless in a society built for cars is one of them. The poor fare substantially better in parts of the United States where access to a car is not a prerequisite to participating in everyday activities.

Racial Injustices

The injustices of US highway policy also disproportionately harm people and communities of color. Much of this harm is historically rooted, but contemporary practices also exacerbate outcomes. As shown in chapters 2 and 3, Black urban communities were particularly likely to lose homes and business to new highways that mostly benefited White suburban car commuters. It was a matter of "White Roads through Black Bedrooms," as protest signs and newspaper columns announced.[22] Racial covenants, zoning regulations, redlining, and targeted violence frequently prevented racial and ethnic minorities from living or working in the booming suburban towns that highway systems and other government programs explicitly supported and subsidized.

Injustices persist, and communities continue to fight displacement from new and widening highways, particularly in places like Texas, where public officials continue tearing down houses, shops, and offices to build ever-wider highways and highway interchanges. Recall from chapter 5 that the Texas Department of Transportation officials' main defense related to the disproportionate, high, and adverse impacts of widening Houston's Interstate 45 on minority communities was to argue that any highway widening would have disproportionate, high, and adverse impacts on minority communities. Somehow showing that the entire public policy is problematic lets the specific project off the hook. And while it is somewhat rare to see these types of public acknowledgments, the disproportionate, high, and adverse impacts of overbuilding show clearly in even a cursory scan of the statistics.

Around a quarter of Black households—self-identified by respondents to the National Household Travel Survey—do not have a car. White households are about four times likelier to have a car and have twice as many vehicles on average as Black households. These differences in vehicle access hold across cities, suburbs, and rural areas. The largest proportional differences occur in low-density areas with poor transit options, where 12.5 percent of Black households do not have cars compared to 3 percent of White households.[23]

Despite driving fewer cars shorter distances on average, Black residents are around 50 percent more likely to die in traffic fatalities than White residents.[24] Differences in cycling and pedestrian fatalities are even higher, particularly when controlling for the amount of travel.[25] Racial characteristics also correlate with income, vehicle quality, trip rates, geography, and the built environment. In a study of traffic safety in Philadelphia, my coauthors and I found statistically significantly higher rates of collisions, injuries, and fatalities in neighborhoods with higher shares of Black residents than White residents while also accounting for differences in poverty rates, roadway design, traffic volumes, and other measures of the built environment.[26] Differences in policing and driver behavior may play an important role. At least two studies, for example, have found that drivers are less likely to yield to Black pedestrians than to White pedestrians.[27] In one study, researchers had six male pedestrians attempt to cross the street at unsignalized midblock crosswalk in downtown Portland, Oregon. The three Black pedestrians waited 32 percent longer and had twice the probability of being passed by one or more cars than the three White pedestrians.

In addition to disproportionately suffering from the unusually elevated traffic fatality rates in the United States (see chapter 7), Black residents are more likely than White residents to live in neighborhoods closer to freeways with substantially worse air quality. Partially as a result, Black residents are disproportionately exposed to small particulate matter, nitrogen oxides, carbon monoxide, and other harmful pollutants.[28] And although air pollution has improved substantially since the 1970s, racial disparities in health outcomes due to pollution increased from 2010 to 2019.[29]

Black residents also experience the transportation system differently from others, with a higher likelihood of being stopped by police for driving or walking and worse experiences using taxis and ride-hailing services.[30] Examining more than one hundred million traffic stops, a large team of researchers found that, relative to the share of the population, Black drivers are substantially more likely to be pulled over than White drivers.[31] These differences diminish after dark, when the authors theorize that it would be harder for police officers to see a driver's skin color.

Racial inequality in the transportation system is neither new nor intrinsically linked to automobility. In her book *Traveling Black: A Story of Race and Resistance*, historian and University of Pennsylvania professor Mia Bay explores the long history of discrimination and inequality faced by Black travelers in stagecoaches, ships, buses, airplanes, and cars.[32] For example, racially segregated railcars did not just force Black people to travel in substantially less comfortable conditions but with substantially less safety. As older wooden railcars were replaced with newer steel ones, Black passengers often found themselves confined to the only wooden cars on a train, a particularly dangerous place to be during the somewhat frequent train crashes of the early twentieth century. The Great Train Wreck of 1918, perhaps the deadliest train crash in the United States, claimed more than one hundred lives when two trains collided one morning in Nashville, Tennessee. More than 70 percent of the victims of the crash were Black. Although Bay argues that advocates have made enormous strides in fighting for transportation equity, she also shows many of the ongoing racial inequities of the contemporary transportation system. For example, one reason Hurricane Katrina hit Black residents of New Orleans so hard was that evacuation planners focused entirely on cars despite the city's high rate of carlessness, particularly in flood-vulnerable Black communities. She cites a statistic that of the 270,000 stranded in New Orleans during the hurricane, more than 90 percent were Black and more than half had no car or other way to evacuate.[33] As she ends her book, "There's no need to travel back in time to travel Black."[34]

Of Soccer Moms and Dad Chauffeurs

The overbuilt roadway system does not always work all that well for an average household. Fully 41.8 percent of households agree or strongly agree that travel is a financial burden.[35] Only one-fourth report that it is not a burden. Similar studies report that gas prices affect how much people travel. According to Experian, Americans owe $1.51 trillion on more than sixty-three million car loans, with an average loan of $23,792.[36] Only home loans account for more US household debt. However, unlike houses, which generally appreciate, cars lose substantial value every year. According to a report by car sales analyst iSeeCars.com, cars lost an average of 38.8 percent of their value in just five years.[37]

As Americans age, there are also substantial challenges related to living in car-oriented towns, cities, and suburbs. In the United States, more than one-fourth of adults older than sixty-five have given up driving due to a medical condition.[38] Many others continue to drive but find driving at night or in heavy traffic to be increasingly difficult. Alex Li, my former PhD student and current professor at the National University of Singapore, focused his dissertation on travel for the growing cohort of older adults in the United States. The probability of becoming carless increases as people age, retire, or become single.[39] Many aging adults would prefer to stay in their neighborhoods, but getting around can be challenging. Although the number of people older than sixty-five is predicted to surpass the number of people younger than eighteen by 2034 there is little in the way of public policy to support the growing mobility needs of this cohort.[40]

Finally, the current system does not even always work all that well for people who easily afford cars and are able to drive with ease. Shuffling kids from activity to activity has become such a prevalent part of American life that terms like soccer mom, hockey mom, and dad chauffeur categorize large swathes of the adult population based on those activities or the act of driving to them. Approximately 13.5 percent of the trips of adults with kids younger than sixteen in the household are to pick up or drop someone off. For comparison, just 14 percent of their trips are going to or from work. Similarly aged adults without kids are picking or dropping someone off for just 3 percent of their trips. Women in particular bear this burden, with 16 percent of their trips to pick up or drop someone off compared to 10 percent for men with kids. Although these trips are frequently combined with other travel, each of these trips takes an average of about fifteen minutes. Picking up and dropping off those without licenses is one of the consequences of an overbuilt highway system where it is frequently dangerous, difficult, and time consuming to get anywhere without a car.

CHAPTER 9
Unbuilding

When you find yourself in a hole, stop digging.—The first law of holes

The first step in addressing an overbuilt transportation system is admitting that the system is overbuilt. New road investments do not solve congestion or spur substantial economic growth. They are not a wholesale investment in America's future, at least not ones that create more wealth than they cost. More and wider roads encourage more driving, which generates more pollution, more traffic fatalities, more sprawling settlement patterns, and more maintenance and reconstruction costs. As Senator Daniel Patrick Moynihan said of US transportation policy in 1991, "We have poured enough concrete."[1]

The second step is to stop digging, to stop pouring more concrete. Expanding roadway infrastructure should be a policy of last resort rather than default public policy, but that's easier said than done. As discussed in chapter 4, the United States has spent more building, rebuilding, and maintaining highways since Moynihan's pronouncement than prior to it. Every single state has added miles of urban highway lanes since 1991's supposedly transformational highway law, the Intermodal Surface

Transportation Efficiency Act (ISTEA). Some of the fastest increases in urban highways came from relatively slow-growing southern states. From 1992 to 2022, the miles of urban Interstate lanes in Mississippi and Arkansas grew four to ten times faster than the population. Faster-growing North Carolina saw its lane miles of urban Interstate nearly triple over the same period.[2] The US highway system is overbuilt, but state and federal agencies keep digging the hole ever deeper.

Shifting trajectories will not be easy. The original Interstate Highway System took four decades to complete. Current land use and transportation systems have developed over nearly a century and cannot be quickly or painlessly reversed. A culture of transportation planning, engineering, and road construction has grown around long-standing finance mechanisms and evaluation metrics. Road-building companies are major political donors. More importantly, driving generates the revenues that fund transportation investments. State departments of transportation thus have a natural incentive to want people to drive more regardless of stated objectives to reduce carbon emissions, improve safety, or foster multimodality. The first year of the COVID-19 pandemic put this reality in stark relief as transportation heads lamented how decreased driving had created large shortfalls in budget projections. Even planners focused on issues like pedestrian safety tend to fear reductions in federal or state transportation funding. Almost every planner, engineer, and public administrator—regardless of whether they favor trains, highways, or bike lanes—wants an ever-larger slice of an ever-larger transportation budget. Large federal transportation bills are celebrated.

In this chapter, I explore some of the interrelated changes to highway finance that are likely needed to move forward and develop a more financially, environmentally, and socially sustainable transportation system. Then, chapter 10 focuses on the tools used to evaluate transportation stems and the role of regulation. Unfortunately, there are no silver bullets, and reversing the effects of an overbuilt road system will take decades of coordinated effort at multiple levels of government.

Fixing Finance

Finance matters. State and federal highway plans languished for decades before the Interstate and Defense Highways Act of 1956 provided highway builders the resources to start building in earnest (chapters 2 and 3). In 1991, ISTEA failed to deliver on its promises to usher in a new era of transportation planning and policy largely because it failed to change finance (chapter 4). State and the federal governments continue to raise dedicated transportation revenues through the gas tax. And they continue to spend most of these funds to build, widen, upgrade, and maintain major highways and arterials.

In the coming years, there will be a critical moment and ideal opportunity for reform. For better or worse, the current transportation finance model is unsustainable and fast approaching a fiscal crisis. The federal gas tax has not increased since 1993. Adjusting for inflation, the gas tax has decreased by more than half. State fuel taxes are similarly difficult to increase and rarely indexed to inflation. When Massachusetts indexed its gas tax to inflation in 2013, for example, voters repealed the law through a ballot initiative the next year. At the same time, vehicles have become substantially more fuel efficient and less likely to rely on gas at all. Drivers are paying substantially less into federal and state coffers for each mile that they drive. The Congressional Budget Office estimates that the Highway Trust Fund will be exhausted by 2028.[3] Following two guiding principles of fiscal reform can reduce the appetite for overbuilding and help set the United States on the path to reducing the high costs of an overbuilt transportation system.

The first principle is to disconnect transportation finance from the amount that people drive. When the roadway system was underbuilt relative to a rapidly growing and rapidly motorizing country in the 1950s and 1960s, the current funding system made a lot of sense. New highways encouraged additional driving that could help quickly fund and build out the national highway system. As the system has expanded and become overbuilt, however, dedicated transportation revenues that are tied to vehicle travel provide too much of an incentive for departments of transportation to facilitate and encourage more driving. The gas tax has also created something of a false impression that drivers have already paid for and carry the costs of the system. As shown in chapter 6, the current costs of the highway system far exceed the tax revenues generated by the gas tax and other sources of dedicated transportation revenues.

At its most basic, this reform could simply eliminate the Highway Trust Fund and move transportation finance to the general budget where transportation would have to compete with other priorities, like education, social services, and public health. The gas tax could be eliminated, converted to a general revenue, or used to offset some of the environmental, public health, or social costs of the transportation system. States could follow suit or choose alternative finance mechanisms.

This reform will likely provoke a few critiques. Transportation officials and highway engineers will likely complain that, without dedicated revenues, the country will struggle to repair and rebuild its degrading infrastructure. Others might argue that having to compete with other programs means that there will be less to invest in transportation. This competition is a good thing. The system is overbuilt. Not everything should be rebuilt, and certainly a lot less should be added. Another critique is that eliminating the gas tax—either intentionally or through its slow degradation as the vehicle fleet increasingly electrifies—will reduce the price of driving and encourage more of it. While that may be true to some degree, the price effect of the gas tax is small relative to the supply effect of new highway infrastructure. My colleague Adam Millard-Ball and I estimated that new infrastructure funded by the federal gas tax from 1981 to 2021 encouraged an additional 153 billion vehicle miles of travel (VMT) in 2021. The higher prices from the 18.5 cent per gallon gas tax, by contrast, likely reduced driving by a much smaller 29 billion VMT.

Another critique is that general revenues are not nearly as closely tied to the use of the transportation system as motor fuel taxes. While that is certainly true, most other industrialized countries have fuel taxes but fund transportation out of general revenues.[4] There is also certainly a solid argument for transportation investments being critical to the national economy. Moreover, there are other ways to raise dedicated transportation revenues that are not as closely connected to driving but are more closely aligned with the benefits of transportation investments than general revenues. Recall from chapter 2 that President Franklin D. Roosevelt initially wanted to fund the Interstate System using the increased value of the land around the system. While somewhat administratively complicated, tying transportation finance to land values would help encourage states to only build roads where the expected effects on land values would outweigh the costs. It would also force them to consider the tremendous value of the land that gets used for roadway—more than $5 trillion in US metropolitan areas in 2024.[5] Prior to the Interstate and Defense Highways Act, tolls, property taxes, and special assessment districts covered the costs of most road building.[6]

While politicians continue to kick the can down the road on resolving the impending collapse of the nation's transportation funding model, taxing the amount that people drive instead of the gasoline that they purchase is perhaps the most widely considered and supported option.[7] The State of Oregon has allowed drivers to opt out of the fuel tax and into a VMT tax since 2015. Program volunteers opt to have their gas tax payments reimbursed and instead pay 1.9 cents per mile driven.[8] The Infrastructure Investment and Jobs Act of 2021 charged the US

Department of Transportation (DOT) with developing a national pilot to test a VMT tax and provided funding for states to test and research programs. At least fourteen states, including Oregon, have developed VMT tax programs or pilots.[9] Around three-fourths of states have funded research into the feasibility of implementing a VMT tax to replace the gas tax. Still, by 2024, fewer than six hundred vehicles had been enrolled in Oregon's program.[10]

Unfortunately, the VMT tax is generally presented as a replacement for the gas tax and a means to preserve the Highway Trust Fund. This simple replacement would be a missed opportunity for reform and a continuation of a mechanism that encourages overbuilding. As long as the distance that people drive determines the budgets and institutional clout of state and federal DOTs, there is too much of an incentive to make investments that encourage more driving and ignore investments that may reduce driving but improve economic performance, public health, and the environment. Recall from chapter 5 that traffic engineers consider any transportation investment an improvement and that the number of improvements is only limited by the size of the budget. For any real progress to be made, transportation finance needs better alignment with the stated goals of ISTEA and subsequent highway laws (chapter 4).

The second principle for financial reform is to favor funding mechanisms that encourage virtuous cycles. Specifically, these mechanisms should raise revenues in ways that reduce the costs of an overbuilt system, such as traffic collisions or pollution, while spending revenues on new projects and programs that do the same. Automated traffic enforcement is a terrific and underutilized example. The City of Philadelphia installed speed cameras on Roosevelt Boulevard, a particularly dangerous arterial where more than a hundred people die in crashes each decade, in June 2020. Since the installation, traffic crashes and fatalities have decreased by around 50 percent relative to other arterials and the rest of Philadelphia.[11] Applying the Pennsylvania DOT estimates of the economic costs of traffic collisions, injuries, and fatalities, the estimated annual safety benefits of enforcement are around six times higher than the $22 million in revenues generated in fiscal year 2021. Moreover, these revenues, have helped fund additional traffic safety projects throughout Philadelphia and the rest of Pennsylvania. While $22 million is a relatively small amount from a transportation investment perspective—roughly enough for one or two lane miles of urban highway—the revenues are from a single dozen-mile corridor and have generated substantial safety benefits independent of how the funds are spent. Creating these kinds of virtuous funding cycles is the best way to raise and spend revenues. Based on the program success, the Pennsylvania state legislature voted in December 2023 to allow expansion of the automated enforcement program to five additional corridors and five school zones. Despite the success of existing programs, only a few cities and states have automated speed enforcement. None have programs that are systematically applied to all major highways and arterials with poor traffic safety records.

More than any other funding mechanism, peak pricing offers the greatest opportunity to disconnect revenues from driving in a way that discourages overbuilding but is directly connected to roadway use. Three years before the Interstate and Defense Highways Act, Nobel Prize–winning economist and Columbia professor William Vickrey proposed variable fares based on passenger demand and system capacity on the New York City subway system.[12] A mayoral commission had asked Vickrey to study how to reduce the effects of transit subsidies on the city's budget. Instead, Vickrey focused on how much more efficient the system would be if fares were steeply reduced or eliminated when there were empty seats on subway cars and increased when high passenger volumes created passenger discomfort or required higher costs in the forms of additional train cars, operators, or tracks.

In a seminal paper extending these ideas to transportation systems more generally, Vickrey started, "I will begin with the proposition that in no other major area are pricing practices so irrational, so out of date, and so conducive to waste as in urban transportation."[13] Instead of charging motorists for the higher costs of travel during the peak and spreading demand to make more efficient use of existing facilities, highway planners and engineers use revenues from all hours of the day to provide facilities for the busiest times of day. That is the essence of the recommended practice of the American Association of State Highway and Transportation Officials (AASHTO) of building highways for the projected thirtieth busiest hour of traffic over the next twenty years. Urban transportation finance has gotten no less irrational, out of date, or wasteful in the years since Vickrey published his critique.

As technologies such as the radio-frequency identification tags in E-ZPass and license-plate detection cameras have made variable pricing of the transportation system easier and less costly, Vickrey's ideas of peak-hour tolling and congestion pricing have gained substantial ground. Peak-hour pricing has been used to manage a variety of transportation systems, including parking in San Francisco, congested bridge facilities, and the Washington, DC, metro system. A much-delayed congestion pricing scheme in New York City would be the first substantial zone-based peak pricing applied to a roadway system in the United States.

Unfortunately, however, peak pricing is most used to increase capacity rather than to manage demand on the existing system. The Dallas metropolitan area, for example, has added around a hundred miles of dynamically priced highway lanes to eight major highway corridors. Prices vary with congestion and are designed to keep traffic flowing at around 50 miles per hour and offer drivers a priced alternative to a non-toll freeway system during congested hours.[14] While Vickrey's original ideas focused on managing peak demand and making better choices about how to manage scarce public resources, like land for the transportation system, most modern applications have focused on providing drivers a secondary overlapping system where they can opt to pay to avoid congestion. Even contemporary academic discussions of congestion pricing focus much more on the costs of congestion to users than the cost of providing infrastructure or the economically optimal amount of roadway.

One of the main points of peak pricing is that traveling at the busiest times of day is fabulously expensive. The lanes that the Texas Department of Transportation is adding at great financial and social expense to Interstate 45 in Houston and Interstate 35 in Austin (chapters 5 and 6) do virtually nothing to benefit anyone driving outside the congested peak hours of travel. Spreading peak demand by raising transportation revenues from tolls collected during congested hours would let Texas meet its forecast travel demands at a fraction of the cost of widening highways. It would also be substantially fairer, not only because it would avoid destroying thousands of homes and businesses in predominantly Black and minority neighborhoods, but also because it would avoid raising revenues from all the trips that are made when there is little or no congestion. AASHTO estimates that the peak demand that planners should build highways for is about 8 to 12 percent of total average daily traffic.[15] Having 90 percent of travel subsidize and encourage travel during the 10 percent of the time that it is most expensive to travel is precisely what makes the US transportation system so irrational, wasteful, and overbuilt. There is no single policy reform that would improve the system's economic, social, and environmental performance than to raise transportation revenues from the peak hours of travel instead of spending revenues primarily to support the peak hours of travel. Doing so would also provide an opportunity to spend transportation dollars differently and start a virtuous cycle slowly unbuilding an overbuilt system.

Freeway Removals and Road Diets

Many urban highways should never have been built. The harm to local neighborhoods, environmental damage, and loss of valuable urban real estate frequently outweigh the benefits to motorists. As shown in chapters 3 and 4, public officials sought to bury Boston's Central Artery almost as soon as the first segments had opened due to the substantial damage it did to surrounding neighborhoods. A movement to downgrade overbuilt roadway systems is already occurring, with some cities and towns choosing to tear down particularly harmful elevated freeways and replace them with at-grade boulevards. As more highways and elevated structures reach the end of their structural lives and require substantial reinvestment, there is a growing opportunity to rebuild differently.

The Embarcadero Freeway removal in San Francisco provides an early, illustrative example of the benefits of highway removals. Like many urban highways, the Embarcadero consumed valuable central land and cut San Francisco off from its waterfront. Moreover, due to freeway revolts in San Francisco, the Embarcadero never connected the northern Golden Gate Bridge to the eastern Bay Bridge as originally intended. There was already a citizen movement and local government support to remove the Embarcadero when the Loma Prieta earthquake hit the Bay Area in 1989, knocking out sections of the structure and forcing officials to close the freeway to traffic.[16] Faced with the enormous costs of rebuilding the structure, state officials opted for the lower-cost solution of replacing the highway with a boulevard with enhanced transit, bicycle, and pedestrian facilities. Despite traffic engineers predicting traffic chaos and reduced safety, neither materialized. People previously using the highways shifted to other highways, transit, or local roadways. Property values also increased near the boulevard relative to other similar properties.[17] Surrounding land uses have also continued to shift over time. For example, the Ferry Building, no longer hemmed in by an elevated freeway, has become one of San Francisco's top destinations for tourists and locals alike.[18]

As part of a series of efforts to revitalize Milwaukee, then mayor John Norquist led an effort modeled on the Embarcadero removal to replace Park East Freeway with a tree-lined boulevard and new houses, shops, and other businesses.[19] Federal highway dollars and a share of the increased local property tax revenues from $1 billion of new real estate investment financed the removal.[20] After completing four terms as mayor, Norquist became president of the Congress for New Urbanism, an urbanist advocacy organization, where he continued advocating for freeway removals. Every few years, the Congress for New Urbanism puts out a list called "Freeways without Futures" that highlights efforts to bury or replace urban highways.[21]

Over time, the list has highlighted projects from thirty-one cities in seventeen states and Washington, DC. Some projects have already been removed and replaced with urban boulevards. For example, officials have begun the process of tearing down portions of Route 34 in New Haven, Connecticut. This highway disconnected parts of downtown New Haven and took up twenty-six valuable acres of centrally located land. In 2019, officials closed the Alaskan Way Viaduct, separating downtown Seattle from its waterfront, and began the process of tearing down the elevated structure, tunneling a new underground highway, and building a surface-level boulevard. And, as illustrated by Boston's Big Dig, burying highways can be extremely expensive. Despite the high costs, federal reserve economists Jeffrey Brinkman and Jeffrey Lin estimate that freeing up land and removing the impacts of surface highways often outweighs these costs. For example, the economists estimate that burying 4.5 miles of Interstate 95 along Philadelphia's waterfront would increase population by 7 percent within a mile of the freeway, boost land values by 2.4 percent, and cover the estimated $500 million per mile in costs.[22] Other projects on the Freeways without Futures list, such as Interstate 35 in Austin, have garnered substantial local and national opposition but appear likely to be widened and rebuilt.[23]

Freeway removals remain somewhat limited in scope and scale. Funding is one major challenge. The Reconnecting Communities Pilot Grant Program provides the first-of-its kind dedicated federal funding aimed at undoing some of the harm created by urban highways. The first $185 million of this $1 billion program went to planning and construction grants supporting forty-five projects to study, cap, sink, replace, or add crossings to existing urban freeways.[24] Several Freeways without Futures projects, including Interstate 35 in Austin, have received funding. A particular emphasis appears to be on funding the removal of highways that separate communities, disconnect cities from bodies of water, and consume substantial amounts of valuable land that can be readily redeveloped into new well-located housing, shops, and offices. For all the program's promise, however, $1 billion is a drop in the bucket. It is roughly one five hundredth of the 2021 federal transportation bill, a fraction of what will be spent on building and widening highways over the same five years, and enough to bury around two miles of urban highway.[25] In short, the program is a promising start but will do little to reduce the overbuilt nature of the US roadway system.

Road diets are another promising, and frequently popular, way to reduce roadway capacity to improve traffic safety and spark local economic development along main streets and other arterials. As state and municipal departments of transportation have spent billions of dollars widening urban arterials to increase capacity and feed the highway system, these major roads have become among the most dangerous and least pleasant. These high-capacity thoroughfares generally make up what cities frequently call their high-injury networks, the roughly 5 percent of roadway that account for 50 percent of serious injuries and fatalities.[26]

The most common road diet is to convert a street with two lanes in each direction to a single lane in each direction and center left-turn-only lane. The removed lane typically makes space for bike lanes, wider sidewalks, or busways. In addition, traffic speeds tend to decrease, and pedestrian crossings get shorter. Studies from California, Virginia, New Jersey, and Rhode Island have all found substantial reductions in crashes, injuries, and fatalities from road diets.[27] Based on the existing research, the Federal Highway Administration recognizes road diets as an effective tool for improving traffic safety, with an expected 19 to 41 percent reduction in crashes after the roadway redesign.[28] In addition to promoting safety, these conversions are also frequently part of a concerted effort to revitalize local main streets and other commercial corridors. They also reflect a pushback against a century of transportation planning and engineering practices that have focused almost exclusively on measuring and prioritizing roadway capacity and traffic speeds.

CHAPTER 10

Fixing What Gets Measured

Garbage in. Garbage out.—Twentieth-century proverb

Management guru Peter Drucker is often quoted as saying, "If you can't measure it, you can't manage it." Regardless of the veracity of the attribution, good measurement is a fundamental component of understanding, improving, and managing systems and institutions.[1] Bad measurement, by contrast, can lead to poor and even dangerous decision-making. Defense secretary Robert McNamara, for example, famously used counts of killed US and North Vietnamese combatants as a measure of which side was winning the military conflict in Vietnam. The McNamara fallacy has come to signify problems created by an overreliance on using easy but incomplete or erroneous metrics to make decisions.

For far too long, highway planners and traffic engineers have been fixated on two measures of the transportation system: how much people are expected to drive and how much roadway capacity is needed to accommodate these drivers. As shown in chapter 5, traffic projections and capacity remain the primary determinant of where highways get built and widened. Indeed, despite limited or even contradictory evidence, transportation engineers conflate safety and capacity.[2] For example, engineering manuals state that traffic lanes should be at least twelve feet wide for safety. This practice, codified in road design manuals, stems from a conjecture made in a 1945 research study about how trucks maneuver on twenty-two-foot roadways relative to twenty-four-foot roadways.[3] Wider lanes allow for faster traffic and more traffic. They also unsurprisingly have more and more serious traffic collisions. The manuals have not been updated, and traffic engineers continue to make claims that widening roadways makes streets safer. Similarly, and despite evidence to the contrary, traffic engineers deem that one-way streets are safer than two-way streets. They are not.[4] They do, however, allow more traffic to move more quickly. In addition to improving safety, there is also a growing body of evidence that converting one-way streets to two-way may be good for local economic development and may reduce the distances that people drive.[5]

Modern US traffic engineering, modeling, and evaluation metrics are substantially based on a series of bogus claims about how and why building wider and wider roadways makes Americans safer, healthier, and more economically productive. In addition to fixing finance, fixing how transportation investments and policies are measured and evaluated is a key component of starting to repair the damage of an overbuilt roadway system.

Moving toward Access

Measuring accessibility—people's ease of getting to the places they are trying to go—instead of mobility—traffic speeds, traffic volumes, and highway capacity—is perhaps the single most important shift that needs to take place to begin to evaluate and assess the impacts of transportation investments properly. Movement and traffic are quite simply the wrong way to measure the transportation system. These measurements almost completely neglect roadways' relationships to other land use and other urban systems. Outside of the occasional joyride or recreational walk, people rarely travel for travel's sake. They travel to get to work, visit a friend, buy groceries, or participate in a range of other activities. The National Household Travel Survey records nineteen different categories of the primary activity being undertaken at each trip's origin and destination. In 2017, for example, an estimated forty-two million trips per day were to go to work. Another forty-nine million trips were to buy goods. These trips involved physical destinations, such as offices, churches, stores, and houses.[6]

In theory, the places with the most destinations nearby and the highest travel speeds would have the highest accessibility. In practice, a larger number of destinations within short distance is also associated with slower travel. In terms of accessibility, the proximity associated with denser urban areas tends to more than offset any reduction in car speeds.[7] Not only do higher speeds tend to spread out origins and destinations, but planners and policymakers tore down tens of thousands of apartments, houses, and businesses to favor higher traffic speeds on highways. Did these investments make it easier for more people to reach their destinations? In some instances, yes, probably. In other instances, no, probably not. No one measured it, but today, the places that have the best access to employment, shops, and homes also frequently have the slowest traffic. They also tend to be the most economically productive.[8]

In a working paper for the Brookings Institution, Gilles Duranton and I argue that accessibility is the most important urban attribute to consider in terms of resource allocation.[9] Housing and transportation are the first and second largest household spending categories, before food, education, health, or any other large household expenditure. We then go on to discuss how difficult accessibility is to measure. Simple measures exist, such as estimates of the number of jobs reachable within some set amount of time by some specific mode, like the ones shown in chapter 8. More complicated measures may assign weights that decay over time so that a job that is ten minutes away is assigned a greater value than a job that is twenty minutes away. Still more complicated measures may consider firm accessibility to workers, as well as household accessibility to jobs. But what does this matter to someone who doesn't work or instead telecommutes? Or if they aren't qualified or interested in the specific job that is twenty minutes away? What about access to restaurants, places of worship, schools, shops, and open space? How do accessibility measures account for variation in preferences? What's the value of a nearby butcher shop to a vegetarian or a mosque to an atheist or Christian? What does car accessibility mean to someone who cannot drive? What about people who just want access to peace and quiet, as far away as possible from all the shops, restaurants, and jobs?

Even for a simple conceptual measure—such as the number of jobs accessible within thirty minutes—evaluating the effects of transportation investments on accessibility requires traffic engineers to develop new skills and methods in addition to shifting perspectives. Perhaps most substantially, accessibility-based measures require integrating land use models into transportation planning and evaluation processes.[10] Imagine, for example, that a state department of transportation wanted to evaluate the effects of a freeway widening on the transportation system. A mobility-based framework would predict future traffic volumes, assign these to the highway network, and look at the effects on speed and traffic based on highway capacity (chapter 5). An accessibility-based measure would require some estimate of how a new highway would potentially affect the location of shops, offices, and households as well. Imagine, for example, that the highway encouraged greater speeds as well as a greater concentration of houses and shops along the highway. The accessibility effects would be quite high. If, by contrast, the highway encouraged new housing developments on the periphery instead of in more centrally located locations, the new widening would have a much smaller, or even potentially negative, predicted effect on accessibility.

In addition to being difficult to measure or even conceptualize, accessibility is somewhat abstract and hardly politically pressing, even invisible.[11] People have a much more personal connection to whether they have an easy time finding parking, whether housing is too expensive, whether a new housing development will strain local school finances, or whether the trains come on time. Mobility measures, such as travel speeds and hours spent in traffic, are also substantially easier to describe and interpret. Partially as a result, professors Jonathan Levine, Joe Grengs, and Louis Merlin argue that "while practitioners have tentatively begun to use the language of accessibility, its application remains largely at the conceptual and visioning levels."[12] Even at this conceptual level, professor Susan Handy argues that federal, state, and local policies often simply conflate accessibility and mobility with "no effort to define or distinguish between the two."[13] Finally, the state departments of transportation that decide what to evaluate and how often have little interest or incentive to move toward accessibility based measures.[14]

For all the challenges of using accessibility measures, there are also some hopeful signs. For one, the measurement and application of accessibility are getting easier, even for the more complicated measures that incorporate preferences and multiple dimensions of accessibility.[15] Levine and his colleagues provide an example application for the San Antonio metropolitan region's long-range transportation plan. As with other regional transportation plans, San Antonio's *Mobility 2040* predicted major increases in traffic congestion without substantial and expensive investments in new highways and arterials. Looking at the effects on job accessibility, by contrast, painted a much more nuanced perspective. First, the predicted net accessibility benefits of the highway investments were negligible. Increased travel speeds in specific locations were offset by predicted losses of jobs and population in more accessible parts of the region, as households and businesses adjusted to the shifting transportation system. In fact, Levine, Grengs, and Merlin estimated that the $17.2 billion plan would decrease residents' overall access to jobs by 0.2 percent despite improving travel speeds by 5.5 percent.[16]

Moreover, the analysis showed how some highway investments might create accessibility benefits exceeding any mobility benefits. For example, Levine and his colleagues predicted that a series of highway investments on the northern peripheral ring road would substantially increase accessibility by concentrating new housing and office developments in a relatively low-density area where existing highway capacity was an impediment to growth.[17]

In addition to getting easier to measure, there is evidence that simpler measures of accessibility are often strongly correlated with more complicated ones.[18] It is certainly much easier to explain the effects of a policy or investment on the jobs that are reachable within thirty minutes than its effects on a gravity-based measure of the number of jobs that are accessible while also accounting for the match between jobs and worker skills and the competition for jobs and workers between firms and employees. Moreover, places with generally better job accessibility are also more likely to have better accessibility to a host of other important destinations, like shops, hospitals, and cultural amenities, though perhaps not open space, or peace and quiet. In this respect, simpler measures are better.[19] Perhaps most importantly, the simplest measures are a marked improvement on the mobility-based measures that are currently used and that continue to encourage overbuilding despite failing to improve accessibility, never mind failing to improve safety, pollution levels, or economic performance.

Accessibility measures also have the distinct advantage of allowing better and integrated measures of the effects of new housing or office development on transportation. From an accessibility perspective, a new development would be net beneficial for the transportation system if the effects on the proximity between households and their destinations outweighed the effects from additional traffic. The current mobility-based measures, by contrast, inevitably make new real estate developments look bad for the transportation system since they lead to more traffic. In many places, new developments get blocked or downsized if they are predicted to increase traffic congestion. And sometimes there is a requirement to offset developments by paying to widen roads or upgrade traffic signals. This requirement can lead to contradictory urban public policies, with one agency trying to promote new offices in the most accessible locations, but another trying to prevent the development because the most accessible locations tend to be the most congested. Taken to their absurd extreme, mobility-based measures would frequently show that razing entire commercial or residential neighborhoods would be beneficial because fewer homes and businesses means less traffic. Garbage in. Garbage out. When it comes to the US transportation system, the cart is leading the horse.

Setting Standards

Setting and enforcing standards is another area where state and federal agencies have an opportunity to offset some of the harm of the transportation system. One of the first places to start is with a thorough review of the minimum roadway safety standards and guidelines that help determine how roadways are designed. Despite being based on decades-old conjecture with little or even contradictory empirical evidence, traffic engineers continue to promote higher speeds, wider lanes, fewer curves, and a host of other treatments in the name of safety. When citizens push back, engineers tend to shut them down and refer to the safety standards in obscure manuals.[20] Safety is the excuse to justify capacity increases when cities, towns, and neighborhoods argue that they do not really want more highway capacity. Worse still, standards can actively prevent cities and towns from providing safer streets. Building narrower streets may be safer, but doing so can open engineers and public officials to tort liability for not meeting minimum industry safety standards.[21] At the very least, liability provides traffic engineers an excuse for following minimum standards.

These supposed safety standards need thorough external scientific review. After centuries of poor practice, state departments of transportation are simply not a credible source of standards or oversight. They understand capacity, traffic volumes, and congestion relatively well, but have chosen to conflate capacity and safety.[22] As I argue in chapter 7, it is difficult to look at US safety practices and not conclude that traffic engineers are incompetent, disingenuous, or a bit of both. The US Department of Health and Human Services or the US Office of Management and Budget are good external candidates for review. The National Academies of Science, Engineering, and Medicine is another, although its Transportation Research Board is perhaps a bit too embedded in the daily practices of state departments of transportation. Even if agencies keep continuing to widen highways, it is well past time to stop lying to citizens and telling them that it is for their own safety.

State and federal agencies also have an opportunity to continue to raise other standards to help offset harm from the transportation system. To date, the biggest successes have come in terms of vehicle design. Despite protests from car manufacturers, state and federal agencies have managed to pass legislation mandating seat belts, safety glass, airbags, and fuel economy standards. In 2020, for example, California mandated that new car sales be 100 percent zero emissions by 2035, and more than a dozen other states have followed suit.[23] One area where additional improvements could be made is in federal vehicle safety standards. Crash testing, for example, focuses entirely on safety within the vehicle during a few specific types of traffic collisions. Larger vehicles with higher bumper heights, however, are more dangerous for other drivers and especially for pedestrians.[24] Children, who have lower centers of gravity, are particularly vulnerable. The increase in SUV and light-duty truck sales have almost certainly contributed to a rapid increase in pedestrian traffic fatalities. In 2009, a low of around 4,100 pedestrians died in traffic collisions, compared to 6,500 to 7,500 in recent years.[25] A recent analysis by *The Economist* found that for every person saved by being in a larger vehicle, like an SUV, a dozen people in smaller vehicles lose their lives.[26]

Beyond vehicle design, state and federal governments can use funding to encourage agencies to track and meet—or have credible plans to meet—air quality, safety, and other standards. Metropolitan planning organizations, for example, must regularly update long-range transportation plans and have credible plans to meet air quality standards. Regions that fail to meet these standards or update transportation plans accordingly risks losing access to federal transportation funds. States such as California require plans to meet greenhouse gas emissions targets. Similar approaches could easily be applied to traffic safety targets. If traffic safety is truly a top state and federal priority, why not tie funding to safety? Why not set targets for things that matter, like how many lives are lost on US roadways, as opposed to abstract measures of level of service that seem purposefully designed to justify more and ever-wider highways?

Cost-Benefit Revolution

Despite some of the skepticism presented in chapter 6, there are opportunities to improve transportation policy through stricter cost-benefit analysis. In his book *The Cost-Benefit Revolution*, Cass Sunstein, legal scholar and former director of the White House Office of Information and Regulatory Affairs, celebrates a quiet revolution that has taken place in US government since President Ronald Reagan signed Executive Order 12291 on federal regulation in 1981.[27] Increasingly, government technocrats have been empowered to provide and enforce policies where measured benefits exceed costs. Sunstein's book even provides examples from the transportation sector. A policy to require rearview backup cameras in new cars is discussed substantially throughout the book. Indeed, the US government has a long history of requiring auto manufacturers to provide safety features.

By contrast, the record on investment policy, as discussed in chapters 5 through 7, is less ideal. One problem is that the technocrats and technocratic tools used in transportation evaluation were primarily developed to encourage and justify investments in greater road capacity. Despite or perhaps due to these challenges, there is a need for external oversight when it comes to transportation evaluation. Public health officials should certainly be more involved in the evaluation of traffic safety. Economists should be more involved in the evaluation of general costs and benefits. The US Government Accounting Office, which has a solid record of evaluating investment policies and regulations, would be a good place to start. As Senator Daniel Patrick Moynihan quoted an MIT colleague in 1960, "Just as war is too important to leave to the generals, so highways are too important to leave to the highway engineers."[28]

CHAPTER 11

The Future Is Now

If we could apply all we know, we could eliminate 98 per cent of all accidents, practically all congestion.—Dr. Miller McClintock, *Fortune,* 1936

Transportation enthusiasts have a long history of placing high hopes in new technologies and innovations. In the early twentieth century, many planners, engineers, and policymakers saw the car as a solution to their contemporary urban woes. Private cars would replace horses, thereby eliminating pollution at a time when horse manure and dead horses were a blight.[1] Private cars would also eliminate the congestion and traffic collisions caused by horses. They would even cure the social ills of the city by allowing decentralization and decongestion.[2] Just a short time later, as automobiles began to proliferate, engineers, enthusiasts, and policymakers began to promote highways as the solution to all the congestion and traffic fatalities that cars were causing (chapters 2 and 3). That a traffic fatality occurred the first day that the first stretch of Germany's Autobahn opened apparently did nothing to dampen claims of superhighways as the solution to all traffic collisions.[3] By 1940, when Norman Bel Geddes published McClintock's safety claims in *Magic Motorways,*[4] they were already demonstrably false.

If the 98 percent improvement figure strikes you as familiar and somewhat contemporary, you are not alone. I have read scores of articles and watched dozens of presentations about self-driving cars that start with a claim that human error causes more than 90 percent of traffic collisions. I have watched a serious and talented academic whom I admire begin his talk by multiplying 94 percent by the 1.35 million people who die globally each year. Never mind that the 94 percent figure is bogus (see chapter 7). Never mind that he believes the technology is decades from full deployment in the United States. Never mind that it is still decades further away in the parts of the world with the highest traffic fatality rates. Never mind that technology fails—repeatedly. It is fundamentally a vision, a hope for the number of lives that new technologies might potentially save. It is also an argument for continued research funding, a justification for public dollars to support automated driving technology. Technology firms, startups, and auto manufacturers sometimes make similar, much stronger, claims. Nissan, for example, announced plans to have a commercially viable and affordable self-driving car on the road by 2020 back in 2014.[5]

In his book *Autonorama: The Illusory Promise of High-Tech Driving*, historian Peter Norton connects the dots between today's interest in automated vehicles and three other periods of technological hype, including McClintock's early planning for cars and Bel Geddes's World Fair *Futurama* exhibit.[6] The third period, not discussed much in this book, includes many of the technologies enabled by improvements in computer processing and showcased through the footage of smart bombs during the first Gulf War in 1991.[7] Think navigation systems, E-ZPass, and dynamic sign boards on the sides of highways. As in earlier waves of technological hype, a coalition of technology firms, car manufacturers, and highway engineers promised massive improvements in traffic safety and traffic congestion that generally failed to materialize. Norton also effectively argues that these waves of hype are a distraction that ultimately serve as excuses to avoid the underlying problems with the US transportation system and continue to justify even more investments in highways.

The fourth wave of hype, what Norton dubs Autonorama, is all about self-driving cars. As with other technologies, like electric vehicles, new technologies present promises and perils. While no one laments the passing of horse-drawn carriages from our streets, mass motorization created a host of new problems. We would do well to avoid betting on technology to save the day. There may be opportunities to offset some of the harm of an overbuilt highway system, but nothing on the horizon appears poised to stop the overbuilding. And the historical track record is far from stellar.

Robot Cars

In the 1990 action film *Total Recall* starring Arnold Schwarzenegger, the main character relies on a robot taxi named Johnny Cab to get around a dystopian future city on the surface of Mars. Pursued by gunmen, Schwarzenegger commands the taxi to just drive—anywhere. Unfamiliar with the destination, Johnny Cab fails to comply. Schwarzenegger curses. Johnny Cab doesn't know where the curse word is located either. Schwarzenegger tears the robot driver Johnny out of the driver's seat, grabs a joystick steering device, and successfully flees his pursuers. Just fourteen years later, the US military's Defense Advanced Research Projects Agency held its first Grand Challenge in the Mojave Desert in 2004 to promote the development of self-driving vehicles. None of the participating teams came remotely close to finishing the 150-mile obstacle course. Just one year later, five cars completed the race, with teams from Stanford University and Carnegie Mellon taking the top finishes. In 2007, the University of Pennsylvania's Ben Franklin Racing

Team, based out of my university, completed the more complicated Urban Challenge with a converted Toyota Prius named Little Ben. So did another half dozen teams.

Today, nearly every major technology firm, every car manufacturer, and a host of startups have gotten into the business of developing self-driving cars. State departments of transportation have developed rules for testing, and there are self-driving vehicles operating on highways and local roads in select cities and states. Waymo, for example, provides fully driverless taxi services—generally without a safety driver—in San Francisco, Los Angeles, Phoenix, and Austin, Texas.[8] Most major car manufacturers already market and sell high-end vehicles with features like automated braking, self-parking, lane-departure warning, and variable-speed cruise control. The future is now.

The future also remains somewhat elusive and uncertain. Despite impressive progress, multiple technological hurdles need to be resolved before a large share of vehicles can drive themselves safely and consistently without human supervision on city streets and highways. Many driverless systems struggle to see consistently well enough for safe operation at night and in poor weather conditions, or to interact safely with pedestrians and bicyclists. As driverless vehicles become more popular, developing systems that are robust to physical and digital hacking will require additional time and effort. Perhaps most importantly, cost is a major impediment. Ricardo Daziano from Cornell University and his colleagues have estimated that consumers are willing to pay an average of $4,500 for a fully self-driving car.[9] Many would pay far less. While companies are cutting costs (and perhaps quality) quickly, the main sensor alone on Waymo's self-driving cars recently cost around $75,000. Sensors and other hardware cost thousands more. Consumers are likely going to want their sensors to last longer and require a lot less maintenance than what is currently required. I do not know what the self-driving version of an electronic window that no longer opens is, but I am nearly certain we will all find out together. In any case, once the technology reaches a marketable price point, the fleet will take at least a decade to turn over. The average car on the road is nearly thirteen years old.[10]

While I remain hopeful that self-driving vehicles ultimately improve safety, the assumption that self-driving cars will eliminate most crashes is naïve at best. Just two weeks before writing this sentence, disturbed neighbors filmed dozens of Waymo's self-driving cars honking at one another in a parking lot in San Francisco.[11] The video is funny, but it is also a stark reminder that self-driving cars are set to introduce a host of new problems. Without regulation, for example, some cars may choose to find the slowest, most congested places and drive in circles because it is cheaper than parking.[12] By making driving less onerous, self-driving cars will almost certainly encourage a lot more driving. An hour-long commute seems a lot more reasonable when you can sleep or take calls. So does that weekend drive to visit relatives. Applying existing behavioral models, metropolitan planners and engineers have estimated a 5 percent to 25 percent increase in driving in their regions once self-driving cars are common.[13] Spend a couple weeks imagining that you have a zero-cost chauffeur and ubiquitous valet parking. I know I would be making a lot more and longer car trips. I would also hope that some of this additional travel will be offset by improved transit services in smaller driverless vehicles that can provide more frequent, reliable services than most bus lines currently do.

In addition to safety, self-driving vehicles have the potential to substantially change the effective capacity of roadways, particularly highways. Platooning vehicles would allow them to drive much more closely together and at higher speeds than is currently possible. In one simulation study, a research team found a possible 300 percent increase in highway capacity if all vehicles had automated systems.[14] Mixed fleets of human- and computer-driven vehicles would likely create more modest increases in capacity.

As with safety, there is a lot of uncertainty about how and when driverless vehicles will influence roadway capacity. But why do we seem to be pinning our safety hopes on new technologies but not our capacity hopes? If anyone truly believes in automated vehicles, why would they continue to project traffic out twenty years into the future to justify demolishing thousands of homes and businesses? How could they justify disproportionate and substantial impacts on minority communities? Why aren't departments of transportation arguing that we should get rid of two-thirds of highway capacity? If the highway system is already overbuilt, it is going to be even more overbuilt as effective roadway capacity increases.

Electric Vehicles

In the same breath stating that driverless cars will nearly eliminate collisions and congestion, proponents also claim that they will eliminate carbon emissions and other forms of pollution. That is because self-driving cars will be electric. Why self-driving cars would be electric but human-driven ones would be gas-powered is beyond me. It is also not the point. By conflating the two, proponents get to claim that self-driving cars eliminate greenhouse gas emissions as well as traffic fatalities. Even if electric cars and self-driving cars had some special synergy—they don't—there are problems with this claim. Electric vehicles may, over time, help address some problems, but just like cars replacing horses, they will likely create others.

First, electric cars are only as clean as the electricity used to produce and power them. If the electricity used to build and power an electric car is powered by coal plants, the cars are hardly doing a world of good for greenhouse gas emissions, especially if a lot of power is lost transmitting electricity. There may still be benefits, though. For example, if very few people live near the coal-fired power plants, fewer people will breathe in harmful air. Regardless of how they are powered, electric cars will help city dwellers breathe easier. A shift to electric vehicles also provides a pathway for cleaner forms of energy production to affect transportation emissions in the future. They do not, however, in and of themselves make the transportation system carbon free.

More problematically, scaling the production and disposal of batteries is going to introduce a suite of new environmental problems.[15] Mining and disposing of lithium will likely produce substantial environmental and social harm. These issues may be resolvable, but currently policymakers and car manufacturers appear blindly optimistic that the day after tomorrow's technological innovations will solve any problems created by today and tomorrow's technological innovations. If history is any kind of guide, electric self-driving cars will not simply eliminate problems coming from the transportation system. They will do nothing to reduce emissions from road building or tire and break wear.[16] The higher weight of electric vehicles also poses specific road safety hazards.[17] Finally, electric and self-driving vehicles do not solve the fundamental problem of an overbuilt transportation system. There is too much roadway without electric self-driving cars. There is too much roadway with them.

Let's Start Today

Electric and self-driving cars are just two technologies that enthusiasts are embracing and conflating as the solution to problems with the current transportation system. High-speed trains, electric scooters, hyperloop, and even flying taxis feature regularly in magazines and on the lips of policymakers and transportation officials. I am not opposed to technology. I have a sweet spot for my robot vacuum cleaner. I also like automated braking, cruise control, backup cameras, digital navigation, and the host of other technologies that make life easier. If automated and electric vehicles improve safety and the environment even by 10 percent, that is a tremendous win for society. What I do oppose is letting the hoped-for benefits of a new technology drive policy decisions and encourage myopia.

I also have a soft spot for other kinds of investments, like trains, buses, bike lanes, and sidewalks. As with new technologies, however, these more classic multimodal transportation investments do nothing to resolve the fundamental, first-order problem of the US transportation system. There are too many and too-high-capacity roadways. Investing hundreds of billions of dollars in transit will not fundamentally change that. If you do not believe me, just wait five years and see. The 2021 Infrastructure Investment and Jobs Act claims to represent the largest ever single federal investment in transit. I am making no claims about whether these investments are needed or will be beneficial. Some may be. Others will not be particularly useful. I am, however, claiming that these transit investments will make little to no difference in the overall US transportation system. You do not solve overbuilding by building something else. To go back to the overeating analogy from chapter 5, adding more vegetables to your diet may have some benefits, but eating more cannot address an overeating problem.

Neither new technologies nor alternative investments will suddenly resolve a decades-old overbuilding problem. It is time to stop passing the buck or hoping for technology to save the day. It is high time to change the finance and evaluation measures that have kept us overbuilding for decades. The goal is not to eliminate driving or make US cities look like European ones. That is as naïve and unrealistic as self-driving electric cars fixing all transportation problems. Instead, we should simply stop making public investments that make the public worse off. Then slowly, over time, we should allow for the unbuilding of an overbuilt system. There is no silver bullet, and it is not glamorous work. But it is well past time to get started.

Acknowledgments

I never would have written *Overbuilt* without teaching Introduction to Transportation Planning to hundreds of bright-eyed first-year graduate students at the University of Pennsylvania since 2013. At least a dozen students helped directly contribute to this book as well, whether by producing a graphic, summarizing a transportation law, or editing a chapter. Apologies if I have left out any names but a special thanks to Promit Chatterjee, Nilo Cobau, Travis Decaminada, Michael Dunst, Khulan Enkhbold, Scott Harris, Nata Kovalova, Alec Pompeo, Riya Saini, Andy Sandweiss, Naomi Tariku, Weslene Uy, Yiping Ying, Ke Zhou, and Jonathan Zisk. Colleagues at the University of Pennsylvania have also been tremendously helpful. Francesca Ammon, Genie Birch, and Domenic Vitiello were particularly generous with their time and provided substantial feedback on early drafts and chapters. Francesca Ammon, Matt Kenyatta, Zhongjie Lin, and Lisa Servon gave me terrific advice and support in rewriting and framing the book's introduction. Gilles Duranton, who has been a terrific collaborator and mentor during my time at Penn, helped me frame and later revise the chapter on economics.

Outside of Penn, Adam Millard-Ball and Eric Morris gave feedback on early drafts of the introduction. Both have also been wonderful collaborators. I am particularly grateful to Eric, who, despite disagreeing with the book's thesis, has given supportive, critical feedback from the start. Scores of researchers and teachers influenced the content and style of this book. One of the great pleasures of writing this book has been reading more and more broadly than the demands of addressing narrower research questions generally allow. I am particularly grateful to my mentors Robert Cervero and Tony Gómez-Ibáñez. I am lucky to have had the chance to learn and attempt to stand on the shoulders of two such giants in the field.

Outside of academia, Bob Cullen from the American Association of State Highway and Transportation Officials and Richard Weingroff from the Federal Highway Administration were extremely generous in providing access to documents in support of the project. Bob generously provided access to photos of Central Artery construction from the Boston Public Library's Leslie Jones Collection on behalf of his family. Thank you to the many librarians who scanned documents, shipped books from other universities, and answered my emails. Many thanks also to Chris Puchalsky, who has always been happy to talk transportation policy and push back on my ideas over a beer on his porch. Heather Boyer from Island Press has been involved in this project from the start and provided constant feedback and support throughout. Thank you, Heather.

Finally, thank you to anyone who has paid the federal gas tax since 1987 when the Surface Transportation and Uniform Relocation Assistance Act created the University Transportation Center program. Like so much transportation research, a University Transportation Center supported not just this book but dozens research projects that I reference throughout. In my case, the Cooperative Mobility for Competitive Megaregions Transportation Center (based out of the University of Texas at Austin), whose management I inherited at Penn, helped inspire and support this project. I am a self-described megaregional skeptic. That does not mean that I do not believe in megaregions. I do. There is so much evidence of metropolitan areas growing along highways into each other and commute patterns connecting neighboring regions, more and more strongly. I am skeptical, however, that this is a good reason for making more and more investments, whether in highways or in high-speed rail. And nearly every time I hear someone mention megaregions, the next sentence is about the need for billions of dollars in new investments. I hope we can spend our tax dollars a bit more wisely.

Notes

Chapter 1: Introduction

1. Fred Salvucci, interview with Fred Salvucci, former Massachusetts secretary of transportation, for "The Big Dig," episode 4 of *Great Projects: The Building of America*, Public Broadcasting Service, 2002, https://www.pbs.org/greatprojects/interviews/salvucci_3.html.
2. Lee Mertz, Interstate Highway Research Project Oral History, interview by John Greenwood, 1988, 57, 60.
3. Federal Highway Administration, "America's Challenge for Highway Transportation in the 21st Century: Interim Report of the Future National Highway Program Task Force," 1988, 1; Earl Swift, *The Big Roads: The Untold Story of the Engineers, Visionaries, and Trailblazers Who Created the American Superhighways* (Boston: Houghton Mifflin Harcourt, 2011), 7; "Celebrating 50 Years: The Eisenhower Interstate Highway System" (Washington, DC: US Government Printing Office, June 27, 2006), 1–3, https://www.transportation.gov/testimony/celebrating-50-years-eisenhower-interstate-highway-system.
4. "Celebrating 50 Years."
5. Federal Highway Administration, "Highway Statistics," accessed July 24, 2024, https://www.fhwa.dot.gov/policyinformation/statistics/.
6. Federal Highway Administration, "Highway Statistics."
7. David Schrank et al., "2021 Urban Mobility Report" (College Station: Texas A&M Transportation Institute, 2021), https://mobility.tamu.edu/umr/report/.

8. US Centers for Disease Control and Prevention, "State-Specific Costs of Motor Vehicle Crash Deaths," Motor Vehicle Safety, November 6, 2020, https://www.cdc.gov/transportationsafety/statecosts/index.html.
9. US Bureau of Labor Statistics, "Consumer Expenditure Survey," 2020, https://www.bls.gov/cex/; Gilles Duranton and Erick Guerra, "Developing a Common Narrative on Urban Accessibility: An Urban Planning Perspective" (Washington, DC: Brookings Institution, 2016).
10. George H. W. Bush, "Remarks to the American Association of State Highway and Transportation Officials" (Washington, DC, June 21, 1991), https://www.presidency.ucsb.edu/documents/remarks-the-american-association-state-highway-and-transportation-officials.

Chapter 2: Out of the Mud and into the Cities

1. Thomas L. Karnes, *Asphalt and Politics: A History of the American Highway System* (Jefferson, NC: McFarland, 2009), chap. 3.
2. Bureau of Public Roads, *Toll Roads and Free Roads*, 76th Cong., 1st Sess. House, Doc. 272 (Washington, DC: US Government Printing Office, 1939), https://catalog.hathitrust.org/Record/001611706.
3. "Statement of General Lucius D. Clay Chairman, President's Advisory Committee on a National Highway Program" (US Senate, March 11, 1955), https://www.fhwa.dot.gov/infrastructure/claytest.cfm.
4. "U.S. Statutes at Large, Volume 27 (1892–1893), 52nd Congress," image (Washington, DC: Library of Congress), accessed February 15, 2022, https://www.loc.gov/item/llsl-v27/.
5. Richard F. Weingroff, "Portrait of a General: General Roy Stone," History of FHWA, n.d., https://www.fhwa.dot.gov/infrastructure/stone.cfm.
6. Maurice O. Eldridge, "Earth Roads," *Farmers' Bulletin* no. 136 (US Department of Agriculture, 1902); Martin Dodge, "Report of the Office of Public Road Inquiries," Department of Agriculture Annual Reports (Washington, DC: Government Printing Office, 1902).
7. Logan Waller Page, "Report of the Director of the Office of Public Roads," Department of Agriculture Annual Reports (Washington, DC: US Government Printing Office, 1905), 429.
8. "U.S. Statutes at Large, Volume 37 (1911–1913), 62nd Congress.," image (Washington, DC: Library of Congress), accessed February 21, 2022, https://www.loc.gov/item/llsl-v37/.
9. US Department of Transportation, "Status of the Nation's Highways, Bridges, and Transit Conditions and Performance," 23rd ed., 2019, fig. A-1, https://www.fhwa.dot.gov/policy/23cpr/index.cfm.

10. "U.S. Statutes at Large, Volume 39 (1915–1916), 64th Congress.," image (Washington, DC: Library of Congress), 355, accessed February 17, 2022, https://www.loc.gov/item/llsl-v39/.
11. Richard F. Weingroff, "Federal Aid Road Act of 1916: Building the Foundation," *Public Roads*, 1996, https://highways.dot.gov/public-roads/summer-1996/federal-aid-road-act-1916-building-foundation-sidebars.
12. Tom Lewis, *Divided Highways: Building the Interstate Highways, Transforming American Life, Divided Highways* (Ithaca, NY: Cornell University Press, 2013), 11, https://doi.org/10.7591/9780801467837.
13. "U.S. Statutes at Large, Volume 42 (1921–1923), 67th Congress.," image (Washington, DC: Library of Congress), accessed June 6, 2023, https://www.loc.gov/item/llsl-v42/.
14. Richard F. Weingroff, "From 1916 to 1939: The Federal-State Partnership at Work," *Public Roads*, 1996, https://highways.dot.gov/public-roads/summer-1996/1916-1939-federal-state-partnership-work.
15. Weingroff, "From 1916 to 1939."
16. Brian D. Taylor et al., *The Drive for Dollars: How Fiscal Politics Shaped Urban Freeways and Transformed American Cities* (New York: Oxford University Press, 2023), chap. 5.
17. Robert Whitten, *Report on a Thoroughfare Plan for Boston* (Boston: City Planning Board, 1930), http://archive.org/details/reportonthorough00bost.
18. Stephen H. Provost, *America's First Highways* (Pleasant Grove, UT: Dragon Crown Books, 2020), 22.
19. Richard F. Weingroff, "A Maximum of Good Results: Martin Dodge and the Good Roads Trains," History of FHWA, accessed February 25, 2022, https://www.fhwa.dot.gov/highwayhistory/dodge/02.cfm.
20. "Celebrating 50 Years: The Eisenhower Interstate Highway System" (Washington, DC: US Government Printing Office, June 27, 2006), https://www.transportation.gov/testimony/celebrating-50-years-eisenhower-interstate-highway-system.
21. Whitten, *Report on a Thoroughfare Plan for Boston*, 4.
22. Whitten, *Report on a Thoroughfare Plan for Boston*, 4; Taylor, Morris, and Brown, *The Drive for Dollars*, 39.
23. Whitten, *Report on a Thoroughfare Plan for Boston*, 1.
24. Whitten, *Report on a Thoroughfare Plan for Boston*, 82.
25. Staff of the Regional Plan, *Regional Plan of New York and Its Environs* (New York: Committee on Regional Plan of New York and Its Environs, 1929), 152–56, 212–13, https://rpa.org/work/reports/regional-plan-of-new-york-and-its-environs.

26. Staff of the Regional Plan, *Regional Plan*, 212.
27. Taylor, Morris, and Brown, *The Drive for Dollars*, chap. 5.
28. Taylor, Morris, and Brown, *The Drive for Dollars*, 149–50.
29. Whitten, *Report on a Thoroughfare Plan for Boston*, 91.
30. Whitten, *Report on a Thoroughfare Plan for Boston*, 91.
31. City of Boston Assessing Department, "Property Tax Facts and Figures FY 2021" (Boston: City of Boston, 2021).
32. John Spelman, "Boston Motordom: Automobiles and the Transformation of the City, 1899–1930" (Charlottesville: University of Virginia, 2014), 221–23, https://doi.org/10.18130/V3WV5W.
33. Robert Whitten, "The Atlanta Zone Plan: Report Outlining a Tentative Zone Plan for Atlanta" (Atlanta: City Planning Commission, 1922), https://catalog.hathitrust.org/Record/100216234.
34. Richard Rothstein, *The Color of Law: A Forgotten History of How Our Government Segregated America* (New York: Liveright, 2017), 46.
35. Lewis, *Divided Highways*, 131.
36. The Texas Highway Department, "From Pioneer Paths to Superhighways—The Texas Highway Department Blazes Texas Trails 1917–1968," accessed March 8, 2022, https://www.tsl.texas.gov/exhibits/highways/contents.html.
37. Lewis, *Divided Highways*, 22–23.
38. Helen Thomas, "Bush: Transportation Law Will Mean 'Jobs, Jobs, Jobs,'" *United Press International*, December 18, 1991, https://www.upi.com/Archives/1991/12/18/Bush-Transportation-law-will-mean-jobs-jobs-jobs/2592693032400/.
39. National Register of Historic Places, "Merritt Parkway" (National Park Service, March 5, 1991), https://npgallery.nps.gov/GetAsset/96eb4fba-acde-4e35-be75-4016e832b170.
40. Lee Mertz, "Origins of the Interstate System," Federal Highway Administration, accessed March 17, 2022, https://www.fhwa.dot.gov/infrastructure/origin01.cfm.
41. Mertz, "Origins of the Interstate System."
42. Norman Bel Geddes, *Magic Motorways* (New York: Random House, 1940), http://archive.org/details/magicmotorways00geddrich.
43. Geddes, *Magic Motorways*, 5.
44. Geddes, *Magic Motorways*, 4.
45. Geddes, *Magic Motorways*, 271.
46. Geddes, *Magic Motorways*, 244–59.

47. "Will Stage Plays in Paris This Spring; Norman-Bel Geddes and Richard Herndon Producers, with Eva Le Gallienne Star," *New York Times*, sec. Archives, March 23, 1925, https://www.nytimes.com/1925/03/23/archives/will-stage-plays-in-paris-this-spring-normanbel-geddes-and-richard.html.
48. Le Corbusier, *The City of To-Morrow and Its Planning*, trans. Frederick Etchells, reissue ed. (New York: Dover, 1987).
49. Mertz, "Origins of the Interstate System."
50. Mark H. Rose and Raymond A. Mohl, *Interstate: Highway Politics and Policy since 1939* (Knoxville: University of Tennessee Press, 2012), 98.
51. Bureau of Public Roads, *Toll Roads and Free Roads.*
52. Taylor, Morris, and Brown, *The Drive for Dollars*, 143–45; Lewis, *Divided Highways*, 53–54.
53. Mertz, "Origins of the Interstate System."
54. Bureau of Public Roads, *Toll Roads and Free Roads*, 93.
55. Rose and Mohl, *Interstate*, 99.
56. Bureau of Public Roads, *Toll Roads and Free Roads*, 94–95.
57. Bureau of Public Roads, *Toll Roads and Free Roads*, 94.
58. Taylor, Morris, and Brown, *The Drive for Dollars*, 113–18.
59. National Interregional Highway Committee, "Interregional Highways" (Washington, DC: US Government Printing Office, 1944).
60. "U.S. Statutes at Large, Volume 58 (1944), 78th Congress, Session 2.," image (Washington, DC: Library of Congress), accessed March 24, 2022, https://www.loc.gov/item/llsl-v58/.
61. Rose and Mohl, *Interstate*, 35.
62. Francesca Russello Ammon, *Bulldozer: Demolition and Clearance of the Postwar Landscape*, illustrated ed. (New Haven, CT: Yale University Press, 2016), 82–85.
63. Mertz, "Origins of the Interstate System."
64. Mertz, "Origins of the Interstate System."
65. Alan Altshuler and David Luberoff, *Mega-Projects: The Changing Politics of Urban Public Investment* (Washington, DC: Brookings Institution Press, 2003), 79.
66. The President's Advisory Committee on a National Highway Program, *A 10-Year National Highway Program*, 84th Cong., 1st Sess. House Document no. 93 (Washington: US Government Printing Office, 1955), https://catalog.hathitrust.org/Record/000968360.
67. "Statement of General Lucius D. Clay."
68. Taylor, Morris, and Brown, *The Drive for Dollars*, 206–9.

Chapter 3: Building the Interstates

1. Ralph A. Gakenheimer, *Transportation Planning as Response to Controversy: The Boston Case* (Cambridge. MA: MIT Press, 1976), 2
2. Boston Public Library, "Boston: Construction [Central Artery]." n.d., https://www.flickr.com/photos/boston_public_library/sets/72157633089829030/.
3. Gakenheimer, *Transportation Planning as Response to Controversy*, 21.
4. Alan Altshuler and David Luberoff, *Mega-Projects: The Changing Politics of Urban Public Investment* (Washington, DC: Brookings Institution Press, 2003), 79.
5. Fred Salvucci, interview with Fred Salvucci, former Massachusetts secretary of transportation, for "The Big Dig," episode 4 of *Great Projects: The Building of America*, Public Broadcasting Service, 2002, https://www.pbs.org/greatprojects/interviews/salvucci_3.html.
6. Charles A. Maguire and Associates, "The Master Highway Plan for the Boston Metropolitan Area" (Boston: Department of Public Works, 1948), v, https://archive.org/details/masterhighwaypla00char.
7. Tom Lewis, *Divided Highways*: *Building the Interstate Highways, Transforming American Life, Divided Highways* (Ithaca, NY: Cornell University Press, 2013), 296.
8. Texas Historical Commission, "Freedman's Cemetery Memorial—Atlas Number 5113006715," 1993, https://atlas.thc.state.tx.us/Details/5113006715/; Charles M. Clow et al., *Freedman's Cemetery: A Legacy of a Pioneer Black Community in Dallas, Texas*, ed. Duane E. Peter et al. (Plano, TX: Geo-Marine, Inc., 2000).
9. Marsha Prior and Robert V. Kemper, "From Freedman's Town to Uptown: Community Transformation and Gentrification In Dallas, Texas," *Urban Anthropology and Studies of Cultural Systems and World Economic Development* 34, no. 2/3 (2005): 177–216.
10. City of Dallas, "Ordinance 21203 Amending Chapter 51A, 'Part II of the Dallas Development Code,' of the Dallas City Code," 1992, https://dallascityhall.com:443/departments/sustainabledevelopment/historicpreservation/Pages/freedman_s_cemetery.aspx.
11. Marsha Prior, "Freedmantown/North Dallas," Texas State Historical Association, 2020, https://www.tshaonline.org/handbook/entries/freedmantownnorth-dallas; James M. Davidson, "Rituals Captured in Context and Time: Charm Use in North Dallas Freedman's Town (1869–1907), Dallas, Texas," *Historical Archaeology* 38, no. 2 (June 1, 2004): 22–54, https://doi.org/10.1007/BF03376641.

12. Vickery Place Neighborhood Association, "North Central Expressway," accessed April 18, 2022, https://www.vickeryplace.com/central-expressway; Megan Kimble, "Forgetful City," *Texas Observer*, September 17, 2021, https://www.texasobserver.org/forgetful-city/.
13. Collin Yarbrough, *Paved A Way: Infrastructure, Policy and Racism in an American City* (Potomac, MD: New Degree Press, 2021), 37.
14. Dallas Chamber of Commerce, *Central Expressway—San Jacinto Street to Fitzhugh Avenue: Dedication August 19, 1949* (Dallas: Dallas Chamber of Commerce, 1949), https://catalog.hathitrust.org/Record/006278509.
15. Davidson, "Rituals Captured in Context and Time"; James M. Davidson, "Freedman's Cemetery (1869–1907): Establishing a Chronology for Exhumed Burials from an African-American Burial Ground, Dallas, Texas," *African Diaspora Archaeology Newsletter* 6, no. 4 (1999): 5.
16. Clow et al., *Freedman's Cemetery*.
17. Texas State Library and Archives Commission, "Before and After Photos of Dallas Central Expressway, 1952 ," accessed April 18, 2022, https://www.tsl.texas.gov/exhibits/highways/greatage/centralexpressway1950s.html.
18. Wilfred Owen, *The New Highways: Challenge to the Metropolitan Region.* (Hartford: Connecticut General Life Insurance Co., 1956), https://catalog.hathitrust.org/Record/010618592.
19. Bernard L. Marsh, "The New Highways: Challenge to the Metro-Politan Region: A Report on a Symposium, Sponsored by Connecticut General Life Insurance Company, Hartford, September 9-12, 1957," *Traffic Engineering* 28 (1957): 15–17.
20. James H. Scheuer, "Highways and People: The Housing Impact of the Highway Program," Technical Bulletin no. 31 (New Haven, CT: Urban Land Institute, 1957), 35.
21. Marsh, "The New Highways"; Richard F. Weingroff, "The Greatest Decade 1956–1966," Interstate System, Highway History, Federal Highway Administration, accessed April 26, 2022, https://www.fhwa.dot.gov/infrastructure/50interstate.cfm.
22. Brian D. Taylor, Eric A. Morris, and Jeffrey R. Brown, *The Drive for Dollars: How Fiscal Politics Shaped Urban Freeways and Transformed American Cities* (New York: Oxford University Press, 2023), 122–32.
23. Weingroff, "The Greatest Decade 1956–1966."
24. Lewis Mumford, "Address of Lewis Mumford," presented at the New Highways: Challenge to the Metropolitan Region, Hartford, CT, September 11, 1957.
25. Lee Mertz, Interstate Highway Research Project Oral History, interview by John Greenwood, 1988, 23.

26. Karl Detzer, "Our Great Big Highway Bungle," *Reader's Digest*, July 1960.
27. Daniel P. Moynihan, "New Roads and Urban Chaos," *The Reporter*, 1960.
28. Moynihan, "New Roads and Urban Chaos."
29. Lee Mertz, "The Bragdon Committee," Interstate System, Highway History, Federal Highway Administration, accessed April 21, 2022, https://www.fhwa.dot.gov/infrastructure/bragdon.cfm#1a; Lewis, *Divided Highways*, 145; Dan McNichol, *The Roads That Built America: The Incredible Story of the U.S. Interstate System*, First Edition (New York: Barnes and Noble, 2003), 139.
30. Mertz, "The Bragdon Committee."
31. Mertz, "The Bragdon Committee."
32. Special Assistant for Public Works Planning, "Progress Review and Analysis: Federal Highway Program: Interim Report," 1960, https://www.enotrans.org/eno-resources/march-1960-interim-report-on-highways-from-john-s-bragdon/.
33. Special Assistant for Public Works Planning, 8.
34. Special Assistant for Public Works Planning, 16.
35. Special Assistant for Public Works Planning, 35.
36. Special Assistant for Public Works Planning, 35–36.
37. Special Assistant for Public Works Planning, 14.
38. Special Assistant for Public Works Planning, 11.
39. American Association of State Highway and Transportation Officials, *The States and the Interstates: Research on the Planning, Design and Construction of the Interstate and Defense Highway System*, 1991, 61.
40. Francesca Russello Ammon, *Bulldozer: Demolition and Clearance of the Postwar Landscape*, Illustrated ed. (New Haven, CT: Yale University Press, 2016).
41. Weingroff, "The Greatest Decade 1956–1966."
42. American Association of State Highway and Transportation Officials, *The States and the Interstates*, xi.
43. Bertram Tallamy, Interstate Highway Research Project Oral History, interview by Darwin Stolzanbach, September 21, 1987, 38.
44. Tallamy, 43.
45. Charles A. Maguire and Associates, "The Master Highway Plan for the Boston Metropolitan Area," v.
46. William Bugge, Interstate Highway Research Project Oral History, interview by John Greenwood, March 28, 1988, 50.
47. Richard M. Zettel, Interstate Highway Research Project Oral History, interview by David Jones, May 24, 1989, 37.

48. Mertz, Interstate Highway Research Project Oral History, 50.
49. Weingroff, "The Greatest Decade 1956–1966."
50. Mertz, Interstate Highway Research Project Oral History, 45–47.
51. Bureau of Public Roads, *General Location of National System of Interstate Highways: Including All Additional Routes at Urban Areas Designated in September 1955*, National System of Interstate Highways (Washington, DC: United States Dept. of Commerce, 1955), https://catalog.hathitrust.org/Record/000968362.
52. Lewis, *Divided Highways*, 161.
53. Mertz, "The Bragdon Committee."
54. B. Drummond Ayres Jr., "Washington; 'White Roads Through Black Bedrooms,'" *New York Times*, sec. Archives, December 31, 1967, https://www.nytimes.com/1967/12/31/archives/washington-white-roads-through-black-bedrooms.html.
55. Leon O. Talbert et al., Interstate Highway Research Project Oral History, interview by Mark Rose and Bruce Seely, n.d., 36.
56. Mark H. Rose and Raymond A. Mohl, *Interstate: Highway Politics and Policy since 1939* (Knoxville: University of Tennessee Press, 2012), 115–16.
57. Zettel, Interstate Highway Research Project Oral History, 36.
58. Rose and Mohl, *Interstate*, 122–27.
59. "Elusive Expressway," *Baltimore Sun*, December 14, 1968.
60. Mertz, Interstate Highway Research Project Oral History, 17.
61. Mertz, Interstate Highway Research Project Oral History, 27.
62. Federal Highway Administration, "Section 4(F)—Highway History," accessed May 5, 2022, https://www.fhwa.dot.gov/infrastructure/50section4f.cfm.
63. Rose and Mohl, *Interstate*, 138.
64. Altshuler and Luberoff, *Mega-Projects*, 84–87; Rose and Mohl, *Interstate*, 155; McNichol, *The Roads That Build America*, 147–52; Gakenheimer, *Transportation Planning as Response to Controversy*, 26–69.
65. Alan Altshuler, Interstate Highway Research Project Oral History, interview by Darwin Stolzanbach, n.d., 8.
66. James Aloisi, "Sargent's Actions 50 Years Ago Resonate Today," *CommonWealth Magazine*, February 9, 2020, https://commonwealthmagazine.org/opinion/sargents-actions-50-years-ago-resonate-today/.
67. Lewis, *Divided Highways*, 223, 230–33; Altshuler and Luberoff, *Mega-Projects*, 87; Altshuler, Interstate Highway Research Project Oral History, 16–20.
68. Altshuler, Interstate Highway Research Project Oral History, 15.

69. Rose and Mohl, *Interstate*, 105.
70. Rose and Mohl, 106; Eric Avila, *The Folklore of the Freeway: Race and Revolt in the Modernist City* (Minneapolis: University of Minnesota Press, 2014), 91–100.
71. Rose and Mohl, *Interstate*, 106–7; Neil R. McMillen, *The Citizens' Council: Organized Resistance to the Second Reconstruction, 1954–64* (Urbana: University of Illinois Press, 1994), 220–21; Avila, *The Folklore of the Freeway*, 47.
72. Avila, *The Folklore of the Freeway*, 109–15; Rose and Mohl, *Interstate*, 118–22.
73. Rose and Mohl, *Interstate*, 137; Altshuler and Luberoff, *Mega-Projects*, 84.
74. Thomas D. Larson, "Rex Whitton—the Man from Missouri," Interstate System, Highway History, Federal Highway Administration, 1990, https://www.fhwa.dot.gov/infrastructure/whitton.cfm.
75. Rose and Mohl, *Interstate*, 152.
76. Karen Stufflebeam Row, Eva LaDow, and Steve Moler, "Glenwood Canyon 12 Years Later," *Public Roads* 67, no. 5 (2004), https://web.archive.org/web/20121108031753/http://www.fhwa.dot.gov/publications/publicroads/04mar/04.cfm.
77. Nathaniel Baum-Snow, "Did Highways Cause Suburbanization?," *Quarterly Journal of Economics* 122, no. 2 (May 1, 2007): 775–805, https://doi.org/10.1162/qjec.122.2.775.
78. Talbert et al., Interstate Highway Research Project Oral History, 68–69.
79. Lewis, *Divided Highways*, 188.
80. Mertz, Interstate Highway Research Project Oral History, 109.
81. Zettel, Interstate Highway Research Project Oral History, 37.
82. Zettel, 29.
83. Lewis, *Divided Highways*, 171.
84. Federal Highway Administration, "Highway Statistics," accessed July 24, 2024, https://www.fhwa.dot.gov/policyinformation/statistics/.

Chapter 4: Sipping the ISTEA

1. Daniel P. Moynihan, "New Roads and Urban Chaos," *The Reporter*, 1960.
2. "Demographic Trends and Transportation Demand" (Washington, DC: US Government Printing Office, 1991), 2, https://catalog.hathitrust.org/Record/010020626.
3. American Association of State Highway and Transportation Officials, *The States and the Interstates: Research on the Planning, Design and Construction of the Interstate and Defense Highway System*, 1991.

4. George H. W. Bush, "Remarks on Signing the Intermodal Surface Transportation Efficiency Act" (Euless, TX, December 18, 1991), https://www.enotrans.org/eno-resources/1991-istea-signing-speeches-statements/.
5. Mark H. Rose and Raymond A. Mohl, *Interstate: Highway Politics and Policy since 1939* (Knoxville: University of Tennessee Press, 2012), 172.
6. Richard F. Weingroff, "Creating a Landmark: The Intermodal Surface Transportation Act of 1991," *Public Roads* 65, no. 3 (2001): 22, https://highways.dot.gov/public-roads/novemberdecember-2001/creating-landmark-intermodal-surface-transportation-act-1991.
7. Weingroff, "Creating a Landmark," 41.
8. *New York Times*, "A New Road for Transportation," sec. Opinion, November 29, 1991, https://www.nytimes.com/1991/11/29/opinion/a-new-road-for-transportation.html.
9. Weingroff, "Creating a Landmark," 48.
10. Federal Highway Administration, "Highway Statistics," accessed July 24, 2024, https://www.fhwa.dot.gov/policyinformation/statistics/.
11. Brian D. Taylor, Eric A. Morris, and Jeffrey R. Brown, *The Drive for Dollars: How Fiscal Politics Shaped Urban Freeways and Transformed American Cities* (New York: Oxford University Press, 2023), 211.
12. Federal Highway Administration, "Highway Statistics."
13. US Census Bureau, "Annual Survey of State and Local Government Finances," Census.gov, accessed October 21, 2022, https://www.census.gov/programs-surveys/gov-finances.html; US Census Bureau, "Census of Governments," Census.gov, accessed October 21, 2022, https://www.census.gov/programs-surveys/cog.html; Federal Highway Administration, "Highway Statistics."
14. Thomas L. Karnes, *Asphalt and Politics: A History of the American Highway System* (Jefferson, NC: McFarland, 2009), 135; Rose and Mohl, *Interstate,* 174–76.
15. Karnes, *Asphalt and Politics,* 135.
16. Taylor, Morris, and Brown, *The Drive for Dollars.*
17. Rose and Mohl, *Interstate,* 174.
18. Weingroff, "Creating A Landmark," 43; Alan Altshuler and David Luberoff, *Mega-Projects: The Changing Politics of Urban Public Investment* (Washington, DC: Brookings Institution Press, 2003), 88.
19. Altshuler and Luberoff, *Mega-Projects,* 115.
20. Tom Lewis, *Divided Highways: Building the Interstate Highways, Transforming American Life, Divided Highways* (Ithaca, NY: Cornell University Press, 2013), 296–99, https://doi.org/10.7591/9780801467837.

21. Lewis, *Divided Highways*, 298; Altshuler and Luberoff, *Mega-Projects*, 88.
22. Altshuler and Luberoff, *Mega-Projects*, 116.
23. Altshuler and Luberoff, *Mega-Projects*, 116–17; Taylor, Morris, and Brown, *The Drive for Dollars*, 223–31.
24. Altshuler and Luberoff, *Mega-Projects*, 91.
25. Altshuler and Luberoff, *Mega-Projects*, 91.
26. Altshuler and Luberoff, *Mega-Projects*, 93; Lewis, *Divided Highways*, 299.
27. Altshuler and Luberoff, *Mega-Projects*, 97.
28. Altshuler and Luberoff, *Mega-Projects*, 101.
29. Lewis, *Divided Highways*, 301; Jeff Davis, "30 Years Ago This Week: Reagan's 1987 Highway Bill Veto," *Eno Transportation Weekly*, March 29, 2017, https://enotrans.org/article/30-years-ago-week-reagans-1987-highway-bill-veto/; Helen Dewar and Lou Cannon, "Reagan Vetoes Highway Bill," *Washington Post*, March 28, 1987, https://www.washingtonpost.com/archive/politics/1987/03/28/reagan-vetoes-highway-bill/033d3806-5612-493a-a9a1-5a53e30f59c3/.
30. Altshuler and Luberoff, *Mega-Projects*, 105.
31. Altshuler and Luberoff, *Mega-Projects*, 119.
32. Altshuler and Luberoff, *Mega-Projects*, 119; Lewis, *Divided Highways*, 303.
33. Leah Brooks and Zachary Liscow, "Infrastructure Costs," *American Economic Journal: Applied Economics* 15, no. 2 (April 2023): 1–30, https://doi.org/10.1257/app.20200398.
34. US Department of Transportation and Massachusetts Department of Public Works, *Third Harbor Tunnel, Interstate 90/Central Artery, Interstate 93, Boston, Massachusetts: Final Environmental Impact Statement/Report and Final Section 4 (f) Evaluation* (Cambridge, MA: Federal Highway Administration, Transportation Systems Center; Massachusetts Department of Public Works, 1985), i, https://catalog.hathitrust.org/Record/100826781.
35. Robert Whitten, "Report on a Thoroughfare Plan for Boston" (Boston: City Planning Board, 1930), http://archive.org/details/reportonthorough00bost; Charles A. Maguire and Associates, "The Master Highway Plan for the Boston Metropolitan Area" (Boston: Department of Public Works, 1948), https://archive.org/details/masterhighwaypla00char.
36. Lewis, *Divided Highways*, 308.
37. North Texas Council of Governments, "Mobility 2010: The Regional Transportation Plan for North Central Texas," April 1991; North Texas Council of Governments, "Mobility 2010 Plan Update Summary: The Regional Transportation Plan for North Central Texas," October 1993; North Texas Council of Governments, "Mobility 2010 Plan Update: The Regional Transportation Plan for North Central Texas," January 1995.

38. Texas Highway Department, "Final Environmental Statement for State Highway 360 From Proposed State Highway 121 South of Grapevine, in Tarrant County to South of U.S. Highway 287, in Ellis County," 1973.
39. North Texas Council of Governments, "Mobility 2010 Plan Update."
40. Texas A&M Transportation Institute, "Congestion Data for Your City—Mobility Division," Urban Mobility Report 2021, August 27, 2020, https://mobility.tamu.edu/umr/congestion-data/.
41. Megan Kimble, *City Limits: Infrastructure, Inequality, and the Future of America's Highways* (New York: Crown, 2024), 107.

Chapter 5: How, Where, and Why Do We Build Roads?

1. "The Resounding Success of the Big Dig," *Places Journal*, accessed July 25, 2023, https://placesjournal.org/workshop-article/the-resounding-success-of-the-big-dig/.
2. Tom Lewis, *Divided Highways: Building the Interstate Highways, Transforming American Life, Divided Highways* (Ithaca, NY: Cornell University Press, 2013), 303, https://doi.org/10.7591/9780801467837.
3. Alaska Department of Transportation and Public Facilities, "Gravina Access Project: Final Environmental Impact Statement," 2004, 1–2, https://dot.alaska.gov/sereg/projects/gravina_access/assets/Final_EIS/COMPLETE_FINALEIS.pdf.
4. US Department of Transportation and Massachusetts Department of Public Works, *Third Harbor Tunnel, Interstate 90/Central Artery, Interstate 93, Boston, Massachusetts: Final Environmental Impact Statement/Report and Final Section 4 (f) Evaluation* (Cambridge, MA: Boston: Federal Highway Administration, Transportation Systems Center; Massachusetts Department of Public Works, 1985), i, https://catalog.hathitrust.org/Record/100826781.
5. Daniel P. Moynihan, "New Roads and Urban Chaos," *The Reporter*, 1960.
6. James Horrox and Andre Delattre, "Highway Boondoggles," US Public Interest Research Group, November 9, 2023, https://pirg.org/edfund/resources/highway-boondoggles/.
7. Pat Forgey, "How a 'Bridge to Nowhere' Became a Road from Nowhere to Nowhere," *Anchorage Daily News*, November 16, 2015, https://www.adn.com/alaska-news/article/how-bridge-nowhere-became-road-nowhere/2015/11/17/.
8. National Research Council, Highway Research Board, Committee on Highway Capacity, *Highway Capacity Manual: Practical Applications of Research* (Washington, DC: US Dept. of Commerce, Bureau of Public Roads, 1950), 1, https://catalog.hathitrust.org/Record/001108733.

9. Joseph Heathcott, "'The Whole City Is Our Laboratory': Harland Bartholomew and the Production of Urban Knowledge," *Journal of Planning History* 4, no. 4 (November 1, 2005): 322–55, https://doi.org/10.1177/1538513205282131.
10. Heathcott, "'The Whole City Is Our Laboratory.'"
11. Heathcott, "'The Whole City Is Our Laboratory'"; "Harland Bartholomew, 100, Dean of City Planners," *New York Times*, accessed August 2, 2023, https://www.nytimes.com/1989/12/07/obituaries/harland-bartholomew-100-dean-of-city-planners.html; Brian D. Taylor and Eric A. Morris, "Public Transportation Objectives and Rider Demographics: Are Transit's Priorities Poor Public Policy?," *Transportation* 42, no. 2 (March 1, 2015): 38, https://doi.org/10.1007/s11116-014-9547-0.
12. Harland Bartholomew, *A Major Street Plan for St. Louis* (St. Louis, MO: Nixon-Jones Printing Co., 1917), http://archive.org/details/cu31924024404927.
13. Bartholomew, *A Major Street Plan*, 14.
14. Miller McClintock, "The Traffic Survey," *The Annals of the American Academy of Political and Social Science* 133, no. 1 (November 1, 1927): 8–18, https://doi.org/10.1177/000271622713300103; Miller McClintock, *Street Traffic Control* (New York: McGraw-Hill, 1925); Miller McClintock, *A Proposed Traffic Ordinance for the City of Los Angeles: With Annotations and Recommendations for the Remedy of Street Traffic Conditions. Oct. 8, 1924*, 1924; Miller McClintock, *Report on San Francisco Citywide Traffic Survey: W.P.A. Project 6108-5863* (San Francisco: Pisani Printing and Publishing, 1937); Committee on Traffic and Public Safety, John Andrew Massen, and Miller McClintock, *Limited Ways: A Plan for the Greater Chicago Traffic Area: A Report to the City Council of the City of Chicago* (Chicago: Chicago City Council, 1933).
15. McClintock, *Street Traffic Control.*
16. McClintock, *Street Traffic Control*, 50–77.
17. Miller McClintock, "Superhighways Needed to Speed Major Traffic Flaws," *Chicago Daily Tribune*, January 29, 1933, sec. part 6.
18. Robert Whitten, *Report on a Thoroughfare Plan for Boston* (Boston: City Planning Board, 1930), 2, 4, http://archive.org/details/reportonthorough00bost.
19. Whitten, *Report on a Thoroughfare Plan for Boston*, 11.
20. Brian D. Taylor, Eric A. Morris, and Jeffrey R. Brown, *The Drive for Dollars: How Fiscal Politics Shaped Urban Freeways and Transformed American Cities* (New York: Oxford University Press, 2023), 150–52.

21. Bureau of Public Roads, *Toll Roads and Free Roads*, 76th Cong., 1st Sess. House, Doc. 272 (Washington, DC: US Government Printing Office, 1939), 35–37, https://catalog.hathitrust.org/Record/001611706.
22. Bureau of Public Roads, *Toll Roads and Free Roads*, 93.
23. Mark H. Rose and Raymond A. Mohl, *Interstate: Highway Politics and Policy since 1939* (Knoxville: University of Tennessee Press, 2012), 19–20; National Interregional Highway Committee, "Interregional Highways" (Washington, DC: US Government Printing Office, 1944); Taylor, Morris, and Brown, *The Drive for Dollars*, 162–64.
24. Taylor, Morris, and Brown, *The Drive for Dollars*, 163; American Association of State Highway Officials, "A Policy on Design Standards: 1. Interstate System. 2. Primary System. 3. Secondary and Feeder Roads. Rev," HathiTrust, 1956, 3, https://hdl.handle.net/2027/mdp.39015021030310?urlappend=%3Bseq=9; Wes Marshall, *Killed by a Traffic Engineer: Shattering the Delusion That Science Underlies Our Transportation System* (Washington, DC: Island Press, 2024), 173–76.
25. Marshall, *Killed by a Traffic Engineer*, 175.
26. North Texas Council of Governments, "Mobility 2010: The Regional Transportation Plan for North Central Texas," April 1991, 4.
27. North Texas Council of Governments, "Mobility 2010 Plan Update: The Regional Transportation Plan for North Central Texas," January 1995, III-3–4.
28. Texas Department of Transportation, "TxDOT Planning Process," 2015.
29. Federal Highway Administration, "Highway Statistics" (Washington, DC: US Department of Transportation), sec. FA-10, accessed July 24, 2024, https://www.fhwa.dot.gov/policyinformation/statistics/.
30. Inga Saffron, interview by Erick Guerra. May 3, 2024.
31. Inga Saffron, "Philly Spent a Decade Reconnecting Neighborhoods to the Waterfront. Widening I-95 Is Repeating Past Mistakes.," *Philadelphia Inquirer*, sec. Opinion, May 19, 2022, https://www.inquirer.com/columnists/i-95-construction-philadelphia-neighborhoods-delaware-river-bike-lanes-20220519.html.
32. Taylor, Morris, and Brown, *The Drive for Dollars*, 211.
33. Saffron, interview.
34. Pennsylvania Department of Transportation, "I-95 Central to South Philadelphia Planning Study," 2023, https://aecomviz.com/I95-CSP-360/.
35. Inga Saffron, "I-95 Reconstruction Is Really a Widening Project That Will Hurt Philly Neighborhoods," *Philadelphia Inquirer*, sec. Opinion, January 22, 2024, https://www.inquirer.com/real-estate/i-95-highways-penn

dot-reconstruction-widening-cities-injustice-mitigate-biden--20240122.html.

36. Saffron, "I-95 Reconstruction."
37. Megan Kimble, *City Limits: Infrastructure, Inequality, and the Future of America's Highways* (New York: Crown, 2024), 91.
38. Texas Department of Transportation, "North Houston Highway Improvement Project, Houston District: Draft Environmental Impact Statement," April 2017, ES-4.
39. Rose and Mohl, *Interstate*, 57–62; Taylor, Morris, and Brown, *The Drive for Dollars*, 38.
40. Rose and Mohl, *Interstate*, 57.
41. Charles McGrath, "Robert Caro's Big Dig," *New York Times*, sec. Magazine, April 12, 2012, https://www.nytimes.com/2012/04/15/magazine/robert-caros-big-dig.html.
42. Taylor, Morris, and Brown, *The Drive for Dollars*, 122–32.
43. Lee Mertz, Interstate Highway Research Project Oral History, interview by John Greenwood, 1988, 55–59.
44. Anthony Downs, *Stuck in Traffic: Coping with Peak-Hour Traffic Congestion* (Washington, DC: Brookings Institution Press, 1992); Anthony Downs, *Still Stuck in Traffic: Coping with Peak-Hour Traffic Congestion*, Revised (Washington, DC: Brookings Institution Press, 2004); Robert Cervero and Mark Hansen, "Induced Travel Demand and Induced Road Investment: A Simultaneous Equation Analysis," *Journal of Transport Economics and Policy* 36, no. 3 (2002): 469–90; Gilles Duranton and Matthew A. Turner, "The Fundamental Law of Road Congestion: Evidence from US Cities," *American Economic Review* 101, no. 6 (October 1, 2011): 2616–52, https://doi.org/10.1257/aer.101.6.2616.
45. Staff of the Regional Plan, "Regional Plan of New York and Its Environs" (New York: Committee on Regional Plan of New York and Its Environs, 1929), 144, https://rpa.org/work/reports/regional-plan-of-new-york-and-its-environs; Taylor, Morris, and Brown, *The Drive for Dollars*, 125, 152; Rose and Mohl, *Interstate*, 57–58.
46. Staff of the Regional Plan, "Regional Plan of New York," 144.
47. Cervero and Hansen, "Induced Travel Demand and Induced Road Investment."
48. Lewis Mumford, "The Roaring Traffic's Boom," *New Yorker*, April 16, 1955.
49. Downs, *Stuck in Traffic*; Downs, *Still Stuck in Traffic*.
50. Anthony Downs, "The Law of Peak-Hour Expressway Congestion," *Traffic*

Quarterly 16, no. 3 (July 1962), https://babel.hathitrust.org/cgi/pt?id=uc1.$b3477&seq=457.

51. Andreas Schafer and David G. Victor, "The Future Mobility of the World Population," *Transportation Research Part A: Policy and Practice* 34, no. 3 (2000): 171–205, https://doi.org/10.1016/S0965-8564(98)00071-8.
52. Mertz, Interstate Highway Research Project Oral History, 38.
53. Marshall Zelinger and Alexander Kirk, "Transportation Secretary Pete Buttigieg on I-70 Congestion, Trucker Crash Impacts," *9NEWS*, February 24, 2022, https://www.9news.com/article/news/local/local-politics/pete-buttigieg-colorado/73-54035201-b23a-4d01-9aa2-67b34a40dd51.
54. Susan Handy, *Shifting Gears: Toward a New Way of Thinking about Transportation* (Cambridge, MA: MIT Press, 2023), 123–29.
55. Jamey M. B. Volker, Amy E. Lee, and Susan Handy, "Induced Vehicle Travel in the Environmental Review Process," *Transportation Research Record*, June 15, 2020, https://journals.sagepub.com/doi/10.1177/0361198120923365.
56. Handy, *Shifting Gears*, 125.
57. Kelcie Ralph et al., "Are Transportation Planning Views Shared by Engineering Students and the Public?," *Journal of Planning Education and Research*, June 9, 2022, 0739456X221097840, https://doi.org/10.1177/0739456X221097840.
58. Handy, *Shifting Gears*, 129.

Chapter 6: The Economic Costs of Overbuilding

1. The Kowloon Walled City was demolished in 1993–1994.
2. John G. Fernald, "Roads to Prosperity? Assessing the Link between Public Capital and Productivity," *American Economic Review* 89, no. 3 (June 1999): 619–38, https://doi.org/10.1257/aer.89.3.619; Sylvain Leduc and Daniel Wilson, "Roads to Prosperity or Bridges to Nowhere? Theory and Evidence on the Impact of Public Infrastructure Investment," *NBER Macroeconomics Annual* 27 (January 2013): 89–142, https://doi.org/10.1086/669173; Marlon G. Boarnet, "Highways and Economic Productivity: Interpreting Recent Evidence," *Journal of Planning Literature* 11, no. 4 (May 1, 1997): 476–86, https://doi.org/10.1177/088541229701100402; Leah Brooks and Zachary Liscow, "Infrastructure Costs," *American Economic Journal: Applied Economics* 15, no. 2 (April 2023): 1–30, https://doi.org/10.1257/app.20200398.
3. US Census Bureau, "Annual Survey of State and Local Government Finances," Census.gov, accessed October 21, 2022, https://www.census

.gov/programs-surveys/gov-finances.html; US Census Bureau, "Census of Governments," Census.gov, accessed October 21, 2022, https://www.census.gov/programs-surveys/cog.html; Federal Highway Administration, "Highway Statistics" (Washington, DC: US Department of Transportation), accessed July 24, 2024, https://www.fhwa.dot.gov/policyinformation/statistics/.

4. Erick Guerra, Gilles Duranton, and Xinyu Ma, "Urban Roadway in America: The Amount, Extent, and Value," *Journal of the American Planning Association* (August 05, 2024): 1–15, https://doi.org/10.1080/01944363.2024.2368260.
5. Lawrence Blincoe et al., "The Economic and Societal Impact of Motor Vehicle Crashes, 2019 (Revised)" (Washington, DC: National Highway Traffic Safety Administration, 2023), https://trid.trb.org/View/2100826.
6. US Environmental Protection Agency, "Inventory of U.S. Greenhouse Gas Emissions and Sinks: 1990–2022," Reports and Assessments, February 8, 2024, 20, https://www.epa.gov/ghgemissions/inventory-us-greenhouse-gas-emissions-and-sinks-1990-2022; Richard S. J. Tol, "Social Cost of Carbon Estimates Have Increased over Time," *Nature Climate Change* 13, no. 6 (June 2023): 532–36, https://doi.org/10.1038/s41558-023-01680-x.
7. David Schrank et al., "2021 Urban Mobility Report" (College Station: Texas A&M Transportation Institute, 2021), https://mobility.tamu.edu/umr/report/.
8. Guerra, Duranton, and Ma, "Urban Roadway in America."
9. Federal Highway Administration, "Highway Statistics"
10. Prottoy Akbar et al., "Mobility and Congestion in Urban India," *American Economic Review* 113, no. 4 (April 2023): 1083–111, https://doi.org/10.1257/aer.20181662; Victor Couture, Gilles Duranton, and Matthew A. Turner, "Speed," *Review of Economics and Statistics* 100, no. 4 (October 1, 2018): 725–39, https://doi.org/10.1162/rest_a_00744.
11. Guerra, Duranton, and Ma, "Urban Roadway in America."
12. Gilles Duranton and Matthew A. Turner, "The Fundamental Law of Road Congestion: Evidence from US Cities," *American Economic Review* 101, no. 6 (October 1, 2011): 2616–52, https://doi.org/10.1257/aer.101.6.2616; Robert Cervero and Mark Hansen, "Induced Travel Demand and Induced Road Investment: A Simultaneous Equation Analysis," *Journal of Transport Economics and Policy* 36, no. 3 (2002): 469–90; Anthony Downs, *Still Stuck in Traffic: Coping with Peak-Hour Traffic Congestion*, rev. ed. (Washington, DC: Brookings Institution Press, 2004).

13. I. W. H Parry, M. Walls, and W. Harrington, "Automobile Externalities and Policies," *Journal of Economic Literature* 45, no. 2 (2007): 373–99.
14. Couture, Duranton, and Turner, "Speed"; Duranton and Turner, "The Fundamental Law of Road Congestion."
15. William S. Vickrey, "Pricing in Urban and Suburban Transport," *American Economic Review* 53, no. 2 (1963): 452–65.
16. William C. Wheaton, "Price-Induced Distortions in Urban Highway Investment," *Bell Journal of Economics* 9, no. 2 (1978): 622–32, https://doi.org/10.2307/3003602.
17. Boarnet, "Highways and Economic Productivity," 476.
18. North Texas Council of Governments, "Mobility 2010 Plan Update: The Regional Transportation Plan for North Central Texas," January 1995, XIV–2.
19. Texas Department of Transportation, "North Houston Highway Improvement Project, Houston District: Draft Environmental Impact Statement," April 2017.
20. Charles L. Marohn Jr., *Confessions of a Recovering Engineer: Transportation for a Strong Town* (Hoboken, NJ: Wiley, 2021), 139.
21. Megan Kimble, *City Limits: Infrastructure, Inequality, and the Future of America's Highways* (New York: Crown, 2024), 255.
22. US Department of Transportation, "Status of the Nation's Highways, Bridges, and Transit Conditions and Performance," 23rd ed., 2019, app. A, https://www.fhwa.dot.gov/policy/23cpr/index.cfm.
23. US Department of Transportation, "Status of the Nation's Highways, Bridges, and Transit Conditions," 10–15.

Chapter 7: Roadkill

1. International Transport Forum, "Transport Statistics" (Paris: Organisation for Economic Co-operation and Development, n.d.), accessed May 29, 2024, http://dx.doi.org/10.1787/trsprt-data-en.
2. International Transport Forum, "Transport Statistics."
3. Richard F. Weingroff, "General Lucius D. Clay—The President's Man," accessed November 15, 2024, https://www.fhwa.dot.gov/infrastructure/clay.cfm.
4. "Celebrating 50 Years: The Eisenhower Interstate Highway System," (Washington, DC: US Government Printing Office, June 27, 2006), https://www.transportation.gov/testimony/celebrating-50-years-eisenhower-interstate-highway-system.
5. Federal Highway Administration, "Highway Statistics" (Washington, DC:

U.S. Department of Transportation), accessed July 24, 2024, https://www.fhwa.dot.gov/policyinformation/statistics/.

6. National Highway Traffic Safety Administration, "Fatality Analysis Reporting System," accessed August 21, 2024, http://www.nhtsa.gov/FARS.
7. International Transport Forum, "Transport Statistics."
8. James David Bean et al., "Fatalities in Frontal Crashes Despite Seat Belts and Air Bags: Review of All CDS Cases Model and Calendar Years 2000–2007 122 Fatalities" (Washington, DC: National Highway Traffic Safety Administration, 2009), https://crashstats.nhtsa.dot.gov/Api/Public/ViewPublication/811102.
9. Bean et al., "Fatalities in Frontal Crashes."
10. Wes Marshall, *Killed by a Traffic Engineer: Shattering the Delusion That Science Underlies Our Transportation System* (Washington, DC: Island Press, 2024).
11. Marshall, *Killed by a Traffic Engineer*, 32.
12. Shima Hamidi and Reid Ewing, "A National Investigation on the Impacts of Lane Width on Traffic Safety: Narrowing Travel Lanes as an Opportunity to Promote Biking and Pedestrian Facilities Within the Existing Roadway Infrastructure" (Baltimore: Johns Hopkins Bloomberg School of Public Health, 2023), https://narrowlanes.americanhealth.jhu.edu/report/JHU-2023-Narrowing-Travel-Lanes-Report.pdf.
13. Douglass Robbins, "Long-Range I-95 CSP Planning—SHCA Feedback," April 19, 2024.
14. Megan Shannon, "PennDot's Survey," Government Transparency Blog, July 28, 2024, https://www.meganshannonrtk.com/blog/penndots-survey; Mike Newall, "South Philly Residents Say PennDot Misled Them about Plans to Remove Ballfields," *Philadelphia Inquirer*, August 10, 2024, https://www.inquirer.com/news/south-philly-baseball-fields-penndot-study-20240810.html.
15. Charles L. Marohn Jr., *Confessions of a Recovering Engineer: Transportation for a Strong Town* (Hoboken, NJ: Wiley, 2021), xxiii.
16. Marohn, *Confessions of a Recovering Engineer*, xxiii.
17. Marohn, *Confessions of a Recovering Engineer* , xxiv.
18. National Highway Traffic Safety Administration, "National Motor Vehicle Crash Causation Survey: Report to Congress" (Washington, DC: US Department of Transportation, 2008).
19. National Highway Traffic Safety Administration, "Fatality Analysis Reporting System."
20. Carolyn Said, "Exclusive: Tempe Police Chief Says Early Probe Shows No Fault by Uber," *San Francisco Chronicle*, March 26, 2018, https://web.arch

ive.org/web/20190830191415/https://www.sfchronicle.com/business/article/Exclusive-Tempe-police-chief-says-early-probe-12765481.php.

21. National Transportation Safety Board, "Collision between Vehicle Controlled by Developmental Automated Driving System and Pedestrian: Tempe, Arizona March 18, 2018," Accident Report, 2019.
22. Lauren Smiley, "The Legal Saga of Uber's Fatal Self-Driving Car Crash Is Over," *Wired*, July 28, 2023, https://www.wired.com/story/ubers-fatal-self-driving-car-crash-saga-over-operator-avoids-prison/.
23. National Transportation Safety Board, "Collision between Vehicle."
24. Marshall, *Killed by a Traffic Engineer*, 48–49.
25. Qinaat Hussain et al., "The Relationship between Impact Speed and the Probability of Pedestrian Fatality during a Vehicle-Pedestrian Crash: A Systematic Review and Meta-Analysis," *Accident Analysis and Prevention* 129 (2019): 241–49; Brian C. Tefft, "Impact Speed and a Pedestrian's Risk of Severe Injury or Death," *Accident Analysis and Prevention* 50 (2013): 871–78; Erik Rosén et al., "Literature Review of Pedestrian Fatality Risk as a Function of Car Impact Speed," *Accident Analysis and Prevention* 43, no. 1 (January 1, 2011): 25–33, https://doi.org/10.1016/j.aap.2010.04.003.
26. National Highway Traffic Safety Administration, "Fatality Analysis Reporting System."
27. Erick Guerra, Xiaoxia Dong, and Michelle Kondo, "Do Denser Neighborhoods Have Safer Streets? Population Density and Traffic Safety in the Philadelphia Region," *Journal of Planning Education and Research*, May 5, 2019, 0739456X19845043, https://doi.org/10.1177/0739456X19845043.
28. Nathaniel Baum-Snow, "Did Highways Cause Suburbanization?," *Quarterly Journal of Economics* 122, no. 2 (May 1, 2007): 775–805, https://doi.org/10.1162/qjec.122.2.775.
29. Guerra, Dong, and Kondo, "Do Denser Neighborhoods Have Safer Streets?"
30. Louis A. Merlin, Erick Guerra, and Eric Dumbaugh, "Crash Risk, Crash Exposure, and the Built Environment: A Conceptual Review," *Accident Analysis and Prevention* 134 (January 1, 2020): 105244, https://doi.org/10.1016/j.aap.2019.07.020.
31. Marshall, *Killed by a Traffic Engineer*, 37.

Chapter 8: The High Costs of Carlessness

1. John Hepp, "SEPTA," in *Encyclopedia of Greater Philadelphia* (Camden, NJ: Mid-Atlantic Regional Center for the Humanities, 2018), https://philadelphiaencyclopedia.org/archive/septa/.

2. Federal Transit Administration, "About FTA," accessed January 29, 2021, https://www.transit.dot.gov/about-fta.
3. Google, "Google Books Ngram Viewer," 2021, https://books.google.com/ngrams#.
4. Louis Keefer et al., "Pittsburgh Area Transportation Study: Final Report in Two Parts. Volume 2 Forecasts and Plans" (Commonwealth of Pennsylvania, County of Allegheny, City of Pittsburgh, and US Department of Commerce: Bureau of Public Roads, February 1963).
5. John Bates, "Case Study VI: Marketing in Marta," Mass Transit Management: Case Studies of the Metropolitan Atlanta Rapid Transit Authority (Athens: University of Georgia, March 1981), 13, https://rosap.ntl.bts.gov/view/dot/527.
6. Keefer et al., "Pittsburgh Area Transportation Study: Final Report in Two Parts. Volume 2 Forecasts and Plans," 58.
7. Erick Guerra, "What the Heck Is a Choice Rider? A Theoretical Framework and Empirical Model," *Journal of Transport and Land Use* 15, no. 1 (2022): 165–82.
8. US Department of Transportation, "National Household Travel Survey," 2017, http://nhts.ornl.gov/; Steve Polzin, Xuehao Chu, and Joel Rey, "Density and Captivity in Public Transit Success: Observations from the 1995 Nationwide Personal Transportation Study," *Transportation Research Record: Journal of the Transportation Research Board* 1735, no. 1 (2000): 10–18, https://doi.org/10.3141/1735-02; Genevieve Giuliano, "Low Income, Public Transit, and Mobility," *Transportation Research Record: Journal of the Transportation Research Board* 1927, no. 1 (January 1, 2005): 63–70, https://doi.org/10.3141/1927-08.
9. Jennifer Rogalsky, "Bartering for Basics: Using Ethnography and Travel Diaries to Understand Transportation Constraints and Social Networks among Working-Poor Women," *Urban Geography* 31, no. 8 (2010): 1018–38; Kristin Lovejoy and Susan Handy, "Social Networks as a Source of Private-Vehicle Transportation: The Practice of Getting Rides and Borrowing Vehicles among Mexican Immigrants in California," *Transportation Research Part A: Policy and Practice* 45, no. 4 (2011): 248–57; Evelyn Blumenberg and Asha Weinstein Agrawal, "Getting around When You're Just Getting By: Transportation Survival Strategies of the Poor," *Journal of Poverty* 18, no. 4 (2014): 355–78, https://doi.org/10.1080/10875549.2014.951905; Evelyn Blumenberg and Michael Smart, "Brother Can You Spare a Ride? Carpooling in Immigrant Neighbourhoods," *Urban Studies* 51, no. 9 (2014): 1871–90.

10. Nicholas J. Klein and Michael J. Smart, "Car Today, Gone Tomorrow: The Ephemeral Car in Low-Income, Immigrant and Minority Families," *Transportation* 44, no. 3 (May 1, 2017): 495–510, https://doi.org/10.1007/s11116-015-9664-4.
11. Guerra, "What the Heck Is a Choice Rider?"
12. Guerra, "What the Heck Is a Choice Rider?"
13. David A. King et al., "The Poverty of the Carless: Toward Universal Auto Access," *Journal of Planning Education and Research*, February 1, 2019, 0739456X18823252, https://doi.org/10.1177/0739456X18823252.
14. Klein and Smart, "Car Today, Gone Tomorrow"; Nicholas J. Klein, "Subsidizing Car Ownership for Low-Income Individuals and Households," *Journal of Planning Education and Research* 44, no. 1 (March 1, 2024): 165–77, https://doi.org/10.1177/0739456X20950428.
15. "Accessibility Observatory: Data Sets," accessed August 22, 2024, https://www.access.umn.edu/data/datasets/index.html.
16. King, Smart, and Manville, "The Poverty of the Carless."
17. Michael J. Smart and Nicholas J. Klein, "Disentangling the Role of Cars and Transit in Employment and Labor Earnings," *Transportation* 47, no. 3 (June 1, 2020): 1275–1309, https://doi.org/10.1007/s11116-018-9959-3.
18. Klein and Smart, "Car Today, Gone Tomorrow."
19. William AV Clark and Wenfei Winnie Wang, "The Automobile, Immigrants, and Poverty: Implications for Immigrant Earnings and Job Access," *Urban Geography* 31, no. 4 (2010): 523–40; Blumenberg and Agrawal, "Getting around When You're Just Getting By."
20. Nicholas J. Klein et al., "'Desperately in Need of Car': Analyzing Crowdfunding Campaigns for Car Purchases and Repairs on Gofundme.Com," preprint (SocArXiv, December 10, 2019), https://doi.org/10.31235/osf.io/8x7d2.
21. Melvin M. Webber, "The Joys of Automobility," in *The Car and the City: The Automobile, the Built Environment, and Daily Urban Life*, ed. Martin Wachs and Margaret Crawford (Ann Arbor: University of Michigan Press, 1992), https://escholarship.org/uc/item/3pb4j3sg.
22. B. Drummond Ayres Jr., "Washington; 'White Roads through Black Bedrooms,'" *New York Times*, sec. Archives, December 31, 1967, https://www.nytimes.com/1967/12/31/archives/washington-white-roads-through-black-bedrooms.html.
23. US Department of Transportation, "NHTS."
24. National Highway Traffic Safety Administration, "Traffic Safety Facts

2021 Data: Race and Ethnicity" (Washington, DC: US Department of Transportation, 2024), https://www.google.com/url?sa=t&source=web&rct=j&opi=89978449&url=https://crashstats.nhtsa.dot.gov/Api/Public/Publication/813572.

25. Matthew A. Raifman and Ernani F. Choma, "Disparities in Activity and Traffic Fatalities by Race/Ethnicity," *American Journal of Preventive Medicine* 63, no. 2 (August 1, 2022): 160–67, https://doi.org/10.1016/j.amepre.2022.03.012.
26. Erick Guerra, Xiaoxia Dong, and Michelle Kondo, "Do Denser Neighborhoods Have Safer Streets? Population Density and Traffic Safety in the Philadelphia Region," *Journal of Planning Education and Research*, May 5, 2019, 0739456X19845043, https://doi.org/10.1177/0739456X19845043.
27. Courtney Coughenour et al., "Examining Racial Bias as a Potential Factor in Pedestrian Crashes," *Accident Analysis and Prevention* 98, supp. C (January 1, 2017): 96–100, https://doi.org/10.1016/j.aap.2016.09.031; Tara Goddard, Kimberly Barsamian Kahn, and Arlie Adkins, "Racial Bias in Driver Yielding Behavior at Crosswalks," *Transportation Research Part F: Traffic Psychology and Behaviour* 33, supp. C (August 1, 2015): 1–6, https://doi.org/10.1016/j.trf.2015.06.002.
28. Abdulrahman Jbaily et al., "Air Pollution Exposure Disparities across US Population and Income Groups," *Nature* 601, no. 7892 (January 2022): 228–33, https://doi.org/10.1038/s41586-021-04190-y; Jiawen Liu et al., "Disparities in Air Pollution Exposure in the United States by Race/Ethnicity and Income, 1990–2010," *Environmental Health Perspectives* 129, no. 12 (December 2021): 127005, https://doi.org/10.1289/EHP8584; Lara P. Clark, Dylan B. Millet, and Julian D. Marshall, "Changes in Transportation-Related Air Pollution Exposures by Race-Ethnicity and Socioeconomic Status: Outdoor Nitrogen Dioxide in the United States in 2000 and 2010," *Environmental Health Perspectives* 125, no. 9 (September 22, 2017): 097012, https://doi.org/10.1289/EHP959.
29. Gaige Hunter Kerr et al., "Increasing Racial and Ethnic Disparities in Ambient Air Pollution-Attributable Morbidity and Mortality in the United States," *Environmental Health Perspectives* 132, no. 3 (March 2024): 037002, https://doi.org/10.1289/EHP11900.
30. Patricia Warren et al., "Driving While Black: Bias Processes and Racial Disparity in Police Stops," *Criminology* 44, no. 3 (2006): 709–38, https://doi.org/10.1111/j.1745-9125.2006.00061.x; Andrew Gelman, Jeffrey Fagan, and Alex Kiss, "An Analysis of the New York City Police Department's

'Stop-and-Frisk' Policy in the Context of Claims of Racial Bias," *Journal of the American Statistical Association* 102, no. 479 (September 1, 2007): 813–23, https://doi.org/10.1198/016214506000001040; Loren Page Ambinder, "Dispelling the Myth of Rationality: Racial Discrimination in Taxicab Service and the Efficacy of Litigation under 42 U.S.C. 1981 Note," *George Washington Law Review* 64, no. 2 (1996 1995): 342–78; Emma Pierson et al., "A Large-Scale Analysis of Racial Disparities in Police Stops across the United States," *Nature Human Behaviour* 4, no. 7 (July 2020): 736–45, https://doi.org/10.1038/s41562-020-0858-1.

31. Pierson et al., "A Large-Scale Analysis of Racial Disparities in Police Stops across the United States."
32. Mia Bay, *Traveling Black: A Story of Race and Resistance* (Cambridge, MA: Belknap Press, 2021).
33. Bay, *Traveling Black*, 312.
34. Bay, *Traveling Black*, 320.
35. US Department of Transportation, "NHTS."
36. Chris Horymski, "Average Auto Loan Debt Grew 5.2% to $23,792 in 2023—Experian," February 13, 2024, https://www.experian.com/blogs/ask-experian/research/auto-loan-debt-study/.
37. ISEECARS, "Top 25 Cars That Hold Their Value the Best—and the 25 Worst—iSeeCars.Com," accessed July 11, 2024, https://www.iseecars.com/cars-that-hold-their-value-study.
38. US Department of Transportation, "NHTS."
39. Shengxiao (Alex) Li, "Vehicle Ownership over the Life Course among Older Americans: A Longitudinal Analysis," *Transportation* 51, no. 1 (February 1, 2024): 247–70, https://doi.org/10.1007/s11116-022-10326-4.
40. Shengxiao (Alex) Li, "Transportation Planning for Older Americans: Challenges, Federal Policies, and Next Steps," *Journal of Aging and Social Policy* 0, no. 0 (n.d.): 1–19, https://doi.org/10.1080/08959420.2023.2238539.

Chapter 9: Unbuilding

1. Richard F. Weingroff, "Creating A Landmark: The Intermodal Surface Transportation Act of 1991," *Public Roads* 65, no. 3 (2001), https://highways.dot.gov/public-roads/novemberdecember-2001/creating-landmark-intermodal-surface-transportation-act-1991.
2. Federal Highway Administration, "Highway Statistics," accessed July 24, 2024, https://www.fhwa.dot.gov/policyinformation/statistics/.
3. "Testimony on The Status of the Highway Trust Fund: 2023 Update"

(Washington, DC: Congressional Budget Office, October 18, 2023), https://www.cbo.gov/publication/59667.

4. Eno Center for Transportation, "How We Pay for Transportation: The Life and Death of the Highway Trust Fund," 2014, https://enotrans.org/wp-content/uploads/2023/02/Highway-Trust-Fund.pdf.
5. Erick Guerra, Gilles Duranton, and Xinyu Ma, "Urban Roadway in America: The Amount, Extent, and Value," *Journal of the American Planning Association* (August 05, 2024): 1–15, https://doi.org/10.1080/01944363.2024.2368260.
6. Brian D. Taylor, Eric A. Morris, and Jeffrey R. Brown, *The Drive for Dollars: How Fiscal Politics Shaped Urban Freeways and Transformed American Cities* (New York: Oxford University Press, 2023).
7. "Testimony on The Status of the Highway Trust Fund"; Taylor, Morris, and Brown, *The Drive for Dollars*; Thomas L. Karnes, *Asphalt and Politics: A History of the American Highway System* (Jefferson, NC: McFarland, 2009); Eno Center for Transportation, "How We Pay for Transportation."
8. Oregon Department of Transportation, "OReGO: Oregon's Road Usage Charge Program," accessed July 30, 2024, https://www.oregon.gov/odot/programs/pages/orego.aspx.
9. Garret Shrode, Jeff Davis, and Robert Puentes, "Driving Change: Advice for the National VMT-Fee Pilot" (Washington, DC: Eno Center for Transportation, 2023), https://enotrans.org/eno-resources/driving-change-advice-for-the-national-vmt-fee-pilot/.
10. Oregon Department of Transportation, "August 2024 Monthly Indicators Report," 2024, https://www.oregon.gov/odot/Data/Documents/Monthly_Indicators_2024.pdf.
11. Erick Guerra et al., "Evaluating the Effectiveness of Speed Cameras on Philadelphia's Roosevelt Boulevard," *Transportation Research Record: Journal of the Transportation Research Board*, February 27, 2024, 03611981241230320, https://doi.org/10.1177/03611981241230320.
12. Fred Knubel, "Vickrey One Year Later: Catching Up with a Thinker Way Ahead of His Time," *Columbia University Record*, October 10, 1997, https://curecordarchive.library.columbia.edu/?a=d&d=cr19971010-01.2.2&e=-------en-20--1--txt-txIN-------; William S. Vickrey, "A Proposal for Revising New York's Subway Fare Structure," *Journal of the Operations Research Society of America* 3, no. 1 (1955): 38–68.
13. William S. Vickrey, "Pricing in Urban and Suburban Transport," *American Economic Review* 53, no. 2 (1963): 452.

14. Texas Department of Transportation, "TEXpress Lanes," accessed July 31, 2024, http://txdot.gov/en/home/discover/express-toll-hov-lanes/managed-lanes/texpress-lanes.html.
15. American Association of State Highway and Transportation Officials. *A Policy on Geometric Design of Highways and Streets*, 7th ed. (Washington, DC: American Association of State Highway and Transportation Officials, 2018).
16. Robert Cervero, J. Kang, and K. Shively, "From Elevated Freeways to Surface Boulevards: Neighborhood and Housing Price Impacts in San Francisco," *Journal of Urbanism: International Research on Placemaking and Urban Sustainability* 2, no. 1 (2009): 31–50; John King, *Portal: San Francisco's Ferry Building and the Reinvention of American Cities* (Norton, 2023).
17. Cervero, Kang, and Shively, "From Elevated Freeways to Surface Boulevards."
18. King, *Portal.*
19. John Norquist, *The Wealth of Cities: Revitalizing the Centers of American Life* (New York: Basic Books, 1999); Congress for New Urbanism, "Completed Highways to Boulevards Projects," text, CNU, June 12, 2015, https://www.cnu.org/our-projects/highways-boulevards/completed-h2b-projects; Cervero, Kang, and Shively, "From Elevated Freeways to Surface Boulevards."
20. City of Milwaukee, "Park East Redevelopment," accessed September 9, 2024, https://city.milwaukee.gov/DCD/Projects/ParkEastredevelopment.
21. Congress for New Urbanism, "Freeways without Futures," text, 2019, https://www.cnu.org/highways-boulevards/freeways-without-futures/2019.
22. Jeffrey Brinkman and Jeffrey Lin, "The Costs and Benefits of Fixing Downtown Freeways," *Economic Insights* 7, no. 1 (2022): 17–22.
23. Megan Kimble, *City Limits: Infrastructure, Inequality, and the Future of America's Highways* (New York: Crown, 2024).
24. US Department of Transportation, "Biden-Harris Administration Announces First-Ever Awards from Program to Reconnect Communities," US Department of Transportation, press release, February 28, 2023, https://www.transportation.gov/briefing-room/biden-harris-administration-announces-first-ever-awards-program-reconnect-communities.
25. Brinkman and Lin, "The Costs and Benefits of Fixing Downtown Freeways"; Federal Highway Administration, "Highway Statistics."
26. Wes Marshall, *Killed by a Traffic Engineer: Shattering the Delusion That*

Science Underlies Our Transportation System (Washington, DC: Island Press, 2024), 179.

27. Kimberly Venegas et al., "Take the High (Volume) Road: Analyzing the Safety and Speed Effects of High-Traffic-Volume Road Diets," *Transportation Research Record* 2678, no. 6 (June 1, 2024): 74–86, https://doi.org/10.1177/03611981231193630; Robert B. Noland et al., "Costs and Benefits of a Road Diet Conversion," *Case Studies on Transport Policy* 3, no. 4 (December 1, 2015): 449–58, https://doi.org/10.1016/j.cstp.2015.09.002; Yuying Zhou et al., "Safety Effectiveness of the Road Diet Treatment in Rhode Island," *Transportation Research Record* 2676, no. 7 (July 1, 2022): 24–31, https://doi.org/10.1177/03611981221076433; Peter B. Ohlms et al., "How's That Diet Working: Performance of Virginia Road Diets," April 1, 2020, https://rosap.ntl.bts.gov/view/dot/54878.
28. Federal Highway Administration, "Road Diets (Roadway Reconfiguration)," accessed August 8, 2024, https://highways.dot.gov/safety/proven-safety-countermeasures/road-diets-roadway-reconfiguration.

Chapter 10: Fixing What Gets Measured

1. Paul Zak, "Measurement Myopia," Drucker Institute, Claremont Graduate University (blog), July 4, 2013, https://drucker.institute/thedx/measurement-myopia/; Andrew McAfee and Erik Brynjolfsson, "Big Data: The Management Revolution," *Harvard Business Review*, October 1, 2012, https://hbr.org/2012/10/big-data-the-management-revolution.
2. Charles L. Marohn Jr., *Confessions of a Recovering Engineer: Transportation for a Strong Town* (Hoboken, NJ: Wiley, 2021); Wes Marshall, *Killed by a Traffic Engineer: Shattering the Delusion That Science Underlies Our Transportation System* (Washington, DC: Island Press, 2024).
3. Marshall, *Killed by a Traffic Engineer*, 181.
4. Marshall, *Killed by a Traffic Engineer*, 184–86.
5. Geoff Boeing and William (Billy) Riggs, "Converting One-Way Streets to Two-Way Streets to Improve Transportation Network Efficiency and Reduce Vehicle Distance Traveled," *Journal of Planning Education and Research*, July 6, 2022, 0739456X221106334, https://doi.org/10.1177/0739456X221106334; William Riggs and Bruce Appleyard, "The Economic Impact of One to Two-Way Street Conversions: Advancing a Context-Sensitive Framework," *Journal of Urbanism: International Research on Placemaking and Urban Sustainability* 11, no. 2 (April 3, 2018): 129–48, https://doi.org/10.1080/17549175.2017.1422535; William Riggs and

John Gilderbloom, "Two-Way Street Conversion: Evidence of Increased Livability in Louisville," *Journal of Planning Education and Research* 36, no. 1 (March 1, 2016): 105–18, https://doi.org/10.1177/0739456X15593147.

6. US Department of Transportation, "National Household Travel Survey," 2017, http://nhts.ornl.gov/.
7. Jonathan Levine et al., "Does Accessibility Require Density or Speed? A Comparison of Fast versus Close in Getting Where You Want to Go in US Metropolitan Regions," *Journal of the American Planning Association* 78, no. 2 (2012): 157–72; Gilles Duranton and Erick Guerra, "Developing a Common Narrative on Urban Accessibility: An Urban Planning Perspective" (Washington, DC: Brookings Institution, 2016), 9; Andrew Mondschein and Brian D. Taylor, "Is Traffic Congestion Overrated? Examining the Highly Variable Effects of Congestion on Travel and Accessibility," *Journal of Transport Geography* 64 (October 1, 2017): 65–76, https://doi.org/10.1016/j.jtrangeo.2017.08.007.
8. Wesley E. Marshall and Eric Dumbaugh, "Revisiting the Relationship between Traffic Congestion and the Economy: A Longitudinal Examination of U.S. Metropolitan Areas," *Transportation* 47, no. 1 (February 1, 2020): 275–314, https://doi.org/10.1007/s11116-018-9884-5; Matthias Sweet, "Traffic Congestion's Economic Impacts: Evidence from US Metropolitan Regions," *Urban Studies* 51, no. 10 (August 1, 2014): 2088–110, https://doi.org/10.1177/0042098013505883.
9. Duranton and Guerra, "Developing a Common Narrative."
10. Jonathan Levine, Joe Grengs, and Louis A. Merlin, *From Mobility to Accessibility: Transforming Urban Transportation and Land-Use Planning* (Ithaca, NY: Cornell University Press, 2019), 62–64.
11. Levine, Grengs, and Merlin, 136; Duranton and Guerra, "Developing a Common Narrative."
12. Levine, Grengs, and Merlin, *From Mobility to Accessibility*, 11.
13. Susan Handy, *Shifting Gears: Toward a New Way of Thinking about Transportation* (Cambridge, MA: MIT Press, 2023), 82.
14. Susan Handy, "Is Accessibility an Idea Whose Time Has Finally Come?," *Transportation Research Part D: Transport and Environment* 83 (June 1, 2020): 102319, https://doi.org/10.1016/j.trd.2020.102319.
15. Duranton and Guerra, "Developing a Common Narrative"; Levine, Grengs, and Merlin, *From Mobility to Accessibility*, 12; Handy, "Is Accessibility an Idea Whose Time Has Finally Come?"

16. Louis A. Merlin, Jonathan Levine, and Joe Grengs, "Accessibility Analysis for Transportation Projects and Plans," *Transport Policy* 69 (October 1, 2018): 35–48, https://doi.org/10.1016/j.tranpol.2018.05.014; Levine, Grengs, and Merlin, *From Mobility to Accessibility*, 64–69.
17. Louis A. Merlin, Jonathan Levine, and Joe Grengs, "Accessibility Analysis for Transportation Projects and Plans"; Levine, Grengs, and Merlin, *From Mobility to Accessibility*, 64–69.
18. Ahmed M. El-Geneidy and David M. Levinson, "Access to Destinations: Development of Accessibility Measures," May 1, 2006, https://hdl.handle.net/11299/638.
19. Ahmed El-Geneidy and David Levinson, "Making Accessibility Work in Practice," *Transport Reviews* 42, no. 2 (March 4, 2022): 129–33, https://doi.org/10.1080/01441647.2021.1975954.
20. Marohn, *Confessions of a Recovering Engineer*; Marshall, *Killed by a Traffic Engineer*.
21. Marshall, *Killed by a Traffic Engineer*, 253–57.
22. Marohn, *Confessions of a Recovering Engineer*; Marshall, *Killed by a Traffic Engineer*.
23. Dan Bosch, "California's Zero Emissions Vehicle Rule and Its Nationwide Impacts," American Action Forum, October 25, 2022, https://www.americanactionforum.org/insight/californias-zero-emissions-vehicle-rule-and-its-nationwide-impacts/.
24. Michael Anderson, "Safety for Whom? The Effects of Light Trucks on Traffic Fatalities," *Journal of Health Economics* 27, no. 4 (July 1, 2008): 973–89, https://doi.org/10.1016/j.jhealeco.2008.02.001; Justin Tyndall, "Pedestrian Deaths and Large Vehicles," *Economics of Transportation* 26–27 (June 1, 2021): 100219, https://doi.org/10.1016/j.ecotra.2021.100219.
25. National Highway Traffic Safety Administration, "Pedestrian Safety," text, accessed August 20, 2024, https://www.nhtsa.gov/book/countermeasures-that-work/pedestrian-safety; National Highway Traffic Safety Administration, "Fatality Analysis Reporting System," accessed August 21, 2024, http://www.nhtsa.gov/FARS.
26. "What to Do about America's Killer Cars," *The Economist*, accessed September 9, 2024, https://www.economist.com/leaders/2024/09/05/what-to-do-about-americas-killer-cars.
27. Cass R. Sunstein, *The Cost-Benefit Revolution* (Cambridge, MA: MIT Press, 2018), 6–26.
28. Daniel P. Moynihan, "New Roads and Urban Chaos," *The Reporter*, 1960, 19.

Chapter 11: The Future Is Now

1. Eric Morris, "From Horse Power to Horsepower," *Access Magazine* 1, no. 30 (2007): 2–10.
2. Jeffrey R. Brown, Eric A. Morris, and Brian D. Taylor, "Planning for Cars in Cities: Planners, Engineers, and Freeways in the 20th Century," *Journal of the American Planning Association* 75, no. 2 (2009): 161–77, https://doi.org/10.1080/01944360802640016.
3. Peter Hall, *Cities of Tomorrow: An Intellectual History of Urban Planning and Design since 1880*, 4th ed. (West Sussex, UK: Wiley, 2014), 332.
4. Norman Bel Geddes, *Magic Motorways* (New York: Random House, 1940), 65, http://archive.org/details/magicmotorways00geddrich.
5. Nissan, "The Future Is Now: Nissan Advances Plans to Have Commercially Viable Autonomous Drive Vehicles on the Road by 2020," 2014, http://www.nissanusa.com/innovations/autonomous-car.article.html.
6. Peter Norton, *Autonorama: The Illusory Promise of High-Tech Driving* (Washington, DC: Island Press, 2021).
7. Norton, *Autonorama*, 107–13.
8. Waymo, "Meet Waymo One: The World's First Autonomous Ride-Hailing Service," accessed November 18 , 2024, https://waymo.com/waymo-one /.
9. Ricardo A. Daziano, Mauricio Sarrias, and Benjamin Leard, "Are Consumers Willing to Pay to Let Cars Drive for Them? Analyzing Response to Autonomous Vehicles," *Transportation Research Part C: Emerging Technologies* 78 (May 2017): 150–64, https://doi.org/10.1016/j.trc.2017.03.003.
10. Jack Fitzgerald, "Average Age of Vehicles in U.S. Continues to Rise," *Car and Driver*, May 23, 2024, https://www.caranddriver.com/news/a60882953/average-age-us-cars-trucks-suvs-rises/.
11. Emily DeLetter, "Video Shows Waymo Self-Driving Cars Honking at Each Other at 4 a.m. in Parking Lot," *USA Today*, accessed August 23, 2024, https://www.usatoday.com/story/tech/2024/08/15/waymo-driverless-cars-honking-parking-lot-video/74810195007/.
12. Adam Millard-Ball, "The Autonomous Vehicle Parking Problem," *Transport Policy* 75 (March 1, 2019): 99–108, https://doi.org/10.1016/j.tranpol.2019.01.003.
13. Erick Guerra, "Planning for Cars That Drive Themselves: Metropolitan Planning Organizations, Regional Transportation Plans, and Autonomous Vehicles," *Journal of Planning Education and Research* 36, no. 2 (2016): 210–24, https://doi.org/10.1177/0739456X15613591.
14. Arash Olia et al., "Traffic Capacity Implications of Automated Vehicles

Mixed with Regular Vehicles," *Journal of Intelligent Transportation Systems* 22, no. 3 (May 4, 2018): 244–62, https://doi.org/10.1080/15472450.2017.1404680.

15. Xiaoning Xia and Pengwei Li, "A Review of the Life Cycle Assessment of Electric Vehicles: Considering the Influence of Batteries," *Science of the Total Environment* 814 (March 25, 2022): 152870, https://doi.org/10.1016/j.scitotenv.2021.152870.
16. Julia C. Fussell et al., "A Review of Road Traffic-Derived Non-Exhaust Particles: Emissions, Physicochemical Characteristics, Health Risks, and Mitigation Measures," *Environmental Science and Technology* 56, no. 11 (June 7, 2022): 6813–35, https://doi.org/10.1021/acs.est.2c01072.
17. Blake Shaffer, Maximilian Auffhammer, and Constantine Samaras, "Make Electric Vehicles Lighter to Maximize Climate and Safety Benefits," *Nature* 598, no. 7880 (October 2021): 254–56, https://doi.org/10.1038/d41586-021-02760-8.

Bibliography

Akbar, Prottoy, Victor Couture, Gilles Duranton, and Adam Storeygard. "Mobility and Congestion in Urban India." *American Economic Review* 113, no. 4 (April 2023): 1083–1111. https://doi.org/10.1257/aer.20181662.

Alaska Department of Transportation and Public Facilities. "Gravina Access Project: Final Environmental Impact Statement," 2004. https://dot.alaska.gov/sereg/projects/gravina_access/assets/Final_EIS/COMPLETE_FINAL EIS.pdf.

Aloisi, James. "Sargent's Actions 50 Years Ago Resonate Today." *CommonWealth Magazine*, February 9, 2020. https://commonwealthmagazine.org/opinion/sargents-actions-50-years-ago-resonate-today/.

Altshuler, Alan. Interstate Highway Research Project Oral History. Interview by Darwin Stolzanbach, n.d.

Altshuler, Alan, and David Luberoff. *Mega-Projects: The Changing Politics of Urban Public Investment*. Washington, DC: Brookings Institution Press, 2003.

Ambinder, Loren Page. "Dispelling the Myth of Rationality: Racial Discrimination in Taxicab Service and the Efficacy of Litigation under 42 U.S.C. 1981 Note." *George Washington Law Review* 64, no. 2 (1996 1995): 342–78.

American Association of State Highway and Transportation Officials. *The States and the Interstates: Research on the Planning, Design and Construction of the Interstate and Defense Highway System*, 1991.

American Association of State Highway Officials. "A Policy on Design Standards: 1. Interstate System. 2. Primary System. 3. Secondary and Feeder

Roads. Rev." HathiTrust, 1956. https://hdl.handle.net/2027/mdp.39015021030310?urlappend=%3Bseq=9.

American Association of State Highway and Transportation Officials. *A Policy on Geometric Design of Highways and Streets*. 7th ed. Washington, DC: American Association of State Highway and Transportation Officials, 2018.

American Transportation Research Institute. "An Analysis of Operational Costs of Trucking: 2020 Update," 2020. https://truckingresearch.org/wp-content/uploads/2020/11/ATRI-Operational-Costs-of-Trucking-2020.pdf.

Ammon, Francesca Russello. *Bulldozer: Demolition and Clearance of the Postwar Landscape*. Illustrated ed. New Haven, CT: Yale University Press, 2016.

Anderson, Michael. "Safety for Whom? The Effects of Light Trucks on Traffic Fatalities." *Journal of Health Economics* 27, no. 4 (July 1, 2008): 973–89. https://doi.org/10.1016/j.jhealeco.2008.02.001.

Avila, Eric. *The Folklore of the Freeway: Race and Revolt in the Modernist City*. Minneapolis: University of Minnesota Press, 2014.

Ayres, B. Drummond, Jr. "Washington; 'White Roads through Black Bedrooms.'" *New York Times*, sec. Archives, December 31, 1967. https://www.nytimes.com/1967/12/31/archives/washington-white-roads-through-black-bedrooms.html.

Baltimore Sun. "Elusive Expressway." December 14, 1968.

Bartholomew, Harland. *A Major Street Plan for St. Louis*. St. Louis, MO: Nixon-Jones Printing Co., 1917. http://archive.org/details/cu31924024404927.

Bates, John. "Case Study VI: Marketing in Marta." Mass Transit Management: Case Studies of the Metropolitan Atlanta Rapid Transit Authority. Athens: University of Georgia, March 1981. https://rosap.ntl.bts.gov/view/dot/527.

Baum-Snow, Nathaniel. "Did Highways Cause Suburbanization?" *Quarterly Journal of Economics* 122, no. 2 (May 1, 2007): 775–805. https://doi.org/10.1162/qjec.122.2.775.

Bay, Mia. *Traveling Black: A Story of Race and Resistance*. Cambridge, MA: Belknap Press: 2021.

Bean, James David, Charles J. Kahane, Mark Mynatt, Rodney W. Rudd, Carla J. Rush, and Chris Wiacek. "Fatalities in Frontal Crashes Despite Seat Belts and Air Bags: Review of All CDS Cases Model and Calendar Years 2000–2007 122 Fatalities." Washington, DC: National Highway Traffic Safety Administration, 2009. https://crashstats.nhtsa.dot.gov/Api/Public/ViewPublication/811102.

Blincoe, Lawrence, Ted R. Miller, Jing-Shiarn Wang, David Swedler, Tom Coughlin, Bruce Lawrence, Feng Guo, Sheila Klauer, and Thomas Dingus.

"The Economic and Societal Impact of Motor Vehicle Crashes, 2019 (Revised)." Washington, DC: National Highway Traffic Safety Administration, 2023. https://trid.trb.org/View/2100826.

Blumenberg, Evelyn, and Asha Weinstein Agrawal. "Getting Around When You're Just Getting By: Transportation Survival Strategies of the Poor." *Journal of Poverty* 18, no. 4 (2014): 355–78. https://doi.org/10.1080/10875549.2014.951905.

Blumenberg, Evelyn, and Michael Smart. "Brother Can You Spare a Ride? Carpooling in Immigrant Neighbourhoods." *Urban Studies* 51, no. 9 (2014): 1871–90.

Boarnet, Marlon G. "Highways and Economic Productivity: Interpreting Recent Evidence." *Journal of Planning Literature* 11, no. 4 (May 1, 1997): 476–86. https://doi.org/10.1177/088541229701100402.

Boeing, Geoff, and William (Billy) Riggs. "Converting One-Way Streets to Two-Way Streets to Improve Transportation Network Efficiency and Reduce Vehicle Distance Traveled." *Journal of Planning Education and Research* 44, no. 3 (July 6, 2022): 1670–78. https://doi.org/10.1177/0739456X221106334.

Bosch, Dan. "California's Zero Emissions Vehicle Rule and Its Nationwide Impacts." American Action Forum, October 25, 2022. https://www.americanactionforum.org/insight/californias-zero-emissions-vehicle-rule-and-its-nationwide-impacts/.

Boston Public Library. "Boston: Construction [Central Artery]," n.d. https://www.flickr.com/photos/boston_public_library/sets/72157633089829030/.

Brinkman, Jeffrey, and Jeffrey Lin. "The Costs and Benefits of Fixing Downtown Freeways." *Economic Insights* 7, no. 1 (2022): 17–22.

Brooks, Leah, and Zachary Liscow. "Infrastructure Costs." *American Economic Journal: Applied Economics* 15, no. 2 (April 2023): 1–30. https://doi.org/10.1257/app.20200398.

Brown, Jeffrey R., Eric A. Morris, and Brian D. Taylor. "Planning for Cars in Cities: Planners, Engineers, and Freeways in the 20th Century." *Journal of the American Planning Association* 75, no. 2 (2009): 161–77. https://doi.org/10.1080/01944360802640016.

Bugge, William. Interstate Highway Research Project Oral History. Interview by John Greenwood, March 28, 1988.

Bureau of Public Roads. *General Location of National System of Interstate Highways: Including All Additional Routes at Urban Areas Designated in September 1955.* National System of Interstate Highways. Washington, DC: United

States Dept. of Commerce, 1955. https://catalog.hathitrust.org/Record/000968362.

———. *Toll Roads and Free Roads.* 76th Cong., 1st Sess. House. Doc. 272. Washington, DC: US Government Printing Office, 1939. https://catalog.hathitrust.org/Record/001611706.

Bush, George H. W. "Remarks on Signing the Intermodal Surface Transportation Efficiency Act." Euless, TX, December 18, 1991. https://www.enotrans.org/eno-resources/1991-istea-signing-speeches-statements/.

———. "Remarks to the American Association of State Highway and Transportation Officials." Washington, DC, June 21, 1991. https://www.presidency.ucsb.edu/documents/remarks-the-american-association-state-highway-and-transportation-officials.

"Celebrating 50 Years: The Eisenhower Interstate Highway System." Washington, DC: US Government Printing Office, June 27, 2006. https://www.transportation.gov/testimony/celebrating-50-years-eisenhower-interstate-highway-system.

Cervero, Robert, and Mark Hansen. "Induced Travel Demand and Induced Road Investment: A Simultaneous Equation Analysis." *Journal of Transport Economics and Policy* 36, no. 3 (2002): 469–90.

Cervero, Robert, J. Kang, and K. Shively. "From Elevated Freeways to Surface Boulevards: Neighborhood and Housing Price Impacts in San Francisco." *Journal of Urbanism: International Research on Placemaking and Urban Sustainability* 2, no. 1 (2009): 31–50.

Charles A. Maguire and Associates. "The Master Highway Plan for the Boston Metropolitan Area." Boston: Department of Public Works, 1948. https://archive.org/details/masterhighwaypla00char.

City of Boston Assessing Department. "Property Tax Facts and Figures FY 2021." Boston: City of Boston, 2021.

City of Dallas. "Ordinance 21203 Amending Chapter 51A, 'Part II of the Dallas Development Code,' of the Dallas City Code," 1992. https://dallascityhall.com:443/departments/sustainabledevelopment/historicpreservation/Pages/freedman_s_cemetery.aspx.

City of Milwaukee. "Park East Redevelopment." Accessed September 9, 2024. https://city.milwaukee.gov/DCD/Projects/ParkEastredevelopment.

Clark, Lara P., Dylan B. Millet, and Julian D. Marshall. "Changes in Transportation-Related Air Pollution Exposures by Race-Ethnicity and Socioeconomic Status: Outdoor Nitrogen Dioxide in the United States in 2000 and 2010." *Environmental Health Perspectives* 125, no. 9 (September 22, 2017): 097012. https://doi.org/10.1289/EHP959.

Clark, William A. V., and Wenfei Winnie Wang. "The Automobile, Immigrants, and Poverty: Implications for Immigrant Earnings and Job Access." *Urban Geography* 31, no. 4 (2010): 523–40.

Clow, Charles M., Victoria G. Clow, James M. Davidson, Melissa M. Green, Victoria M. Owens, Duane E. Peter, Marsha Prior, Terry Anne Schulte, and Angela L. Tine. *Freedman's Cemetery: A Legacy of a Pioneer Black Community in Dallas, Texas*. Edited by Duane E. Peter, Marsha Prior, Melissa M. Green, and Victoria G Clow. Plano, TX: Geo-Marine, Inc., 2000.

Committee on Traffic and Public Safety. John Andrew Massen, and Miller McClintock. *Limited Ways: A Plan for the Greater Chicago Traffic Area: A Report to the City Council of the City of Chicago*. Chicago: Chicago City Council, 1933.

Congress for New Urbanism. "Completed Highways to Boulevards Projects." Text, June 12, 2015. https://www.cnu.org/our-projects/highways-boulevards/completed-h2b-projects.

———. "Freeways without Futures." Text, 2019. https://www.cnu.org/highways-boulevards/freeways-without-futures/2019.

Corbusier, Le. *The City of To-Morrow and Its Planning*. Translated by Frederick Etchells. Reissue ed. New York: Dover, 1987.

Coughenour, Courtney, Sheila Clark, Ashok Singh, Eudora Claw, James Abelar, and Joshua Huebner. "Examining Racial Bias as a Potential Factor in Pedestrian Crashes." *Accident Analysis and Prevention* 98, supp. C (January 1, 2017): 96–100. https://doi.org/10.1016/j.aap.2016.09.031.

Couture, Victor, Gilles Duranton, and Matthew A. Turner. "Speed." *Review of Economics and Statistics* 100, no. 4 (October 1, 2018): 725–39. https://doi.org/10.1162/rest_a_00744.

Dallas Chamber of Commerce. *Central Expressway—San Jacinto Street to Fitzhugh Avenue: Dedication August 19, 1949*. Dallas: Dallas Chamber of Commerce, 1949. https://catalog.hathitrust.org/Record/006278509.

Davari, Mehraneh. "The Resounding Success of the Big Dig." *Places Journal*, December 2021. https://placesjournal.org/workshop-article/the-resounding-success-of-the-big-dig/.

Davidson, James M. "Freedman's Cemetery (1869-1907): Establishing a Chronology for Exhumed Burials from an African-American Burial Ground, Dallas, Texas." *African Diaspora Archaeology Newsletter* 6, no. 4 (1999): 5.

———. "Rituals Captured in Context and Time: Charm Use in North Dallas Freedman's Town (1869–1907), Dallas, Texas." *Historical Archaeology* 38, no. 2 (June 1, 2004): 22–54. https://doi.org/10.1007/BF03376641.

Davis, Jeff. "30 Years Ago This Week: Reagan's 1987 Highway Bill Veto." *Eno*

Transportation Weekly, March 29, 2017. https://enotrans.org/article/30-years-ago-week-reagans-1987-highway-bill-veto/.

Daziano, Ricardo A., Mauricio Sarrias, and Benjamin Leard. "Are Consumers Willing to Pay to Let Cars Drive for Them? Analyzing Response to Autonomous Vehicles." *Transportation Research Part C: Emerging Technologies* 78 (May 2017): 150–64. https://doi.org/10.1016/j.trc.2017.03.003.

DeLetter, Emily. "Video Shows Waymo Self-Driving Cars Honking at Each Other at 4 a.m. in Parking Lot." *USA TODAY*. Accessed August 23, 2024. https://www.usatoday.com/story/tech/2024/08/15/waymo-driverless-cars-honking-parking-lot-video/74810195007/.

"Demographic Trends and Transportation Demand." Washington, DC: US Government Printing Office, 1991. https://catalog.hathitrust.org/Record/010020626.

Detzer, Karl. "Our Great Big Highway Bungle." *Reader's Digest*, July 1960.

Dewar, Helen, and Lou Cannon. "Reagan Vetoes Highway Bill." *Washington Post*, March 28, 1987. https://www.washingtonpost.com/archive/politics/1987/03/28/reagan-vetoes-highway-bill/033d3806-5612-493a-a9a1-5a53e30f59c3/.

Dodge, Martin. "Report of the Office of Public Road Inquiries." Department of Agriculture Annual Reports. Washington, DC: Government Printing Office, 1902.

Downs, Anthony. "The Law of Peak-Hour Expressway Congestion." *Traffic Quarterly* 16, no. 3 (July 1962). https://babel.hathitrust.org/cgi/pt?id=uc1.$b3477&seq=457.

———. *Stuck in Traffic: Coping with Peak-Hour Traffic Congestion*. Washington, DC: Brookings Institution Press, 1992.

———. *Still Stuck in Traffic: Coping with Peak-Hour Traffic Congestion*. Rev. ed. Washington, DC: Brookings Institution Press, 2004.

Duranton, Gilles, and Erick Guerra. "Developing a Common Narrative on Urban Accessibility: An Urban Planning Perspective." Washington, DC: Brookings Institution, 2016.

Duranton, Gilles, and Matthew A. Turner. "The Fundamental Law of Road Congestion: Evidence from US Cities." *American Economic Review* 101, no. 6 (October 1, 2011): 2616–52. https://doi.org/10.1257/aer.101.6.2616.

Eldridge, Maurice O. "Earth Roads." *Farmer's Bulletin* no. 136. US Department of Agriculture, 1902.

El-Geneidy, Ahmed, and David Levinson. "Making Accessibility Work in Practice." *Transport Reviews* 42, no. 2 (March 4, 2022): 129–33. https://doi.org/10.1080/01441647.2021.1975954.

El-Geneidy, Ahmed M., and David M. Levinson. "Access to Destinations: Development of Accessibility Measures," May 1, 2006. https://hdl.handle.net/11299/638.

Eno Center for Transportation. "How We Pay for Transportation: The Life and Death of the Highway Trust Fund," 2014. https://enotrans.org/wp-content/uploads/2023/02/Highway-Trust-Fund.pdf.

Federal Highway Administration. "America's Challenge for Highway Transportation in the 21st Century: Interim Report of the Future National Highway Program Task Force," 1988.

———. "Highway Statistics." Accessed July 24, 2024. https://www.fhwa.dot.gov/policyinformation/statistics/.

———. "Road Diets (Roadway Reconfiguration)." Accessed August 8, 2024. https://highways.dot.gov/safety/proven-safety-countermeasures/road-diets-roadway-reconfiguration.

———. "Section 4(F)—Highway History." Accessed May 5, 2022. https://www.fhwa.dot.gov/infrastructure/50section4f.cfm.

Federal Transit Administration. "About FTA." Accessed January 29, 2021. https://www.transit.dot.gov/about-fta.

Fernald, John G. "Roads to Prosperity? Assessing the Link between Public Capital and Productivity." *American Economic Review* 89, no. 3 (June 1999): 619–38. https://doi.org/10.1257/aer.89.3.619.

Fitzgerald, Jack. "Average Age of Vehicles in U.S. Continues to Rise." *Car and Driver*, May 23, 2024. https://www.caranddriver.com/news/a60882953/average-age-us-cars-trucks-suvs-rises/.

Forgey, Pat. "How a 'Bridge to Nowhere' Became a Road from Nowhere to Nowhere." *Anchorage Daily News*, November 16, 2015. https://www.adn.com/alaska-news/article/how-bridge-nowhere-became-road-nowhere/2015/11/17/.

Fussell, Julia C., Meredith Franklin, David C. Green, Mats Gustafsson, Roy M. Harrison, William Hicks, Frank J. Kelly, Franceska Kishta, Mark R. Miller, Ian S. Mudway, et al. "A Review of Road Traffic-Derived Non-Exhaust Particles: Emissions, Physicochemical Characteristics, Health Risks, and Mitigation Measures." *Environmental Science and Technology* 56, no. 11 (June 7, 2022): 6813–35. https://doi.org/10.1021/acs.est.2c01072.

Gakenheimer, Ralph A. *Transportation Planning as Response to Controversy: The Boston Case*. Cambridge, MA: MIT Press, 1976.

Geddes, Norman Bel. *Magic Motorways*. New York: Random House, 1940. http://archive.org/details/magicmotorways00geddrich.

Gelman, Andrew, Jeffrey Fagan, and Alex Kiss. "An Analysis of the New York

City Police Department's 'Stop-and-Frisk' Policy in the Context of Claims of Racial Bias." *Journal of the American Statistical Association* 102, no. 479 (September 1, 2007): 813–23. https://doi.org/10.1198/016214506000001040.

Giuliano, Genevieve. "Low Income, Public Transit, and Mobility." *Transportation Research Record: Journal of the Transportation Research Board* 1927, no. 1 (January 1, 2005): 63–70. https://doi.org/10.3141/1927-08.

Goddard, Tara, Kimberly Barsamian Kahn, and Arlie Adkins. "Racial Bias in Driver Yielding Behavior at Crosswalks." *Transportation Research Part F: Traffic Psychology and Behaviour* 33, supp. C (August 1, 2015): 1–6. https://doi.org/10.1016/j.trf.2015.06.002.

Google. "Google Books Ngram Viewer," 2021. https://books.google.com/ngrams#.

Guerra, Erick. "Planning for Cars That Drive Themselves: Metropolitan Planning Organizations, Regional Transportation Plans, and Autonomous Vehicles." *Journal of Planning Education and Research* 36, no. 2 (2016): 210–24. https://doi.org/10.1177/0739456X15613591.

———. "What the Heck Is a Choice Rider? A Theoretical Framework and Empirical Model." *Journal of Transport and Land Use* 15, no. 1 (2022): 165–82.

Guerra, Erick, Xiaoxia Dong, and Michelle Kondo. "Do Denser Neighborhoods Have Safer Streets? Population Density and Traffic Safety in the Philadelphia Region." *Journal of Planning Education and Research*, May 5, 2019, 0739456X19845043, https://doi.org/10.1177/0739456X19845043.

Guerra, Erick, Gilles Duranton, and Xinyu Ma. "Urban Roadway in America: The Amount, Extent, and Value." *Journal of the American Planning Association* (August 5, 2024): 1–15. https://doi.org/10.1080/01944363.2024.2368260.

Guerra, Erick, Christopher Puchalsky, Nata Kovalova, Yihong Hu, Qi Si, Jiamin Tan, and Gillian Zhao. "Evaluating the Effectiveness of Speed Cameras on Philadelphia's Roosevelt Boulevard." *Transportation Research Record: Journal of the Transportation Research Board*, February 27, 2024, 03611981241230320. https://doi.org/10.1177/03611981241230320.

Hall, Peter. *Cities of Tomorrow: An Intellectual History of Urban Planning and Design since 1880.* 4th ed. West Sussex, UK: Wiley, 2014.

Hamidi, Shima, and Reid Ewing. "A National Investigation on the Impacts of Lane Width on Traffic Safety: Narrowing Travel Lanes as an Opportunity to Promote Biking and Pedestrian Facilities within the Existing Roadway Infrastructure." Baltimore, MD: Johns Hopkins Bloomberg School of Public

Health, 2023. https://narrowlanes.americanhealth.jhu.edu/report/JHU-2023-Narrowing-Travel-Lanes-Report.pdf.

Handy, Susan. "Is Accessibility an Idea Whose Time Has Finally Come?" *Transportation Research Part D: Transport and Environment* 83 (June 1, 2020): 102319. https://doi.org/10.1016/j.trd.2020.102319.

———. *Shifting Gears: Toward a New Way of Thinking about Transportation*. Cambridge, MA: MIT Press, 2023.

Heathcott, Joseph. "'The Whole City Is Our Laboratory': Harland Bartholomew and the Production of Urban Knowledge." *Journal of Planning History* 4, no. 4 (November 1, 2005): 322–55. https://doi.org/10.1177/1538513205282131.

Hepp, John. "SEPTA." In *Encyclopedia of Greater Philadelphia*. Camden, NJ: Mid-Atlantic Regional Center for the Humanities, 2018. https://philadelphiaencyclopedia.org/archive/septa/.

Horrox, James, and Andre Delattre. "Highway Boondoggles." US Public Interest Research Group, November 9, 2023. https://pirg.org/edfund/resources/highway-boondoggles/.

Horymski, Chris. "Average Auto Loan Debt Grew 5.2% to $23,792 in 2023—Experian," February 13, 2024. https://www.experian.com/blogs/ask-experian/research/auto-loan-debt-study/.

Hussain, Qinaat, Hanqin Feng, Raphael Grzebieta, Tom Brijs, and Jake Olivier. "The Relationship between Impact Speed and the Probability of Pedestrian Fatality during a Vehicle-Pedestrian Crash: A Systematic Review and Meta-Analysis." *Accident Analysis and Prevention* 129 (2019): 241–49.

International Transport Forum. "Transport Statistics." Paris: Organisation for Economic Co-operation and Development, n.d. Accessed May 29, 2024. http://dx.doi.org/10.1787/trsprt-data-en.

ISEECARS. "Top 25 Cars That Hold Their Value the Best—and the 25 Worst—iSeeCars.Com." Accessed July 11, 2024. https://www.iseecars.com/cars-that-hold-their-value-study.

Jbaily, Abdulrahman, Xiaodan Zhou, Jie Liu, Ting-Hwan Lee, Leila Kamareddine, Stéphane Verguet, and Francesca Dominici. "Air Pollution Exposure Disparities across US Population and Income Groups." *Nature* 601, no. 7892 (January 2022): 228–33. https://doi.org/10.1038/s41586-021-04190-y.

Karnes, Thomas L. *Asphalt and Politics: A History of the American Highway System*. Jefferson, NC: McFarland, 2009.

Keefer, Louis, David Witheford, Sarah Jane Thomas, Arthur Schwartz, E. Richard Kolesar, Roy Cominsky, Sheldon Sullivan, Robert Irwin, George Luster, William G. Blake, et al. "Pittsburgh Area Transportation Study:

Final Report in Two Parts. Volume 2 Forecasts and Plans." Commonwealth of Pennsylvania, County of Allegheny, City of Pittsburgh; US Department of Commerce: Bureau of Public Roads, February 1963.

Kerr, Gaige Hunter, Aaron van Donkelaar, Randall V. Martin, Michael Brauer, Katrin Bukart, Sarah Wozniak, Daniel L. Goldberg, and Susan C. Anenberg. "Increasing Racial and Ethnic Disparities in Ambient Air Pollution—Attributable Morbidity and Mortality in the United States." *Environmental Health Perspectives* 132, no. 3 (March 2024): 037002. https://doi.org/10.1289/EHP11900.

Kimble, Megan. *City Limits: Infrastructure, Inequality, and the Future of America's Highways*. New York: Crown, 2024.

———. "Forgetful City." *Texas Observer*, September 17, 2021. https://www.texasobserver.org/forgetful-city/.

King, David A., Michael J. Smart, and Michael Manville. "The Poverty of the Carless: Toward Universal Auto Access." *Journal of Planning Education and Research* 42, no. 3 (February 1, 2019): 464–81. https://doi.org/10.1177/0739456X18823252.

King, John. *Portal: San Francisco's Ferry Building and the Reinvention of American Cities*. Norton, 2023.

Klein, Nicholas J. "Subsidizing Car Ownership for Low-Income Individuals and Households." *Journal of Planning Education and Research* 44, no. 1 (March 1, 2024): 165–77. https://doi.org/10.1177/0739456X20950428.

Klein, Nicholas J., and Michael J. Smart. "Car Today, Gone Tomorrow: The Ephemeral Car in Low-Income, Immigrant and Minority Families." *Transportation* 44, no. 3 (May 1, 2017): 495–510. https://doi.org/10.1007/s11116-015-9664-4.

Klein, Nicholas J., Minh Tran, and Sarah Riley. "'Desperately in Need of Car': Analyzing Crowdfunding Campaigns for Car Purchases and Repairs on Gofundme.Com." Preprint. SocArXiv, December 10, 2019. https://doi.org/10.31235/osf.io/8x7d2.

Knubel, Fred. "Vickrey One Year Later: Catching Up with a Thinker Way Ahead of His Time." *Columbia University Record* 23, no. 6 (October 10, 1997). https://curecordarchive.library.columbia.edu/.

Larson, Thomas D. "Rex Whitton—The Man from Missouri." Interstate System, Highway History, Federal Highway Administration, 1990. https://www.fhwa.dot.gov/infrastructure/whitton.cfm.

Leduc, Sylvain, and Daniel Wilson. "Roads to Prosperity or Bridges to Nowhere? Theory and Evidence on the Impact of Public Infrastructure Investment." *NBER Macroeconomics Annual* 27 (January 2013): 89–142. https://doi.org/10.1086/669173.

Levine, Jonathan, Joe Grengs, and Louis A. Merlin. *From Mobility to Accessibility: Transforming Urban Transportation and Land-Use Planning.* Ithaca, NY: Cornell University Press, 2019.

Levine, Jonathan, Joe Grengs, Qingyun Shen, and Qing Shen. "Does Accessibility Require Density or Speed? A Comparison of Fast versus Close in Getting Where You Want to Go in US Metropolitan Regions." *Journal of the American Planning Association* 78, no. 2 (2012): 157–72.

Lewis, Tom. *Divided Highways: Building the Interstate Highways, Transforming American Life. Divided Highways.* Ithaca, NY: Cornell University Press, 2013.

Li, Shengxiao (Alex). "Transportation Planning for Older Americans: Challenges, Federal Policies, and Next Steps." *Journal of Aging and Social Policy* (July 24, 2023): 1–19. https://doi.org/10.1080/08959420.2023.2238539.

———. "Vehicle Ownership over the Life Course among Older Americans: A Longitudinal Analysis." *Transportation* 51, no. 1 (February 1, 2024): 247–70. https://doi.org/10.1007/s11116-022-10326-4.

Liu, Jiawen, Lara P. Clark, Matthew J. Bechle, Anjum Hajat, Sun-Young Kim, Allen L. Robinson, Lianne Sheppard, Adam A. Szpiro, and Julian D. Marshall. "Disparities in Air Pollution Exposure in the United States by Race/Ethnicity and Income, 1990–2010." *Environmental Health Perspectives* 129, no. 12 (December 2021): 127005. https://doi.org/10.1289/EHP8584.

Lovejoy, Kristin, and Susan Handy. "Social Networks as a Source of Private-Vehicle Transportation: The Practice of Getting Rides and Borrowing Vehicles among Mexican Immigrants in California." *Transportation Research Part A: Policy and Practice* 45, no. 4 (2011): 248–57.

Marohn, Charles L., Jr. *Confessions of a Recovering Engineer: Transportation for a Strong Town.* Hoboken, NJ: Wiley, 2021.

Marsh, Bernard L. "The New Highways: Challenge to the Metro-Politan Region: A Report on a Symposium, Sponsored by Connecticut General Life Insurance Company, Hartford, September 9–12, 1957." *Traffic Engineering* 28 (1957): 15–17.

Marshall, Wes. *Killed by a Traffic Engineer: Shattering the Delusion That Science Underlies Our Transportation System.* Washington, DC: Island Press, 2024.

Marshall, Wesley E., and Eric Dumbaugh. "Revisiting the Relationship between Traffic Congestion and the Economy: A Longitudinal Examination of U.S. Metropolitan Areas." *Transportation* 47, no. 1 (February 1, 2020): 275–314. https://doi.org/10.1007/s11116-018-9884-5.

McAfee, Andrew, and Erik Brynjolfsson. "Big Data: The Management Revolution." *Harvard Business Review*, October 1, 2012. https://hbr.org/2012/10/big-data-the-management-revolution.

McClintock, Miller. *A Proposed Traffic Ordinance for the City of Los Angeles: With Annotations and Recommendations for the Remedy of Street Traffic Conditions. Oct. 8, 1924*. Los Angeles: Traffic Commission of the City and County of Los Angeles, 1924.

———. *Report on San Francisco Citywide Traffic Survey: W.P.A. Project 6108-5863*. San Francisco: Pisani Printing and Publishing, 1937.

———. *Street Traffic Control*. New York: McGraw-Hill, 1925.

———. "Superhighways Needed to Speed Major Traffic Flaws." *Chicago Daily Tribune*, sec. part 6, January 29, 1933.

———. "The Traffic Survey." *Annals of the American Academy of Political and Social Science* 133, no. 1 (November 1, 1927): 8–18. https://doi.org/10.1177/000271622713300103.

———. "Unfit for Modern Motor Traffic." *Fortune* 14, no. 2 (August 1936): 85–92, 94, 96, 99.

McGrath, Charles. "Robert Caro's Big Dig." *New York Times*, sec. Magazine, April 12, 2012. https://www.nytimes.com/2012/04/15/magazine/robert-caros-big-dig.html.

McMillen, Neil R. *The Citizens' Council: Organized Resistance to the Second Reconstruction, 1954–64*. Urbana: University of Illinois Press, 1994.

McNichol, Dan. *The Roads That Built America: The Incredible Story of the U.S. Interstate System*. New York: Barnes and Noble, 2003.

Merlin, Louis A., Erick Guerra, and Eric Dumbaugh. "Crash Risk, Crash Exposure, and the Built Environment: A Conceptual Review." *Accident Analysis and Prevention* 134 (January 1, 2020): 105244. https://doi.org/10.1016/j.aap.2019.07.020.

Merlin, Louis A., Jonathan Levine, and Joe Grengs. "Accessibility Analysis for Transportation Projects and Plans." *Transport Policy* 69 (October 1, 2018): 35–48. https://doi.org/10.1016/j.tranpol.2018.05.014.

Mertz, Lee. Interstate Highway Research Project Oral History. Interview by John Greenwood, 1988.

———. "The Bragdon Committee." Interstate System, Highway History, Federal Highway Administration. Accessed April 21, 2022. https://www.fhwa.dot.gov/infrastructure/bragdon.cfm#1a.

———. "Origins of the Interstate System." Federal Highway Administration. Accessed March 17, 2022. https://www.fhwa.dot.gov/infrastructure/origin01.cfm.

Millard-Ball, Adam. "The Autonomous Vehicle Parking Problem." *Transport Policy* 75 (March 1, 2019): 99–108. https://doi.org/10.1016/j.tranpol.2019.01.003.

Millard-Ball, Adam, and Erick Guerra. "Should Environmentalists Support the Gasoline Tax?" *Journal of the American Planning Association* (September 24, 2024): 1–4. https://doi.org/10.1080/01944363.2024.2394058.

Mondschein, Andrew, and Brian D. Taylor. "Is Traffic Congestion Overrated? Examining the Highly Variable Effects of Congestion on Travel and Accessibility." *Journal of Transport Geography* 64 (October 1, 2017): 65–76. https://doi.org/10.1016/j.jtrangeo.2017.08.007.

Morris, Eric. "From Horse Power to Horsepower." *Access Magazine* 1, no. 30 (2007): 2–10.

Moynihan, Daniel P. "New Roads and Urban Chaos." *The Reporter*, 1960.

Mumford, Lewis. "Address of Lewis Mumford." Presented at the New Highways: Challenge to the Metropolitan Region, Hartford, CT, September 11, 1957.

———. "The Roaring Traffic's Boom." *New Yorker*, April 16, 1955.

National Highway Traffic Safety Administration. "Fatality Analysis Reporting System." Accessed August 21, 2024. http://www.nhtsa.gov/FARS.

———. "National Motor Vehicle Crash Causation Survey: Report to Congress." Washington, DC: US Department of Transportation, 2008.

———. "Pedestrian Safety." Text. Accessed August 20, 2024. https://www.nhtsa.gov/book/countermeasures-that-work/pedestrian-safety.

———. "Traffic Safety Facts 2021 Data: Race and Ethnicity." Washington, DC: US Department of Transportation, 2024. https://www.google.com/url?sa=t&source=web&rct=j&opi=89978449&url=https://crashstats.nhtsa.dot.gov/Api/Public/Publication/813572.

National Interregional Highway Committee. "Interregional Highways." Washington, DC: US Government Printing Office, 1944.

National Register of Historic Places. "Merritt Parkway." National Park Service, March 5, 1991. https://npgallery.nps.gov/GetAsset/96eb4fba-acde-4e35-be75-4016e832b170.

National Research Council, Highway Research Board, Committee on Highway Capacity. *Highway Capacity Manual: Practical Applications of Research*. Washington, DC: US Department of Commerce, Bureau of Public Roads, 1950. https://catalog.hathitrust.org/Record/001108733.

National Transportation Safety Board. "Collision between Vehicle Controlled by Developmental Automated Driving System and Pedestrian: Tempe, Arizona March 18, 2018." Accident Report, 2019.

Newall, Mike. "South Philly Residents Say PennDot Misled Them about Plans to Remove Ballfields." *Philadelphia Inquirer*, August 10, 2024. https://www.inquirer.com/news/south-philly-baseball-fields-penndot-study-20240810.html.

New York Times. "Harland Bartholomew, 100, Dean of City Planners." Accessed August 2, 2023. https://www.nytimes.com/1989/12/07/obituaries/harland-bartholomew-100-dean-of-city-planners.html.

New York Times. "A New Road for Transportation," sec. Opinion, November 29, 1991. https://www.nytimes.com/1991/11/29/opinion/a-new-road-for-transportation.html.

New York Times. "Will Stage Plays in Paris This Spring; Norman-Bel Geddes and Richard Herndon Producers, with Eva Le Gallienne Star," sec. Archives, March 23, 1925. https://www.nytimes.com/1925/03/23/archives/will-stage-plays-in-paris-this-spring-normanbel-geddes-and-richard.html.

Nissan. "The Future Is Now: Nissan Advances Plans to Have Commercially Viable Autonomous Drive Vehicles on the Road by 2020," 2014. http://www.nissanusa.com/innovations/autonomous-car.article.html.

Noland, Robert B., Dong Gao, Eric J. Gonzales, and Charles Brown. "Costs and Benefits of a Road Diet Conversion." *Case Studies on Transport Policy* 3, no. 4 (December 1, 2015): 449–58. https://doi.org/10.1016/j.cstp.2015.09.002.

Norquist, John. *The Wealth of Cities: Revitalizing the Centers of American Life*. New York: Basic Books, 1999.

North Texas Council of Governments. "Mobility 2010 Plan Update Summary: The Regional Transportation Plan for North Central Texas," October 1993.

———. "Mobility 2010 Plan Update: The Regional Transportation Plan for North Central Texas," January 1995.

———. "Mobility 2010: The Regional Transportation Plan for North Central Texas," April 1991.

Norton, Peter. *Autonorama: The Illusory Promise of High-Tech Driving*. Washington, DC: Island Press, 2021.

Ohlms, Peter B., Lance E. Dougald, Hannah E MacKnight, and Virginia Transportation Research Council (VTRC). "How's That Diet Working: Performance of Virginia Road Diets," April 1, 2020. https://rosap.ntl.bts.gov/view/dot/54878.

Olia, Arash, Saiedeh Razavi, Baher Abdulhai, and Hossam Abdelgawad. "Traffic Capacity Implications of Automated Vehicles Mixed with Regular Vehicles." *Journal of Intelligent Transportation Systems* 22, no. 3 (May 4, 2018): 244–62. https://doi.org/10.1080/15472450.2017.1404680.

Oregon Department of Transportation. "August 2024 Monthly Indicators Report," 2024. https://www.oregon.gov/odot/Data/Documents/Monthly_Indicators_2024.pdf.

———. "OReGO: Oregon's Road Usage Charge Program." Accessed July 30, 2024. https://www.oregon.gov/odot/programs/pages/orego.aspx.

Owen, Wilfred. *The New Highways: Challenge to the Metropolitan Region.* Hartford: Connecticut General Life Insurance Co., 1956. https://catalog.hathitrust.org/Record/010618592.

Page, Logan Waller. "Report of the Director of the Office of Public Roads." Department of Agriculture Annual Reports. Washington, DC: US Government Printing Office, 1905.

Parry, I. W. H., M. Walls, and W. Harrington. "Automobile Externalities and Policies." *Journal of Economic Literature* 45, no. 2 (2007): 373–99.

Pennsylvania Department of Transportation. "I-95 Central to South Philadelphia Planning Study," 2023. https://aecomviz.com/I95-CSP-360/.

Pierson, Emma, Camelia Simoiu, Jan Overgoor, Sam Corbett-Davies, Daniel Jenson, Amy Shoemaker, Vignesh Ramachandran, Phoebe Barghouty, Cheryl Phillips, Ravi Shroff, and Sharad Goel. "A Large-Scale Analysis of Racial Disparities in Police Stops across the United States." *Nature Human Behaviour* 4, no. 7 (July 2020): 736–45. https://doi.org/10.1038/s41562-020-0858-1.

Polzin, Steve, Xuehao Chu, and Joel Rey. "Density and Captivity in Public Transit Success: Observations from the 1995 Nationwide Personal Transportation Study." *Transportation Research Record: Journal of the Transportation Research Board* 1735, no. 1 (2000): 10–18. https://doi.org/10.3141/1735-02.

President's Advisory Committee on a National Highway Program. *A 10-Year National Highway Program.* 84th Cong., 1st Sess. House Document no. 93. Washington, DC: US Government Printing Office, 1955. https://catalog.hathitrust.org/Record/000968360.

Prior, Marsha. "Freedmantown/North Dallas." Texas State Historical Association, 2020. https://www.tshaonline.org/handbook/entries/freedmantownnorth-dallas.

Prior, Marsha, and Robert V. Kemper. "From Freedman's Town to Uptown: Community Transformation and Gentrification in Dallas, Texas." *Urban Anthropology and Studies of Cultural Systems and World Economic Development* 34, no. 2/3 (2005): 177–216.

Provost, Stephen H. *America's First Highways.* Pleasant Grove, UT: Dragon Crown Books, 2020.

Raifman, Matthew A., and Ernani F. Choma. "Disparities in Activity and Traffic Fatalities by Race/Ethnicity." *American Journal of Preventive Medicine* 63, no. 2 (August 1, 2022): 160–67. https://doi.org/10.1016/j.amepre.2022.03.012.

Ralph, Kelcie, Nicholas J. Klein, Calvin Thigpen, and Anne Brown. "Are Transportation Planning Views Shared by Engineering Students and the Public?" *Journal of Planning Education and Research*, June 9, 2022, 0739456X221097840. https://doi.org/10.1177/0739456X221097840.

Riggs, William, and Bruce Appleyard. "The Economic Impact of One to Two-Way Street Conversions: Advancing a Context-Sensitive Framework." *Journal of Urbanism: International Research on Placemaking and Urban Sustainability* 11, no. 2 (April 3, 2018): 129–48. https://doi.org/10.1080/17549175.2017.1422535.

Riggs, William, and John Gilderbloom. "Two-Way Street Conversion: Evidence of Increased Livability in Louisville." *Journal of Planning Education and Research* 36, no. 1 (March 1, 2016): 105–18. https://doi.org/10.1177/0739456X15593147.

Robbins, Douglass. "Long-Range I-95 CSP Planning - SHCA Feedback," April 19, 2024.

Rogalsky, Jennifer. "Bartering for Basics: Using Ethnography and Travel Diaries to Understand Transportation Constraints and Social Networks among Working-Poor Women." *Urban Geography* 31, no. 8 (2010): 1018–38.

Rose, Mark H., and Raymond A. Mohl. *Interstate: Highway Politics and Policy since 1939*. Knoxville: University of Tennessee Press, 2012.

Rosén, Erik, Helena Stigson, and Ulrich Sander. "Literature Review of Pedestrian Fatality Risk as a Function of Car Impact Speed." *Accident Analysis and Prevention* 43, no. 1 (January 1, 2011): 25–33. https://doi.org/10.1016/j.aap.2010.04.003.

Rothstein, Richard. *The Color of Law: A Forgotten History of How Our Government Segregated America*. New York: Liveright, 2017.

Saffron, Inga. "I-95 Reconstruction Is Really a Widening Project That Will Hurt Philly Neighborhoods." *Philadelphia Inquirer*, sec. Opinion, January 22, 2024. https://www.inquirer.com/real-estate/i-95-highways-penndot-reconstruction-widening-cities-injustice-mitigate-biden--20240122.html.

———. "Philly Spent a Decade Reconnecting Neighborhoods to the Waterfront. Widening I-95 Is Repeating Past Mistakes." *Philadelphia Inquirer*, sec. Opinion, May 19, 2022. https://www.inquirer.com/columnists/i-95-construction-philadelphia-neighborhoods-delaware-river-bike-lanes-20220519.html.

———. Interview by Erick Guerra, May 3, 2024.

Said, Carolyn. "Exclusive: Tempe Police Chief Says Early Probe Shows No Fault by Uber." *San Francisco Chronicle*, March 26, 2018. https://web.archive.org/web/20190830191415/https://www.sfchronicle.com/business/article/Exclusive-Tempe-police-chief-says-early-probe-12765481.php.

Salvucci, Fred. Interview with Fred Salvucci, former Massachusetts secretary of transportation, for "The Big Dig," episode 4 of *Great Projects: The Building of America*. Public Broadcasting Service, 2002. https://www.pbs.org/greatprojects/interviews/salvucci_3.html.

Schafer, Andreas, and David G. Victor. "The Future Mobility of the World Population." *Transportation Research Part A: Policy and Practice* 34, no. 3 (2000): 171–205. https://doi.org/10.1016/S0965-8564(98)00071-8.

Scheuer, James H. "Highways and People: The Housing Impact of the Highway Program." Technical Bulletin no. 31, 35–42. New Haven, CT: Urban Land Institute, 1957.

Schrank, David, Luke Albert, Bill Eisele, and Tim Lomax. "2021 Urban Mobility Report." College Station: Texas A&M Transportation Institute, 2021. https://mobility.tamu.edu/umr/report/.

Shaffer, Blake, Maximilian Auffhammer, and Constantine Samaras. "Make Electric Vehicles Lighter to Maximize Climate and Safety Benefits." *Nature* 598, no. 7880 (October 2021): 254–56. https://doi.org/10.1038/d41586-021-02760-8.

Shannon, Megan. "PennDot's Survey." Government Transparency Blog, July 28, 2024. https://www.meganshannonrtk.com/blog/penndots-survey.

Shrode, Garret, Jeff Davis, and Robert Puentes. "Driving Change: Advice for the National VMT-Fee Pilot." Washington, DC: Eno Center for Transportation, 2023. https://enotrans.org/eno-resources/driving-change-advice-for-the-national-vmt-fee-pilot/.

Smart, Michael J., and Nicholas J. Klein. "Disentangling the Role of Cars and Transit in Employment and Labor Earnings." *Transportation* 47, no. 3 (June 1, 2020): 1275–1309. https://doi.org/10.1007/s11116-018-9959-3.

Smiley, Lauren. "The Legal Saga of Uber's Fatal Self-Driving Car Crash Is Over." *Wired*, July 28, 2023. https://www.wired.com/story/ubers-fatal-self-driving-car-crash-saga-over-operator-avoids-prison/.

Special Assistant for Public Works Planning. "Progress Review and Analysis: Federal Highway Program: Interim Report," 1960. https://www.enotrans.org/eno-resources/march-1960-interim-report-on-highways-from-john-s-bragdon/.

Spelman, John. "Boston Motordom: Automobiles and the Transformation of the City, 1899–1930." Charlottesville: University of Virginia, 2014. https://doi.org/10.18130/V3WV5W.

Staff of the Regional Plan. *Regional Plan of New York and Its Environs*. New York: Committee on Regional Plan of New York and Its Environs, 1929. https://rpa.org/work/reports/regional-plan-of-new-york-and-its-environs.

"Statement of General Lucius D. Clay Chairman, President's Advisory

Committee on a National Highway Program." US Senate, March 11, 1955. https://www.fhwa.dot.gov/infrastructure/claytest.cfm.

Stufflebeam Row, Karen, Eva LaDow, and Steve Moler. "Glenwood Canyon 12 Years Later." *Public Roads* 67, no. 5 (2004). https://web.archive.org/web/20121108031753/http://www.fhwa.dot.gov/publications/publicroads/04mar/04.cfm.

Sunstein, Cass R. *The Cost-Benefit Revolution*. Cambridge, MA: MIT Press, 2018.

Sweet, Matthias. "Traffic Congestion's Economic Impacts: Evidence from US Metropolitan Regions." *Urban Studies* 51, no. 10 (August 1, 2014): 2088–110. https://doi.org/10.1177/0042098013505883.

Swift, Earl. *The Big Roads: The Untold Story of the Engineers, Visionaries, and Trailblazers Who Created the American Superhighways*. Boston: Houghton Mifflin Harcourt, 2011.

Talbert, Leon O., John B. Ellis, Finley Byrd, and G. Albert Weese. Interstate Highway Research Project Oral History. Interview by Mark Rose and Bruce Seely, n.d.

Tallamy, Bertram. Interstate Highway Research Project Oral History. Interview by Darwin Stolzanbach, September 21, 1987.

Taylor, Brian D., and Eric A. Morris. "Public Transportation Objectives and Rider Demographics: Are Transit's Priorities Poor Public Policy?" *Transportation* 42, no. 2 (March 1, 2015): 347–67. https://doi.org/10.1007/s11116-014-9547-0.

Taylor, Brian D., Eric A. Morris, and Jeffrey R. Brown. *The Drive for Dollars: How Fiscal Politics Shaped Urban Freeways and Transformed American Cities*. New York: Oxford University Press, 2023.

Tefft, Brian C. "Impact Speed and a Pedestrian's Risk of Severe Injury or Death." *Accident Analysis and Prevention* 50 (2013): 871–78.

"Testimony on The Status of the Highway Trust Fund: 2023 Update." Washington, DC: Congressional Budget Office, October 18, 2023. https://www.cbo.gov/publication/59667.

Texas A&M Transportation Institute. "Congestion Data for Your City—Mobility Division." Urban Mobility Report 2021, August 27, 2020. https://mobility.tamu.edu/umr/congestion-data/.

Texas Department of Transportation. "North Houston Highway Improvement Project, Houston District: Draft Environmental Impact Statement," April 2017.

———. "TEXpress Lanes." Accessed July 31, 2024. http://txdot.gov/en/home/discover/express-toll-hov-lanes/managed-lanes/texpress-lanes.html.

———. "TxDOT Planning Process," 2015.

Texas Highway Department. "Final Environmental Statement for State Highway 360 from Proposed State Highway 121 South of Grapevine, in Tarrant County to South of U.S. Highway 287, in Ellis County," 1973.

———. *From Pioneer Paths to Superhighways—The Texas Highway Department Blazes Texas Trails 1917–1968.* Exhibit. Accessed March 8, 2022. https://www.tsl.texas.gov/exhibits/highways/contents.html.

Texas Historical Commission. "Freedman's Cemetery Memorial—Atlas Number 5113006715," 1993. https://atlas.thc.state.tx.us/Details/5113006715/.

Texas State Library and Archives Commission. "Before and After Photos of Dallas Central Expressway, 1952." Accessed April 18, 2022. https://www.tsl.texas.gov/exhibits/highways/greatage/centralexpressway1950s.html.

Thomas, Helen. "Bush: Transportation Law Will Mean 'Jobs, Jobs, Jobs.'" *United Press International*, December 18, 1991. https://www.upi.com/Archives/1991/12/18/Bush-Transportation-law-will-mean-jobs-jobs-jobs/2592693032400/.

Tol, Richard S. J. "Social Cost of Carbon Estimates Have Increased over Time." *Nature Climate Change* 13, no. 6 (June 2023): 532–36. https://doi.org/10.1038/s41558-023-01680-x.

Tyndall, Justin. "Pedestrian Deaths and Large Vehicles." *Economics of Transportation* 26–27 (June 1, 2021): 100219. https://doi.org/10.1016/j.ecotra.2021.100219.

University of Minnesota Accessibility Observatory. "Access Across America." Accessed August 22, 2024. https://www.access.umn.edu/data/datasets/index.html.

US Bureau of Labor Statistics. "Consumer Expenditures (Annual) News Release," August 29, 2017. https://www.bls.gov/news.release/archives/cesan_08292017.htm.

———. "Consumer Expenditure Survey," 2020. https://www.bls.gov/cex/.

———. "Real Average Hourly Earnings up 1.4 Percent for the Year Ending March 2016." *Economics Daily*, April 19, 2016. https://www.bls.gov/opub/ted/2016/real-average-hourly-earnings-up-1-4-percent-for-the-year-ending-march-2016.htm.

US Census Bureau. "Annual Survey of State and Local Government Finances." Census.gov. Accessed October 21, 2022. https://www.census.gov/programs-surveys/gov-finances.html.

———. "Census of Governments." Census.gov. Accessed October 21, 2022. https://www.census.gov/programs-surveys/cog.html.

US Centers for Disease Control and Prevention. "State-Specific Costs of Motor

Vehicle Crash Deaths." Motor Vehicle Safety, November 6, 2020. https://www.cdc.gov/transportationsafety/statecosts/index.html.

US Department of Transportation. "Biden-Harris Administration Announces First-Ever Awards from Program to Reconnect Communities." US Department of Transportation, press release, February 28, 2023. https://www.transportation.gov/briefing-room/biden-harris-administration-announces-first-ever-awards-program-reconnect-communities.

———. "National Household Travel Survey," 2017. http://nhts.ornl.gov/.

US Department of Transportation. "National Transportation Statistics: Truck Profile," 2019. https://doi.org/10.21949/1503663.

———. "Status of the Nation's Highways, Bridges, and Transit Conditions and Performance." 23rd ed. 2019. https://www.fhwa.dot.gov/policy/23cpr/index.cfm.

US Department of Transportation and Massachusetts Department of Public Works. *Third Harbor Tunnel, Interstate 90/Central Artery, Interstate 93, Boston, Massachusetts: Final Environmental Impact Statement/Report and Final Section 4 (f) Evaluation*. Cambridge, MA: Federal Highway Administration, Transportation Systems Center; Massachusetts Department of Public Works, 1985. https://catalog.hathitrust.org/Record/100826781.

US Environmental Protection Agency. "Inventory of U.S. Greenhouse Gas Emissions and Sinks: 1990–2022." Reports and Assessments, February 8, 2024. https://www.epa.gov/ghgemissions/inventory-us-greenhouse-gas-emissions-and-sinks-1990-2022.

"U.S. Statutes at Large, Volume 27 (1892–1893), 52nd Congress." Image. Washington, DC: Library of Congress. Accessed February 15, 2022. https://www.loc.gov/item/llsl-v27/.

"U.S. Statutes at Large, Volume 37 (1911–1913), 62nd Congress." Image. Washington, DC: Library of Congress. Accessed February 21, 2022. https://www.loc.gov/item/llsl-v37/.

"U.S. Statutes at Large, Volume 39 (1915–1916), 64th Congress." Image. Washington, DC: Library of Congress. Accessed February 17, 2022. https://www.loc.gov/item/llsl-v39/.

"U.S. Statutes at Large, Volume 42 (1921–1923), 67th Congress." Image. Washington, DC: Library of Congress. Accessed June 6, 2023. https://www.loc.gov/item/llsl-v42/.

"U.S. Statutes at Large, Volume 58 (1944), 78th Congress, Session 2." Image. Washington, DC: Library of Congress. Accessed March 24, 2022. https://www.loc.gov/item/llsl-v58/.

Venegas, Kimberly, Brian D. Taylor, Severin Martinez, and Yu Hong Hwang. "Take the High (Volume) Road: Analyzing the Safety and Speed Effects of High-Traffic-Volume Road Diets." *Transportation Research Record* 2678, no. 6 (June 1, 2024): 74–86. https://doi.org/10.1177/03611981231193630.

Vickery Place Neighborhood Association. "North Central Expressway." Accessed April 18, 2022. https://www.vickeryplace.com/central-expressway.

Vickrey, William S. "Pricing in Urban and Suburban Transport." *American Economic Review* 53, no. 2 (1963): 452–65.

———. "A Proposal for Revising New York's Subway Fare Structure." *Journal of the Operations Research Society of America* 3, no. 1 (1955): 38–68.

Volker, Jamey M. B., Amy E. Lee, and Susan Handy. "Induced Vehicle Travel in the Environmental Review Process." *Transportation Research Record*, June 15, 2020. https://journals.sagepub.com/doi/10.1177/0361198120923365.

Warren, Patricia, Donald Tomaskovic-Devey, William Smith, Matthew Zingraff, and Marcinda Mason. "Driving While Black: Bias Processes and Racial Disparity in Police Stops." *Criminology* 44, no. 3 (2006): 709–38. https://doi.org/10.1111/j.1745-9125.2006.00061.x.

Waymo. "Meet Waymo One: The World's First Autonomous Ride-Hailing Service." Accessed November 18, 2024. https://waymo.com/waymo-one/.

Webber, Melvin M. "The Joys of Automobility." In *The Car and the City: The Automobile, the Built Environment, and Daily Urban Life*, edited by Martin Wachs and Margaret Crawford. Ann Arbor: University of Michigan Press, 1992. https://escholarship.org/uc/item/3pb4j3sg.

Weingroff, Richard F. "Creating A Landmark: The Intermodal Surface Transportation Act of 1991." *Public Roads* 65, no. 3 (2001). https://highways.dot.gov/public-roads/novemberdecember-2001/creating-landmark-intermodal-surface-transportation-act-1991.

———. "Federal Aid Road Act of 1916: Building The Foundation." *Public Roads*, 1996. https://highways.dot.gov/public-roads/summer-1996/federal-aid-road-act-1916-building-foundation-sidebars.

———. "From 1916 to 1939: The Federal-State Partnership at Work." *Public Roads*, 1996. https://highways.dot.gov/public-roads/summer-1996/1916-1939-federal-state-partnership-work.

———. "General Lucius D. Clay—The President's Man." Accessed November 15, 2024. https://www.fhwa.dot.gov/infrastructure/clay.cfm.

———. "The Greatest Decade 1956–1966." Interstate System, Highway History, Federal Highway Administration. Accessed April 26, 2022. https://www.fhwa.dot.gov/infrastructure/50interstate.cfm.

———. "A Maximum of Good Results: Martin Dodge and the Good Roads Trains." History of FHWA. Accessed February 25, 2022. https://www.fhwa.dot.gov/highwayhistory/dodge/02.cfm.

———. "Portrait of a General: General Roy Stone." History of FHWA, n.d. https://www.fhwa.dot.gov/infrastructure/stone.cfm.

"What to Do about America's Killer Cars." *The Economist*. September 5, 2024. https://www.economist.com/leaders/2024/09/05/what-to-do-about-americas-killer-cars.

Wheaton, William C. "Price-Induced Distortions in Urban Highway Investment." *Bell Journal of Economics* 9, no. 2 (1978): 622–32. https://doi.org/10.2307/3003602.

Whitten, Robert. "The Atlanta Zone Plan: Report Outlining a Tentative Zone Plan for Atlanta." Atlanta: City Planning Commission, 1922. https://catalog.hathitrust.org/Record/100216234.

———. *Report on a Thoroughfare Plan for Boston*. Boston: City Planning Board, 1930. http://archive.org/details/reportonthorough00bost.

Xia, Xiaoning, and Pengwei Li. "A Review of the Life Cycle Assessment of Electric Vehicles: Considering the Influence of Batteries." *Science of the Total Environment* 814 (March 25, 2022): 152870. https://doi.org/10.1016/j.scitotenv.2021.152870.

Yarbrough, Collin. *Paved A Way: Infrastructure, Policy and Racism in an American City*. Potomac, MD: New Degree Press, 2021.

Zak, Paul. "Measurement Myopia." Drucker Institute, Claremont Graduate University (blog), July 4, 2013. https://drucker.institute/thedx/measurement-myopia/.

Zelinger, Marshall, and Alexander Kirk. "Transportation Secretary Pete Buttigieg on I-70 Congestion, Trucker Crash Impacts." *9NEWS*, February 24, 2022. https://www.9news.com/article/news/local/local-politics/pete-buttigieg-colorado/73-54035201-b23a-4d01-9aa2-67b34a40dd51.

Zettel, Richard M. Interstate Highway Research Project Oral History. Interview by David Jones, May 24, 1989.

Zhou, Yuying, Scott Himes, Thanh Le, Jeff Gooch, Kayla Northup, and Peter Pavao. "Safety Effectiveness of the Road Diet Treatment in Rhode Island." *Transportation Research Record* 2676, no. 7 (July 1, 2022): 24–31. https://doi.org/10.1177/03611981221076433.

About the Author

Erick Guerra, PhD, is professor of regional planning and associate dean for research at the Weitzman School at the University of Pennsylvania, where he teaches courses in transportation planning and quantitative planning methods. His research focuses on relationships between land use, transportation systems, and travel behavior, with an emphasis on rapidly motorizing cities, public health outcomes, and transportation technologies. He has published dozens of peer-reviewed journal articles on various topics, including land use and transportation in Mexico and Indonesia, highway policy, public transport policy, automated traffic enforcement, land use and traffic safety, and contemporary planning for self-driving vehicles. His 2017 book, *Beyond Mobility*, with Robert Cervero and Stefan Al explores global challenges and opportunities to creating safer, healthier, and more productive cities. He holds a PhD in city and regional planning from the University of California, Berkeley; a master's in urban planning from Harvard University; and a bachelor of arts from the University of Pennsylvania. He served as a Peace Corps volunteer in Gabon from 2002 to 2004.

Index

Note: page numbers followed by f, t, and n refer to figures, tables, and footnotes, respectively.